D1064729

The Antitrust Dilemma

Conference in Industrial Organization, Southern Illinois Univ., Edwardsville, 1973.

The Antitrust Dilemma

James A. Dalton
University of South Florida

Stanford L. Levin
Southern Illinois University
at Edwardsville

Lexington Books
D.C. Heath and Company
Lexington, Massachusetts
Toronto   London

Library
I.U.P.
Indiana, Pa.

338.82   C76a

c.1

Library of Congress Cataloging in Publication Data

Conference in Industrial Organization, Southern Illinois University,
Edwardsville, 1973.
The antitrust dilemma.

Bibliography: p.
1. Trusts, Industrial—United States—Congresses. 2. Monopolies—United
States—Congresses. I. Dalton, James A., ed. II. Levin, Stanford L., ed.
III. Southern Illinois University, Edwardsville, IV. Title.
HD2795.C62   338.8'2'0973   74-17111
ISBN 0-669-96529-4

Copyright © 1974 by D.C. Heath and Company.

All rights reserved. No part of this publication may be reproduced or
transmitted in any form or by any means, electronic or mechanical,
including photocopy, recording, or any information storage or retrieval
system, without permission in writing from the publisher.

Published simultaneously in Canada.

Printed in the United States of America.

International Standard Book Number: 0-669-96529-4

Library of Congress Catalog Card Number: 74-17111

To June and Sharon

Contents

List of Figures

List of Tables

Preface

Industrial organization economists have few occasions to confer regularly among themselves as do economists in other areas of research. This problem is further accented since research is conducted both in academic institutions and in the government. In view of this, we felt that there might be a latent desire for a gathering for economists to present and discuss both research and practical experience gained in the planning and evaluating of antitrust activity. Therefore, in the fall of 1973 an invitation was sent to many antitrust economists to determine if they would be interested in such a conference and if they would be willing to participate by presenting a paper dealing with some aspect of antitrust.

The response to these letters was positive. Many economists offered to present papers. As a consequence, a Conference in Industrial Organization was held at Southern Illinois University at Edwardsville, April 26-27, 1973. We were fortunate to be able to arrange a program of papers of the highest quality by economists prominent in antitrust research, including economists from both government and academia, along with discussants of equal stature for each of the papers. The theme of each paper focused on some aspect of policy planning in antitrust.

The program began with a talk on current issues in antitrust by Willard Mueller followed by three conference sessions, each comprising two papers and discussions on each paper, in addition to questions and comments from the audience. Howard Dye, William Wait, and George Hay each moderated a session. All of the people in attendance contributed to the conference with their questions and discussion.

The Research and Projects Committee of the School of Business provided the substantial financial support to enable the conference to take place. In addition, we would like to thank Jerome Hollenhorst, James Miller, Paul Sultan, Gilbert Rutman, and Marshall Burak for their advice and support. We would also like to acknowledge invaluable assistance from Sharon Rhodes, Dorothy Ladd, Linda Kapilla, and Francine Marti.

Part I
Introduction

1 Allocative and Distributive Effects of Monopoly

James A. Dalton and Stanford L. Levin

The purpose of this volume is to direct attention toward a rational and comprehensive approach to antitrust policy. Consequently, the focus is on approaches to planning and evaluating antitrust policy, on the implementation of policy, and on the remedies and penalties thereof.

Any debate on the allocation of resources by a public agency must begin by focusing on the net benefits to the public from these expenditures. Thus the efforts of the antitrust agencies—the Federal Trade Commission (FTC) and the Antitrust Division of the Department of Justice—should be directed to restoring competitive vigor in those markets where the payoff per dollar expended is greatest. Beginning economics students are exposed to the proposition that the exercise of monopoly power results in higher prices and lower outputs than the prices and outputs that would be generated under more competitive market conditions. Few would deny that there is monopoly power at the local, regional, and national market levels. Moreover, the empirical evidence overwhelmingly supports the proposition that profit rates and seller concentration are positively related.[1] The higher the profits are, the higher are the prices and the lower are the output levels.

The economic distortions generated by the exercise of monopoly power affect the allocation of resources and the distribution of income. The first part of this presentation will discuss the analytical and empirical ramifications of the allocative and distributive effects. Readers familiar with this analysis may wish to skip to the discussion at the end of the chapter relating to the theme of this volume—namely, the planning, evaluation, and implementation of antitrust policy.

The one effect of monopoly that has received virtually all of the attention of economists, perhaps to the detriment of other important aspects of the problem, is the misallocation of resources. This misallocation can be separated into a price and a cost effect. The traditional method for analyzing the price effect involves welfare triangles and the deadweight welfare loss. However, resource misallocation may no longer be the only major disadvantage of monopoly, if indeed it ever was. Therefore this analysis used by itself as a basis for antitrust decisions, as it often is, probably neglects other important aspects of monopoly from consideration. In addition, the restrictive assumptions accompanying this analysis render it of questionable usefulness when attempting to use it as a basis for antitrust decisions made under conditions often vastly differing from those of the assumptions. As a starting point, however, it is useful to set forth the traditional welfare triangle analysis since much of the analysis in the subsequent chapters uses it as a takeoff.[2]

The price effect can be illustrated initially and intuitively through a simple comparison in Figure 1-1 of competitive industry (C) with monopolistic industry (M). The effects on consumer welfare operate through the transfer of resources from the monopolistic to the competitive industry. The monopolistic price and output are $15 and 5 units, respectively, while price and output in the competitive industry are $8 and 30 units, respectively. If the output of M is to be expanded, resources must be drawn from C. Assume that $4 worth of resources are transferred, resulting in a sacrifice of 1/2 unit of C. The $4 worth of resources results in an additional 4/10 of M when $10 is needed to produce a unit of M. The value of the additional 4/10 of M to consumers is (0.4 x $12) or $4.80, assuming that price had to be reduced to $12 to sell the extra 4/10 M.[3] At the same time, the sacrifice to consumers of C is $4 (0.5 x $8).[4] There is a net gain of $.80 in the value of output as measured by society: $4.80 − $4.00 = $.80.

A consequence of the initial situation was an overallocation to the production of C. Indeed, as long as M is monopolized and barriers to entry are high, entry will not occur sufficient to drive price down to $10, the competitive price.

As long as P_M exceeds the unit cost of production including a normal profit, there will be a net gain from the reallocation of resources from any competitive

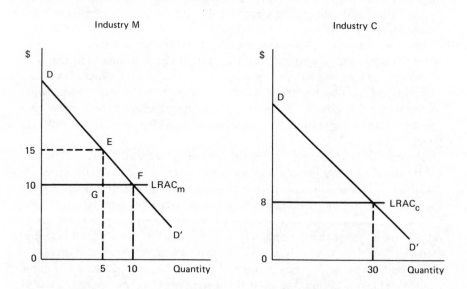

Figure 1-1. Price Effect of Monopoly

to any monopolistic industry. If P_M falls below the competitive price, resources should be transferred from M to C.

This simple analysis suggests that there are gains in value to consumers from the reduction of price in monopolistic industries, *ceterus paribus*. The gain stems from the elimination of the triangle *EFG* in Figure 1-1.[5] The situation can be summarized with the aid of Figure 1-2. Unit costs are assumed to be constant over the relevant ranges of output and the demand curve is assumed to be linear. The subscripts C and M refer to competitive and monopolistic industries. If the industry were monopolized, the profit-maximizing price and output would be P_M and Q_M respectively. P_M reflects the value to the consumer of obtaining an additional unit of the commodity. If the competitive outcome existed, the value of the Q_Mth unit would be P_M but only P_C would have been paid. The latter situation results in a surplus value to the consumer of *EG* or the difference

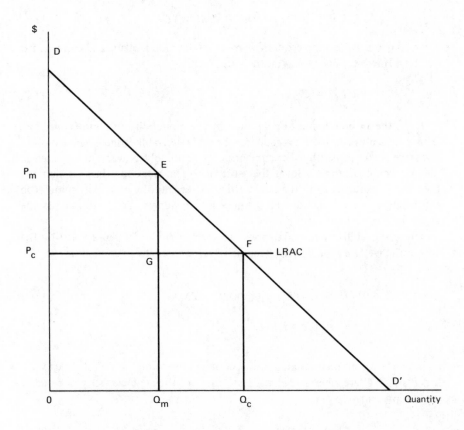

Figure 1-2. Gains From Eliminating Monopoly

between P_M and P_C. Furthermore, the surplus extends to all units sold at P_C except the last or Q_Cth unit. Thus the total consumer surplus is the area of the triangle bounded by the demand curve, the price ordinate, and the horizontal price line.

The consumer surplus under the monopoly structure (CS_M) is the area DEP_M, whereas the surplus under competitive conditions (CS_C) is the area DFP_C. The total loss in consumer surplus (L_T) is

$$L_T = CS_C - CS_M \qquad (1.1)$$

which includes the monopoly profit rectangle $P_M EGP_C$ and the welfare triangle EFG. The welfare triangle represents the surplus that is removed from the consumer by the monopolist but not enjoyed by him. This deadweight or net loss in consumer welfare (L_N) is specified as

$$L_N = (CS_C - CS_M) - (\Pi_M - \Pi_C) \qquad (1.2)$$

where Π_M and Π_C are the economic profits of the monopolistic and competitive markets. However, since long-run $\Pi_C = 0$,

$$L_N = CS_C - CS_M - \Pi_M. \qquad (1.3)$$

L_N is the surplus that is not captured by the monopolist or by the consumer. It thus indicates the total net economic benefits derivable from a reallocation of resources accompanied by the elimination of monopoly power. As indicated in the numerical example above, the existence of a monopoly implies that the transfer of resources from the competitive sector into the monopoly induces an expansion in the production valued more by consumers and a reduction in the production valued less by consumers.[6]

The actual dollar value of the deadweight welfare loss is represented by the area of the welfare triangle. The benefits (B) from reallocation would be

$$B = 1/2 (P_M - P_C)(Q_C - Q_M) \qquad (1.4)$$

or

$$B = 1/2 \, \Delta P \, \Delta Q.[7] \qquad (1.5)$$

Equation (1.5) can be translated into economic dimensions in the following way. If ΔP and ΔQ are small and if signs are ignored, then the elasticity of demand (E) is approximately

$$E = (\Delta Q/Q) \,/\, (\Delta P/P)G. \qquad (1.6)$$

and, through rearrangement,

$$\Delta Q = E (\Delta P/P)Q. \tag{1.7}$$

Since $\Delta P = P(\Delta P/P)$, substituting (1.7) into (1.5) yields

$$B = 1/2 \, PQE \, (P/\Delta P)^2. \tag{1.8}$$

It is accepted that the relative distortion in price is equivalent to the ratio of economic profit to sales: Π/S. Recognizing that PQ is equal to sales, the measure of deadweight welfare loss (or gain through reallocation) is

$$B = 1/2 \, (\frac{\Pi}{S})^2 \, SE.^8 \tag{1.9}$$

There have been several empirical studies of the welfare loss embodied in the triangle. The study most frequently alluded to is that of Harberger,[9] who used Equation (1.9) to compute the welfare loss from monopoly power. He facilitated his computations by assuming $E = 1$. He suggested that the elimination of monopolistic misallocations would yield an increase in welfare of approximately 0.1 percent of GNP. In a trillion dollar economy, the Harberger estimate translates into a welfare loss of $10 billion per year. Swartzman employed somewhat different techniques.[10] Using an $E = 2$, he found that the welfare loss is probably no greater than 0.06 percent of GNP. For the 1972 economy, this would amount to a little more than $6 billion per year. The Harberger-Swartzman efforts thus yield losses of between $30 and $50 per capita.[11]

The Harberger-Swartzman estimates of welfare loss are probably too low because, according to Stigler:

A monopolist does not operate where his marginal revenue is zero. A loosely coordinated set of oligopolies might operate where *industry* marginal revenues is zero, but only because their monopoly power was weak—and it seems undesirable in such a study to *assume* that oligopolies are competitive. In any event, the assumption seems empirically objectionable: most industries have long-run demand curves which are elastic.[12]

A study by Kamerschen[13] employs higher estimates of elasticity. Scherer[14] made adjustments to what he felt were unrealistically low estimates in the Harberger-Swartzman studies and an unrealistic high estimate by Kamerschen. His estimate of monopolistic resource misallocation is 1.5 percent of GNP. (This is felt to be a conservative estimate by Scherer and the present writers.)

The discussion of monopoly-induced welfare losses has focused thus far only on the "price effect." As a monopolist raises price above the competitive price, the deadweight loss occurs. An implicit assumption in constructing empirical estimates of the dollar magnitude of the welfare triangle is that the unit costs present in the monopoly are those that would obtain if the industry were competitive. But such estimates may *understate* welfare losses because of the "cost effect" of monopoly power. If competitive pressures are absent, costs may be higher than those consistent with intense competition. (1) The oligopolistic umbrella may protect high-cost producers that would be eliminated in a competitive market. (2) In the absence of intense pressures on firm profits, management and employees may not discipline themselves to keep costs to a minimum. Thus the higher costs are a source of allocative inefficiency and reduce the consumer surplus.

Figure 1-3 can be used to illustrate the cost effect.[15] If the existing costs, $LRAC_M$, are assumed to be efficient, the welfare loss is the area of the triangle *EFG*. If the economic (competitive) costs are $LRAC_C$ (and are less than $LRAC_M$), the competitive price and output would be P'_C and Q'_C, respectively. The actual welfare triangle would be *EHJ*. Thus the calculated loss in *allocative efficiency* would have understated the true welfare loss by the area *GFHJ* if costs are inflated above competitive levels. Furthermore, a shift from a monopolistic to a competitive structure would induce an added welfare gain through a more efficient use of the monopolistic inputs. This actual loss is indicated by the area of the rectangle $P_C P'_C JG$.[16]

There are several possible sources of inflated costs. The monopoly profits can induce "organizational slack" which, in the absence of pressures to minimize costs, results in waste. This waste could take the form of protecting suboptimal, excess, or obsolete capacity;[17] and management may satisfy its preference for higher income and certain amenities.[18] In addition, wages may be higher, other things being equal, in monopolistic vis-à-vis competitive industries; promotional outlays may be inflated beyond the informative level; and higher costs are associated with delivered pricing systems which encourage cross-hauling and foster nonoptimal plant-location decisions.

Scherer has attempted to adjust the overstatement of competitive costs stemming from the above sources.[19] In conjunction with his earlier estimate of a 1.5 percent deadweight loss, the additional costs bring the total welfare loss to 6.2 percent of GNP.

The above estimate does not include an adjustment for two additional sources of higher cost curves in monopolistic industries. First, costs could be higher due to capitalization of monopoly gains. If firms with monopoly power had been acquired in the past, the value of the monopoly power at the time of the acquisition would be capitalized in the purchase price.[20] The observed economic profit (Π) would be

$$\Pi = \Pi_a - \gamma K \qquad\qquad (1.10)$$

where Π_a is the observed total profit, γ the normal rate of return, and K the invested capital. If K is inflated by the capitalization of acquired monopoly gains, the economic profit would be understated.[21]

Another element of the cost effect is the social cost of the effort to protect the transfer of the economic profits from the hands of the monopolist to those of the consumer and/or a rival firm. In other words, the firm with market power may invest resources to protect or gain economic profits.[22] Large legal staffs and lobbyists may be maintained by the companies; skilled management may invest considerable time in protecting or building a monopoly; existing capacity may not be designed for optimum efficiency but to protect its position. Indeed,

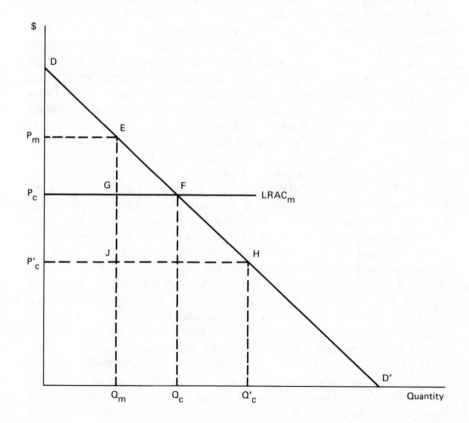

Figure 1-3. Cost Effect of Monopoly

since the size of the potential transfer is large, the costs may be high not only because of the efforts of the successful monopolist, but also because of the resources invested by those who fail.[23]

As a final comment on the analysis of welfare losses, it must be remembered that the estimates of welfare losses, which are not all-inclusive, are only for single years. The losses (benefits) from the exercise (elimination) of monopoly power will flow over time. If the discount rate is 8 percent, an acceptable estimate of the normal rate of return, and the average annual rate of growth is 5 percent, then the present value of the discounted stream of losses (equal to 6 percent of GNP) for the fifteen-year period 1972-87 is approximately $750 billion.

A critical assumption implicit in the foregoing discussion of the effects of monopoly power concerns the "neutralized" effects of monopoly profit.[24] Antitrust authorities concerned with the effects of monopoly must consider both the allocative *and* distributive effects of monopoly power; that is, both the welfare triangle and the monopoly profit rectangle of Figure 1-2. When observing Figure 1-2, one can see that the triangle *EFG* could exist with different levels of monopoly profits.[25] But economists have failed to provide analyses of the effects of monopoly on the distribution of income. Traditionally, economists have argued that they were not in a position to determine whether consumer welfare would rise more than the reduction in welfare of the owners whose income has been redistributed. On the other hand, this should not have prevented economists from providing evidence on the inequality generated by the distribution of monopoly profits over time. Indeed, monopoly profits amount to approximately 3 percent of GNP per year.[26]

The pioneering effort in this area is that of Comanor and Smiley who have focused on the effects of monopoly on the distribution of wealth. The following is a summary of their results.[27] Less than 0.3 percent of all the households control 18.5 percent of total household wealth, of which monopoly profits have contributed between 10.5 and 15.5 percentage points. The wealthiest 2.4 percent of the households account for roughly 40 percent of the wealth. Without the distribution of monopoly profits, their share would be between 16.6 and 27.5 percent—a drop of nearly 50 percent. As one would expect, they found that the 93.3 percent with the least wealth would have improved in wealth in the absence of monopoly. In fact, the net wealth of the "poorest" 28 percent would move from the negative into the positive category.

An alternative measure of benefits would include the redistributive effects of monopoly. The ultimate measure would be a weighted average of the welfare loss triangle EGF and the excess profits rectangle $P_M EGP_C$. The result could be a return from antitrust action encompassing the assumption that the loss of income from consumers due to higher prices was weighed much more heavily by antitrust officials than the reduction in utility to stockholders formerly enjoying the higher profit. The weights placed on the two dimensions would reflect the relative concern of the authorities for deadweight welfare losses versus income redistribution from consumers to monopoly shareholders.

The success of such a program may be limited because of the considerable influence of the industries and companies which could be the targets of the antitrust agencies. The evidence may suggest that an antitrust case should be brought against an ITT, a GM, or the automobile industry. However, since the decisions are made in the political arena, the proposed actions may be rejected.

Large conglomerates, oligopolists, and multinational firms wield tremendous influence beyond the sphere of their respective industrial activities. Of late, one has been reminded repeatedly that such companies exert influence on public policy through their political contributions, lobbyists, lawyers, and former/future employees. The resulting political influence can be used to insulate their market power from attack by regulatory authorities[28] (and from domestic and foreign competition). This mosaic is certainly at odds with the hypothetical operation of our economy and political system.

Nevertheless, these noneconomic considerations should not be included in the calculus of the antitrust economist as policy advisor. Not only do such aspects defy quantification, but also they are not the concern of an economist as economist. Rather, they are the concern of the economist as a member of society. The solution appears to lie in the regulatory process itself rather than at the input stage.[29]

It has been suggested that because of economic theory, economists find it easier to recommend against rather than for implementation of a policy proposal. The cause of this asymmetric influence stems from the need to simplify reality when constructing economic models. William Baumol has suggested that because the model's representativeness may be suspect, the economists may lack confidence in policy proposals developed from the theory.[30]

The experience of many economists appears to suggest that it is easier to argue against rather than for policy proposals. But there is one area in which economists have been arguing forcefully for changes in public policy; industrial organization economists have been arguing for thrusts into new areas of antitrust policy. Whereas there is a lack of unanimity of opinion regarding the direction of antitrust policy, there appears to be a basic agreement that the direction of antitrust policy should be altered and the implementation made more forceful.

The major focus of this volume is on the evaluation of the processes involved in an antitrust action—policy planning, enforcement, and penalties and remedies. Part II focuses on policy planning by the antitrust agencies and contains a jointly authored chapter by H. Michael Mann and James W. Meehan. The third part assesses the enforcement activities of the anti-trust agencies and contains chapters by Leonard W. Weiss and Richard O. Zerbe. In Part IV, dealing with penalties and remedies, there are again two chapters, one by Michael Glassman, the other by William Breit and Kenneth G. Elzinga. The final section presents an overview of the antitrust process with a chapter by Willard F. Mueller. With the exception of the last chapter and this introductory chapter, each chapter is accompanied by a commentary written by a respected economist.

Chapter 2, by Mann and Meehan, has as its central theme the proper allocation of resources by antitrust agencies. In the early part of the chapter, Mann and Meehan outline a conceptual framework for determining where the largest social gain from antitrust activity lies. The model is based on the deadweight welfare loss concept outlined earlier in this chapter. Rather than elaborate on the basic concepts of the model, they evaluate its utility for planning purposes in light of weaknesses in the model and the data and of recent criticism of the framework's presumption. The second major section of their chapter presents speculation on the probable success of policy planning based on criteria of economic efficiency. They are pessimistic regarding the likelihood that consumer welfare will be the prime concern of the decisionmakers and legal staffs in the antitrust arena.

Weiss estimates the gain to consumers from antitrust actions by the Antitrust Division in Chapter 3. Using data from Antitrust Division cases for 1968-70, he estimates gains from prosecution in ten areas encompassing collusion, mergers, structural cases, and leverage. A secondary focus of this chapter is on the deadweight loss associated with monopoly power. He concludes that the distributive or allocative gains by themselves exceeded the costs of litigation in each of the areas considered.

In Chapter 4, Zerbe has employed opinions in major antitrust cases in an effort to determine the quality of economic analysis in antitrust. Zerbe's analysis leads him to conclude that antitrust opinions as a whole have not been sound. These opinions generated several observations: prosecutors and judges have ignored economic theory, competitors have been favored at the expense of competition, and even with a government victory, the courts failed to offer adequate remedies.

In Chapter 5, Glassman focuses on the real costs that society must bear if good economic analysis is absent or ignored in the selection of cases for litigation and in designing the appropriate remedy. Glassman, with the aid of several cases, suggests that without economic input in the planning of cases and the shaping of remedies, the act of "winning" a case may be fruitless.

The primary focus by Breit and Elzinga in Chapter 6 is on the efficiency of each antitrust penalty regarding its deterrence impact, social cost, and the likelihood of avoiding bureaucratic inefficiency. Their analysis prompts the conclusion that the instruments of antitrust enforcement be severely reduced and that the sole weapon should be a severe financial penalty for antitrust violators.

In the final chapter, Mueller paints a bleak picture of the antitrust scene. He believes the areas requiring action are the problems associated with large domestic and multinational conglomerate corporations, the restructuring of oligopolistic industries, and reforms in the antitrust agencies. Mueller discusses the facets of each problem and outlines appropriate courses of action.

**Part II
Policy Planning**

2 Policy Planning for Antitrust Activities: Present Status and Future Prospects

H. Michael Mann and James W. Meehan, Jr.

The purpose of this chapter is to examine the effort being made at the Federal Trade Commission (FTC) to allocate its resources so as to maximize social benefit. This commitment, now institutionalized in an Office of Policy Planning and Evaluation, clearly provides a vehicle for dealing with the persistent criticism that the FTC is immersed in matters of little "public importance."[1] The central issue raised by this indictment is how the FTC should determine which matters promise large social gains and which do not. Over the last year and a half, economists and lawyers at the FTC have addressed themselves to this question. The next section of the chapter will briefly outline the conceptual framework, with its heavy emphasis on allocative efficiency, for planning policy approaches to antitrust activities.[2] The flaws in the theoretical models and in the data that must be used will be discussed along with some recent writings questioning the presumptions of this framework. Lastly, there is speculation about whether a policy planning effort that gives important weight to considerations of allocative efficiency will succeed.

An essential task of the Commission is to encourage effective competition in the marketplace. The cost to consumers of departures from competitive equilibrium can be estimated, at least in theory, by the familiar deadweight welfare loss equation: $W = 1/2\ PQet^2$, where PQ is industry sales, e is elasticity of demand, and t is extent to which price exceeds unit cost, including the opportunity cost of capital.[3] These computations provide a way of ranking all industries with respect to the welfare loss created.[4] This is, of course, only the beginning. Various refinements are called for to give the model greater practical use. Two important refinements are: (1) the multiplication of the welfare loss by an estimate of the probability of success from an effort to introduce greater competition so that a measure of expected benefit is obtained; (2) revision of the basic equation to recognize that there will be only partial recovery of the welfare loss in most instances and that the Commission's principal antitrust effort tries to prevent additional welfare losses arising from movements away from the industry's present price-output combination—for example, a horizontal merger.

Conceivably, the end product of this undertaking could be a matrix. The

The views expressed in this chapter do not necessarily reflect the official views of the Federal Trade Commission.

vertical would list industries and the horizontal would list various categories for Commission action: monopoly, merger, price discrimination, vertical restrictions, and reciprocity, to name some. The matrix's cells would contain a calculation of estimated net benefits (benefit minus cost of obtainment). Such a scheme does appear to have a quality of a "delusion of grandeur." There are, at present, two severe limitations to the development of a rigorous policy-planning model. First, there are not enough good data to measure welfare losses for more than a handful of industries. The welfare loss equation requires an estimate of excess[5] profit to sales for the firms in a relevant economic market.

Profitability calculations do not exist for meaningful economic markets. Industry profitability can be computed for the Internal Revenue Service's minor industries, but these are too aggregative to fit the definition of a theoretical industry: one in which all sellers produce substitute products and sell them to a common group of buyers and exclude all sellers not fitting this description. The commonly used industry is the Standard Industrial Classification System's four-digit industry, although this level of detail varies, sometimes considerably, from the boundaries of an economic market. But there are no profit data for these groupings, and attempts to assign firms on the basis of their most important four-digit activity in order to generate profitability measures have foundered because of the great diversification of most of our large corporations.[6]

The second hindrance to the development of the matrix is the state of economic theory. In order to estimate the incremental welfare loss which may occur from some particular practice, two pieces of information are needed. First, knowledge is needed regarding the extent to which concentration and barriers to entry will change from their present levels. Second, given levels of concentration and of barriers to entry, it is necessary to know how a particular anticompetitive practice will enhance agreements on a noncompetitive price. Knowledge about these would permit determining the change in the current welfare loss caused by the practice.[7] The obvious difficulty with this procedure is that, with the possible exception of a horizontal merger, how much certain behavior will change the allocative performance of an industry or even the direction of change cannot be predicted. Unanimity is lacking in the profession about whether certain forms of conduct, price discrimination, reciprocity, and conglomerate mergers, to name some, are procompetitive—decreasing price toward competitive levels—or are anticompetitive—allowing established firms to move, or hold, price further away from the competitive level.

Recognition of these serious drawbacks introduces considerable caution into how much useful advice about the allocation of its resources can be given to the Commission. However, the basic propositions of the model remain: that social benefit is best conceived in terms of deadweight welfare loss and that a key structural variable affecting the size of these losses is concentration. That is, other things being equal, the model will direct the Commission's attention toward industries with high concentration or industries with rapidly increasing concentration because economic theory and a great deal of evidence[8] leads one to expect that departures from competitive equilibrium, and consequently welfare losses, are tied to levels of concentration.

This structural focus of the model faces two kinds of criticism. The first is that recent evidence calls into question the emphasis on a link between concentration and allocative inefficiency. The findings of recent research suggest that: (1) there is no connection between concentration and allocative inefficiency;[9] (2) if a positive relationship exists, the deadweight loss will dissipate without antitrust action;[10] and (3) if a positive relationship exists, it is potentially the result of a socially desirable phenomenon such as economies of scale.[11] The first two call for the end to the kind of model being constructed. The third advises caution in the advice given the Commission about the employment of its antitrust resources because of tradeoffs among various dimensions of performance.

The second basic criticism argues that, although the goal of the model is sound, identification of industries which restrict output is done best by observation of conduct rather than structure.[12] These two sets of criticism will be discussed in turn.

There is no doubt that any empirical test of the relationship between concentration and profitability is hindered by a variety of liabilities, the most notable of which is poor data.[13] All the hindrances, however, tend to work in the same direction: to make it difficult to reject the null hypothesis that there is no relationship between concentration and profitability. Yet, in one count of thirty-two tests, all but one[14] find that seller concentration has a positive, but weak, impact on profitability. This evidence, especially since it reflects a wide range of sample sizes, time periods, and data led one scholar to state: "In general we can probably conclude that any relationship between profit and concentration, business, and/or output change that we observe are real and are probably badly understated."[15] How, then, should the results of one analysis, that of Yale Brozen's cited above, which calls into question one of the thirty-one tests[16] that found a positive relationship, be weighed? The judgment, which goes to the heart of statistical testing, is that it should not be weighed at all.

Economic theory leads us to expect a positive relationship between concentration and profitability. Empirical tests, then, are expected, using the conventional 0.05 rule, to permit rejection of the null hypothesis 95 out of 100 times and a failure to reject 5 in 100 times. Evidence of no relationship in one experiment is not unexpected, especially when contrasted with the nearly unanimous findings favoring rejection of the null hypothesis.[17] The evidence for the structuralist underpinnings to the policy-planning model remains convincing in the sense that the odds are less than 5 in 100 that the thirty-one tests would have observed a positive relationship between concentration and profitability by chance.

It would be comforting if Brozen's analysis, cited above, unambiguously suggested that the high profitability observed in highly concentrated industries was a short-lived phenomenon attributable to temporary advantages derivable from economies of scale or innovational activity and that market growth and the spread of knowledge about the efficiency of large-scale operation and about the innovations to actual and potential competitors will dissipate the above competitive returns. Brozen's investigation does not appear to support this hypothesis. Rather, it seems to demonstrate the sensitivity of group averages to the movement of a few observations, particularly when samples are small, as a close look at the three studies he reviews shows.[18]

The closeness of the means for Bain's sample of industries with concentration above 70 percent and for those with concentration below 70 percent in 1957-58 as opposed to 1936-40 is largely explained by substantial rises for six of the unconcentrated twenty-one industries,[19] not the group which is the focus of Brozen's argument. The decline in the average profitability for George Stigler's seventeen concentrated industries between 1953-57 and 1962-66 is due almost entirely to sharp decreases in five industries.[20] And the drop in the average profitability of those concentrated industries with high barriers to entry between 1950-60 and 1961-66 in Michael Mann's work is nearly totally attributable to a steep decline for two of the eight observations in that class.[21]

The changes over time observed by Brozen among concentrated industries are too dependent upon the happenings in a few cases to be a convincing demonstration that high concentration and high barriers to entry are not critical elements in permitting firms to engage in persistent monopolistic pricing, especially in circumstances where "high prices may induce high costs, perhaps because they protect suboptimal, excess, or obsolete capacity, perhaps because of internal or union-induced incentives to pay high wages, or perhaps because of managerial preferences for certain expenses."[22] There is certainly no reason to presume that decreases in profitability are a sign of intensified price competition as opposed to an upward shift of the cost curve, unless concentration and barriers to entry are falling as well. Brozen makes no such claim.

As a guide for action, the policy-planning model is limited by its emphasis on one dimension of performance—allocative efficiency. A large welfare loss may occur along with a superb record of innovation, a better adaptation to risk, or a full exploitation of economies of scale. It clearly may not be to society's net benefit to bring antitrust action in such circumstances. This contention certainly has merit and brings into focus Oliver Williamson's admonition: "a sensitivity to variance as well as average tendencies is important. Enforcement officials, whose natural posture is one of advocacy, may need to be cautioned in this regard lest empirical results be 'used' with excessive zeal."[23] Caution, therefore, is advisable, but not to the point of inaction, because the evidence in favor of a substantial deficiency in pricing performance being more than offset by superiority in other areas is not very convincing. High concentration generally does not seem to be dictated by the imperative of efficient scale relative to market size[24] or of adaptation to a risky environment.[25] Very little is known about market structure's impact on progressiveness because actual records of innovation cannot (or have not) been compared to what could have been. Nevertheless, it seems to be a common judgment that high concentration is not necessary to insure a satisfactory degree of progress.[26]

Thus a review of some recent work does not indicate an alteration in the structuralist foundation of the policy-planning model. It is a sound presumption that high levels of concentration and rapid increases in concentration are going to be associated with welfare losses which should not be ignored because they will turn out to be temporary or more than offset by superior performance in other dimensions. This judgment does not preclude recognition of genuine exceptions. It should be understood that policy planning only points toward areas where the competitive process seems deficient. That is only the beginning of a careful assessment of whether the Commission can, or should, take action.

Posner rejects the notion that the policy-planning model should highlight industries with high concentration or with rapid increases in concentration as candidates for the use of the Commission's investigatory and possibly litigating resources. This is partly due to his acceptance of Brozen's work, reviewed above. He further argues, though, that there is a consensus about the kind of characteristics which will cause serious losses in economic efficiency: fixed relative market shares, exchanges of price information, regional price variations, identical bids, price-output and capacity changes at the formation of the cartel, retail price maintenance, declining market share of the leaders, and the amplitude and fluctuations of price changes.[27] As Posner recognizes, there is a very elusive quality to most of these criteria. There are several interpretations other than price fixing and output restriction that might explain the data collected about the above characteristics. In fact, given the state of economic theory, observations about behavior just do not have any certain connection with noncompetitive pricing and the resultant output restriction.[28]

To expend time attempting to collect information about each item on Posner's list of characteristics in order to sort out important from unimportant markets for attention would be an immense undertaking with questionable benefit. Market structure, particularly as measured by the concentration ratio, is theoretically and empirically a better and more certain predictor of the likelihood of anticompetitive performance. Even if welfare losses cannot be computed with any precision, it is sensible for the Commission to presume that the consumer interest is served by worrying about high levels of, and instances of rapidly increasing, concentration. The issue, however, is whether allocative efficiency will be accorded any weight in decisions about where to direct enforcement resources.

There appears to be a consensus that the enforcement of the antitrust laws has been primarily concerned "with complaints filed by affected business firms seeking protection of their own individual interests."[29] An alternative goal, offered by a number of economists and lawyers,[30] including the authors,[31] is that the enforcement of the antitrust laws ought to be primarily concerned with economic efficiency. Yet the antitrust agencies continue to pursue the same type of cases they have followed in the past. The issues, then, are why the antitrust agencies have failed to be guided by the goal of economic efficiency and what hope there is for getting them to employ a policy-planning model which uses economic efficiency as the main criterion for allocating the antitrust agencies' scarce resources.

The tradition of a growing body of literature[32] attempts to explain the behavior of economic organizations[33] by the use of a model which assumes that the decisionmakers in these organizations maximize their utility subject to some set of constraints. First, the model will be applied to the Federal Trade Commission.[34] Then the model will be applied to the Department of Justice because Posner predicts that the Antitrust Division of the Department of Justice will perform better than the Commission in the antitrust area. He recommends that the Commission be abolished and its antitrust responsibilities be turned over to the Antitrust Division.[35] This recommendation will be evaluated.

Recently, an increasing number of economists have begun to explain the performance of the regulatory commissions by examining the incentives influencing regulators' judgments.[36] In particular, they assume that the regulators maximize their utility function subject to constraints externally imposed upon them by the political process and the laws governing the agency. Ross Eckert has suggested that the regulator's utility is usually a function of such items as his future stream of income, the size of the budget of the agency, the ease of managing an agency, his personal prestige within the regulator's chosen profession, and his view of the public interest.[37] Eckert also suggests that these constraints become operative by making it more costly to pursue some behavior patterns and making it more rewarding to pursue other behavior patterns. The regulator will engage in more of a particular kind of behavior the lower the cost and the greater the rewards of pursuing that kind of behavior.[38]

An examination of the incentive structure of the Commission is necessary in order to predict how the FTC will behave with respect to antitrust policy. Posner[39] has suggested that since the FTC is responsible to Congress, it is likely to be very sensitive to the interest and complaints of members of Congress. Since congressional members represent small districts, and since each congressional district will have its share of small- and medium-sized retail stores, gas stations, auto dealers, auto parts jobbers, wholesalers, and so forth, they are likely to be very sensitive to the interests of small businesses.

Congressmen, on the other hand, are much less sensitive to the interest of the consumer. The reason is rather straightforward. Voters are likely to lobby quite vigorously for or against a particular action if that action affects an activity from which they earn a substantial part of their income. Therefore the voter as a producer will lobby quite hard for his interests, whereas the voter's interest as a consumer is likely to be so diffuse that the effect of any particular action directed at his purchases as a consumer is likely to be very small.[40] Another factor that works in favor of protecting the voter's interest as a producer rather than as a consumer is that it is less costly to organize voters to protect their interests as producers since they are likely to belong to a trade association or a union made up of a number of voters, all of whom share the same interest. Voters in their roles as consumers are likely to belong to many clubs and organizations that have very divergent interests, and therefore the cost of organizing a sufficient number of them to have an impact on Congress is bound to be high.

The congressional pressure to produce certain kinds of antitrust actions coincides with the incentives of the commissioners and the staff. Since all of the recent commissioners[41] have been lawyers and since a good number of them have returned to private practice, it is likely that they place heavy weight on their reputation within the legal profession. A reasonable prediction, therefore, is that this leads commissioners to be conservative in the kinds of cases which they institute, that is, the cases would not be novel, but rather follow along rather closely with existing interpretations of the law. This is not to say that the commissioners would not like to initiate a couple of important or precedent setting cases, but the precedents would only be modest extensions of the existing interpretations of the law rather than a radical departure.[42] Therefore, as long as congressmen put no pressure on the commissioners to pursue a more liberal interpretation of the law,[43] they will probably stay close to established interpretations of the law. This means that the Commission will bring cases primarily concerned with conduct and unfair practices and therefore will seldom confront directly the effect of market power on consumers.

Given the Commission incentives, the staff has little alternative but to follow the same pattern of cases because they will not be rewarded for suggesting actions which do not conform with those that maximize the utility function of the commissioners. In addition, it appears that the weight the staff puts on various elements in their utility function is not much different from the factors and weights employed by the commissioners. Information about staff turnover indicates that in the last four years, the average attorney remains at the Commission 3.8 years and approximately 20 percent of the legal staff turns over each year.[44] The attorney who plans to enter private practice after his service at the FTC will be rewarded for his trial experience and "not the social payoff from [his] . . . litigation."[45] Cases involving the questions of economic efficiency are usually complex, and therefore there is usually a long time lag from the beginning of an investigation to complaint and then to trial.[46] An innovative monopoly case may be of some value to a young lawyer's future stream of income, but if he works exclusively on one of these cases and gets no trial experience, its value will be limited. The tradeoff would probably work in favor of the trial experience and against the monopoly case.[47]

Besides the barrier of incentives, considerations of allocative efficiency are apt to be accorded small weight because it is especially difficult to measure the output of the commission if the output is measured with respect to its impact on economic efficiency.[48] Since the evaluation of output in terms of gains in economic efficiency is going to be imprecise and complicated, Congress will judge output in terms of numbers of cases.[49] The emphasis on numbers, in turn, puts pressure on the Commission to increase its activity. Since efficiency cases are likely to involve complex economic issues, they take longer to prepare and to litigate with the consequent reduction in the number of cases, assuming a fixed budget.

It appears then that even if the technical problems associated with development of a rigorous policy-planning model were overcome, there are serious obstacles to implementation at the Commission. Can the Antitrust Division be expected to utilize such a model?

Since the assistant attorneys general usually have the same background as FTC commissioners, we must assume that their utility functions are similar. Therefore any difference in performance will occur because the constraints operative on the Antitrust Division are different than the constraints operative on the FTC. These constraints will be examined in an effort to determine how different, if any, they are. If they are different, the Antitrust Division will give greater attention to economic efficiency than to protecting competitors. If the constraints are not significantly different, the Antitrust Division's performance should be not much different from that of the FTC.

There are two differences between the FTC and the Antitrust Division that might lead to a different antitrust output. First, the Antitrust Division is directly responsible to the President rather than to Congress. This, according to Posner, is likely to make the Antitrust Division much bolder since "major policy initiatives are rarely taken without the backing of the President."[50] Responsibility to the President is important only if the President would give greater weight to the consumers' interest than to producers' interests. Although it could be argued that congressmen represent small districts with parochial interests and the President represents the whole country, the belief is that producers are more efficient in lobbying for their interests than consumers, and therefore these interests are likely to receive more weight than those of the consumer. Furthermore, since the Antitrust Division must have its budget approved by Congress, it inevitably will give some weight to the complaints of congressmen. The Nader Study Group, which studied the Antitrust Division's enforcement of the antitrust laws, found that:

The Division also answers Congressional correspondence, some 650 letters per year. . . . The Official Manual stresses that "All Congressional correspondence must be acknowledged or answered in full within 48 hours." Policy Planning Director Donnem explains why: "They can destroy us with the stroke of a pen."[51]

In short, responsibility to the President does not exempt the Antitrust Division from the same congressional pressures exerted on the FTC.

The second important difference between the FTC and the Antitrust Division lies in the laws that both agencies enforce. The Antitrust Division has sole responsibility for the Sherman Act and the FTC has sole responsibility for Section 5 of the FTC Act. Both agencies share responsibility for Sections 2, 3, 7, and 8 of the Clayton Act although the Antitrust Division has left the enforcement of Section 2, as amended by the Robinson-Patman Act, to the FTC.

It might be that since the primary concern of the Sherman Act is to prevent losses in economic efficiency[52] and the primary purpose of the Robinson-Patman Act is to protect competitors, the Antitrust Division will be likely to bring cases concerned with economic efficiency, whereas the FTC probably will bring cases concerned with protecting competitors. Although the enforcement of different laws will probably have some impact on the performance of the respective agencies, it is not likely that there will be a significant effect. The reason is that Congress also demonstrated a concern with values other than economic efficiency in the debates about passage of the Sherman Act.[53] And it appears that the courts, especially the Warren Court, have recognized Congress's concern and given a very large weight to the protection of competitors. Thomas Kauper, currently the Assistant Attorney General in Charge of Antitrust, has argued:

The Court has often seemed less concerned with economically necessary level of rivalry within the market than with what may be described as the rights of the individual firms which comprise the market: Their independence and right to be treated as other firms are treated have become values to be protected as ends in themselves.[54]

The courts' interest in protecting competitors is found not only in its findings in Robinson-Patman cases, but in Sherman Act Section 1 and 2 cases, and in Clayton Act Section 7 cases. Almarin Phillips cites the doctrine in *American Tobacco*[55] to demonstrate that injury to competitors or hotel meetings are sufficient to find a violation of the Sherman Act, but injury to consumers is not even a necessary condition to apply the Sherman Act.[56] Kauper argues that a number of cases involving vertical price constraints, tie-in agreements, and territorial restrictions were decided on the basis of injury to competitors without considering the affect of these conduct patterns on economic efficiency.[57] A number of commentators have cited the *Brown Shoe*[58] and the *Vons' Grocery*[59] cases to demonstrate that the courts have been primarily concerned with protecting competitors in Section 7 cases, even those involving horizontal mergers.[60]

Given the emphasis placed on the protection of competitors by the courts, especially the Supreme Court, and assuming that an Assistant Attorney General in Charge of Antitrust is reluctant to see his cases overturned by the courts, the prediction is that the Antitrust Division would file cases that have an emphasis on injury to competitors rather than an emphasis on economic efficiency.[61]

Two final considerations insure that the Division's record will be similar to the FTC's. The first is that the incentives for the legal staff at Antitrust Division are not any different from the incentives of the legal staff at the FTC. That is, the young lawyers are primarily interested in getting trial experience[62] rather than instituting cases concerned with consumer interests. Thus the staff will bring cases where the law is well defined: conduct cases involving some evidence of intent to injure competitors, rather than cases concerned with economic efficiency that are likely to take five or six years to get into court. The second is that, like the FTC, it is difficult to measure the gains to society from cases brought by the Antitrust Division. Therefore Congress, and consequently the Antitrust Division, puts heavy emphasis on the "numbers game." The Ralph Nader Study Group indicated that Representative John Rooney of the House Appropriations Subcommittee always asks about the number of cases and the win and loss record, but never asks about the impact of the Division's cases.[63] Since budget approval is critical, it is likely that the Division will put greater emphasis on the number of cases and the won/loss record rather than the effect of the case on economic efficiency.[64] Such criteria will encourage traditional cases rather than novel cases concerned with economic efficiency.[65]

The above analysis suggests that although there are some differences in the constraints affecting the Antitrust Division, there is no reason to expect a significant difference between the two agencies. Abolition of the FTC will not end the effort to protect competitors. It will only shift the focus to the Antitrust Division with the result that more Robinson-Patman enforcement will be substituted for Sherman Act litigation.

It is clear that policy planning requires the measurement of the social benefit achievable from alternative courses of action. Conceptually, this task is possible, although there are severe technical problems to be overcome. The effort will inevitably place heavy weight upon allocative efficiency as a primary goal of antitrust policy and will emphasize the role of high market concentration in the creation and maintenance of deadweight losses.

The success of the undertaking does not turn upon the fact that recent research indicates that high concentration is not connected with allocative inefficiency, that deadweight losses will dissipate without antitrust action, or that allocative inefficiency is more than compensated for by the superior performance of oligopolies in other dimensions. The evidence underlying these contentions is simply not persuasive. Rather, success will depend upon whether there are any incentives to support the policy-planning undertaking and to utilize the results at the Federal Trade Commission and the Antitrust Division. The theorizing, sprinkled with some evidence, suggests that there are serious obstacles.[66] The combination of the more easily organized producer interests,

Library
I.U.P.
Indiana, Pa,

25 338.82 C76a
C. 1

the incentives of federal trade commissioners and assistant attorneys general in charge of antitrust and their staffs to be conservative with respect to marked departures from established avenues of antitrust litigation, and the difficulty of measuring antitrust output in terms of efficiency gains, makes success unlikely for a bold undertaking in behalf of rigorous policy planning at the Commission. If directing antitrust toward areas which will most benefit the consumer is costly to the policymaker and confers little or no rewards, one can hardly expect antitrust to depart from its historical role of settling equity disputes among businessmen rather than promoting consumer welfare.

Comment

John M. Blair

These remarks will be directed toward only one part of the chapter by Mann and Meehan: their discussion of the loss to consumers of departures from competition as measured by the "deadweight welfare loss equation." With some of their qualitative arguments, there is no disagreement: for example, the deplorable tendency to evaluate performance in terms of number of cases, the desire of many antitrust lawyers to avoid novelty, and the sensitivity of members of Congress to the interests of small business. With others there is disagreement: for example, their repeated assumption that an inherent conflict exists between cases that benefit small business and those that benefit consumers and a corollary conflict between cases involving conduct and those that promote competition. The opportunities for conflict are certainly present in the law, but they can be avoided. It should be the function of the economic staff of the Federal Trade Commission to see to it that cases brought involving conduct (which represent most of the Commission's opportunities for action) not only benefit small business but also promote competition generally. There is no shortage of such possible cases, but it takes constant harassment by the economic staff to see that they are the ones brought.

This writer has no quarrel with the authors' fundamental objective; the orientation of antitrust enforcement toward minimizing departures from competitive equilibrium.[1] But while strongly supporting the need for planning antitrust, there are some questions regarding the workability, relevance, and conceptual propriety of the fundamental approach proposed by Mann and Meehan for this purpose, the Harberger deadweight welfare loss equation: $W = 1/2\,PQet^2$ (where W is the welfare loss, PQ industry sales, e elasticity of demand, and t the margin between price and full costs).[2] For the purpose for which it is intended—that is, of providing a guide for antitrust enforcement in terms of cost to consumers—the formula suffers from four types of deficiencies. These deficiencies are not peculiar to this particular formula alone but are applicable to many of the attractive but simplistic models occupying the economic journals today.

Mann and Meehan fully recognize the inadequacy of data for a critical component of their formula. This is the absence of profit data for meaningful economic markets, a problem which each passing conglomerate merger renders more difficult of solution. As Mann has emphasized elsewhere, this problem would be met at least in part by a systematic divisional financial reporting program, the prospects for which he regards as "encouraging."[3] But even if such a program were introduced, problems would still remain. Thus under any conceivable classification system, the profit data obtained for most product-line

27

categories will encompass nonsubstitutable products and thus in varying degrees be unsuitable for measuring the welfare loss occasioned by departure from competitive equilibrium in particular markets. Moreover, with its vulnerability to antitrust depending so greatly on the profitability shown by its various divisions, a multiline company will have a powerful incentive to minimize profitability in its more profitable divisions by the use of "creative accounting" (e.g., using profitability as the basis of allocating the company's total overhead costs).

There is another area of data inadequacy not commented on by Mann and Meehan—the elasticity of demand. Even in the case of consumer goods such as automobiles, the authorities differ on the proper methodology to be employed, the time period to be covered, and the type of data to be used.[4] For products with derived demand such as steel, the problems are even more complex. It is hard, for example, to reconcile the general consensus of a very low price elasticity for steel with the fact that between 1955 and 1968—both years of high economic activity—industrial production rose by 71 percent while the available domestic supply of steel (domestic shipment plus imports minus exports) increased by only 32 percent. Illustrative of the methodological difficulties is the interesting question of how much greater the increase in the domestic supply of steel and how much less the increase in the supply of competitive materials (plastics, fiberglass, etc.) would have been had the price increase of the former and the price decrease of the latter been less. The "solution" by Mann and Meehan is to ignore the problem by assuming for each industry the same coefficient of elasticity, unity.

In measuring "excess profits," that is, net income minus the amount necessary for a competitive return, the welfare loss equation requires, according to the authors, a figure representing the "extent to which price exceeds full costs, including the opportunity cost of capital." But they do not explain why a formula designed to yield an estimate of the cost to consumers of the departure from competition should itself depart from competitive price theory by employing the margin between price and full costs rather than the margin between price and variable or direct costs. Certainly, it has long been recognized that the seller of a nondifferentiated product in a free competitive market model has neither any selling costs nor any occasion to incur them. As Edward H. Chamberlin observed, "selling costs are very naturally passed over in competitive theory since they are at odds with the assumptions of pure competition. . . ."[5] Why, for example, should "excess profit" be defined in such a way as to exclude automatically such unnecessary and wasteful costs as annual model changes in automobiles, promotion by detail men in drugs, and the expenses of Washington lobbyists in oil. Moreover, what is the opportunity cost for capital in a world where the rates of return on capital reflect varying degrees of control of the market.

It is no criticism of the technique to recognize that any econometric model, to be operational, must exclude some (usually many) possibly relevant variables.

But a model does become subject to valid criticism if what it excludes are variables of critical importance to the issue at hand. By taking them as given, the deadweight welfare loss equation in effect excludes two variables of very great importance to consumer welfare. It assumes, in effect, that the level of costs and the pace of invention and innovation will be the same under monopoly as under competition. On the one hand, it can be argued that costs will tend to be lower under competition than under monopoly—that competition, in effect, exerts a constant downward pressure on costs. And, similarly, that the rate of invention and innovation will be more rapid under competition, since (a) the smaller enterprise is more conducive to the creative temperament, (b) there are more potential adoptors, and (c) the active rivalry among competing firms makes them more interested in—and willing to adopt—new products and processes. On the other hand, it can be contended that, because of economies of scale and the opportunity to secure managerial economics, costs will be lower under monopoly, and similarly, that inventors and innovation will proceed more rapidly under monopoly because research today requires the expensive laboratories and teams of specialists that only the largest companies can afford.

Determining the welfare cost of a loss of competition necessitates an evaluation of these conflicting arguments. Happily, such an evaluation can now be based on a very considerable body of information, the very existence of which makes almost incomprehensible the authors' statement: "We know very little about market structure's impact on progressiveness because actual records of innovation cannot (or have not) been compared to what could have been." But actual records of innovation by large companies have been compared to actual records of small companies and independent inventors, and the results certainly do not support the assertion, "We know very little about market structure's impact on progressiveness. . . ." Perhaps the real problem is not the absence of information but, owing to its very nature, the inability to compress it into a single numerical value suitable for handy incorporation into a simplistic mathematical formula.

Like most econometric models, the deadweight welfare loss equation assumes the functions to be continuous: the larger the sales, the higher the elasticity; and the wider the margin between price and full costs, the greater the welfare loss. But nature abounds with phenomena whose functions are discontinuous: water does not tend to boil as temperature moves up toward 212F. nor tend to freeze as it moves down toward 32F. There can be a proclivity but no tendency toward pregnancy. Continuous functions, whether linear or curvilinear, are fundamental to such physical sciences as physics, chemistry, and astronomy, but play a very unimportant role in such other physical sciences as agronomy, anatomy, biology, botany, geology, and pharmacology. In these disciplines the questions of interest are not the extent to which one variable varies with given variations in one or more other variables. In pharmacology, it has been found that the effects of certain drugs are not dose-related. Rather, within broad limits, their effects are the same regardless of the quantity.

Similarly, assumptions of continuity have played virtually no role in the development of the body of theory concerning the economic effects of monopoly. The issue of concern in imperfect competition theory has always been whether there is a significant difference in price behavior between industries which on the one hand are oligopolistic and those which on the other are competitive; for example, do prices of concentrated industries during periods of falling demand tend to decline less than prices of unconcentrated industries, remaining relatively "rigid" or "inflexible"? The point at issue has never been whether differences exist in the price behavior of oligopolistic industries that differ only in the degree to which they are oligopolistic. The focusing of attention on deviations from an actual or inferred central tendency, once the point of oligopoly has been reached, tends merely to divert attention away from the essential question of whether, in general, a significant difference in price behavior exists between the two different types of industries. Under the logic of imperfect competition theory, once the condition has been established that each of a small group of producers accounts for a sufficient proportion of the total output and that his actions can materially affect the price, the argument that further increases in concentration would make for even less price flexibility must rest upon the improbable assumption that each oligopolist will become *progressively* more aware of, and concerned with, his rival's probable reaction to a price cut and thus be progressively more reluctant to make one. Similarly, there is no conceptual reason why price behavior should differ significantly among competitive industries that differ only in the degree to which they are unconcentrated. On theoretical grounds, there is no reason to expect any difference in price behavior as long as the various producers are unable to affect the price significantly by varying their output and therefore have no reason to be concerned with the reactions of their competitors.

In retrospect, it is easy to see how the above remarks could be interpreted as an attack upon model-building per se. They are not so intended. Where the data are adequate and suitable to the purpose at hand, where the concepts employed are appropriate to the issue under examination, where variables critical to the issue are not excluded, and where, if appropriate, the analysis is made in terms of discrete intervals rather than continuous functions, multivariate analysis can be a highly useful tool for most fields of economic inquiry, including the effects of concentration. Indeed, new opportunities for the application of this methodology are being opened up by the "industry-sector" price series being published by the Bureau of Labor Statistics, which for the first time makes possible an exact match between the census concentration ratios and the BLS price indexes.

Another promising area are studies of the relation of concentration to margins above direct costs. Studies of this type by Norman Collins and Lee Preston[6] and by Howard N. Ross[7] have two compelling attributes: (a) comparability of the independent and dependent variables, since both are derived from the same source (the census), and (b) derivation from reports by manufacturers on specific items that largely reflect actual transactions (shipments, wages and salaries, cost of materials and supplies). Careful use of these bodies of data will reveal some of the welfare costs of the departure from competition. But efforts to derive one workable model, which will measure all of these costs or even just the principal costs, are likely to prove about as fruitful (and occasion as much waste of valuable economists' resources) as attempts to quantify the marginal utilities of consumers.

Part III
Enforcement

3

An Analysis of the Allocation of Antitrust Division Resources

Leonard W. Weiss

This is an attempt to evaluate the allocation of resources within the Antitrust Division of the Department of Justice. The project was suggested by recent work by Posner[1] and the Hales[2] and by the author's experience in the Division. The analysis is applied to the broad types of activities in which the division is engaged and is based on many very rough estimates. As a result, the conclusions drawn are bound to be inaccurate in detail and incorrect even in the broad for atypical cases in each category. The considerations introduced seem to be the appropriate ones, however, and the procedure outlined might be useful in evaluating particular cases.

The basic method involves an estimate of the gain to the public from the prosecution of a particular sort of case and an attempt to balance that against the Division's legal resources employed in each such case. The gains to the public from eliminating a monopolistic practice or preventing an anticompetitive change in market structure involve both improvements in economic efficiency and the redistribution of income and wealth. This chapter focuses mainly upon the distributive effects. Some attempt will be made to estimate the effects on allocative efficiency for the broad classes of antitrust action, but such estimates almost certainly understate the efficiency losses due to monopoly. The main effects of antitrust on efficiency may be in reducing the protection that monopolistic structure or practices can offer to high-cost methods of production and distribution,[3] but the gains to the public from eliminating such a shield are not easy to estimate.

The distributive effects of monopolistic practices seem to be one of the major motives for the antitrust laws in any event. It seems doubtful whether Congress gave much if any weight to allocative efficiency when formulating the antitrust laws, while the prevention of large capital gains to those who organized monopolistic cartels or mergers is probably a major concern of the public in its commitment to competition. To the extent that antitrust is thought of as a means of protecting consumers against excessive prices charged by monopolists, it seems appropriate to measure the gains from antitrust in terms of the "excess profits" avoided. From this point of view, the efficiency losses due to monopoly that can be estimated should be added to the distributive effect since they represent additional losses to consumers. Another purpose of the antitrust laws—the maintenance of "fair" business methods—is ignored here. It may be

35

appropriate to revise the final conclusions for those cases where fairness is a major issue.

While the distributive effect is probably the primary motivation for the antitrust laws, a dollar redistributed is not really comparable with a dollar of public expenditure. This chapter first will take the Antitrust Division budget as given and attempt to evaluate its allocation among competing activities on the basis of the distributive effects of those activities. Later, when some attempt to estimate allocative effects of antitrust is made, the more conventional benefit-cost question of whether antitrust is worthwhile can be considered.

The particular classes of antitrust actions considered are listed in the first column of Table 3-1. The analyses in Tables 3-1 through 3-6 are meant to apply to the efforts of the Antitrust Division to enforce existing law. They are not meant to refer to weak cases (e.g., merger cases where concentration is so low that little or no monopolistic effect can be expected) or to cases which are brought primarily for their precedent value, though such cases should be analyzed individually, using the same considerations. The estimated gains from a weak case would be lower than those suggested in Table 3-1. Indeed, some cases may reduce competition (e.g., a suit against a small acquisition which might facilitate an important entrant) or may result in higher costs (e.g., a suit against a horizontal merger among suboptimal firms). The gain to consumers would be negative in such cases. The estimated deterrent effects of a precedent case would be higher than those presented in Table 3-1. Precedent cases might well be worthwhile even where policing cases seemed to yield only small gains.

The specific types of cases envisioned in the ten categories listed in Table 3-1 can be described in more detail. Criminal collusion is meant to include the whole range of conventional per se prohibitions under Section 1 of the Sherman Act. These include price-fixing, market-sharing, bid-rigging, and boycotts.

Civil collusion refers to practices that are illegal under Section 1 but which are not secret so that criminal conspiracy is seldom charged. Such practices are usually easy to detect. Included are various restrictive patent license provisions, resale price maintenance practices, the allocation of territories or classes of customers to distributors by manufacturers, and formal agreements of a sort where illegality has not previously been established, such as the allocation of territories for wholesale sales of power by bulk power producers or agreements among real estate agents on commissions on jointly listed properties. It is almost impossible to exclude precedent-setting cases from this category, so the deterrent effect is high.

Horizontal mergers refer to mergers among firms that sell on the same market. To be a strong case, the merger must be in a concentrated market or in one where there are strong indications that concentration will become serious in the near future. The parties to the merger also must be of at least minimum efficient scale.

Vertical mergers refer to mergers where one firm supplies or could easily supply important inputs of the other from existing facilities. To be a "strong" case, at least one of the markets involved should be concentrated, a large part of one of the two markets should be integrated with the other either as a result of the merger or of a clear trend of which the merger is a part, and there should be clear evidence that nonintegrated firms would be at a serious strategic disadvantage if integration became widespread. Vertical mergers that yield clear-cut social economies, mergers in industries that are already largely integrated, and foothold acquisitions should all be excluded from the class of strong cases.

Potential entry mergers refer to mergers between one of the most likely entrants into a market and a leading firm in the same market. To be a strong case, the affected market should be concentrated, the potential entrant should be one of a very few firms that are much more likely to enter than any others, and the acquired firm should be one of a few leaders. Mergers that yield clear economies and foothold acquisitions would not be strong cases.

"Pure" conglomerate mergers refer to mergers among large firms in markets that are only distantly related. A "strong" case would require a very large firm merging with a leading firm in a concentrated industry. Theoretically, precedent cases should be excluded, but in fact all cases to date have been test cases.

Structural monopoly cases are Section 2 cases where a major purpose is to change market structure. The main cases would be those seeking dissolution or divestiture as part of relief, but the category also includes suits attempting to revise the terms of joint ventures that exclude competitors (e.g., some pipeline cases). This category should be distinguished from Section 2 cases where the remedies sought involve conduct only, since a structural case can seldom have much positive effect on firms not involved, while conduct cases can have extensive deterrent effects. A special category for Section 2 conduct cases was initially investigated, but this proved to be so heterogeneous that even the rough estimates used here were impractical. Certain conduct cases are treated in the leverage category. The remaining fairly small "miscellaneous" category is ignored.

Leverage cases include tying agreements, long-term requirements contracts, and reciprocity practice cases (but not merger cases based on potential tying or reciprocity effect).

Regulation mergers refer to merger cases argued by the Antitrust Division before regulatory agencies such as Penn-Central and Northern Lines before the ICC, ITT-ABC before the FCC, American-Eastern Airlines before the CAB, or public utility holding company act cases before the SEC. Section 7 cases involving regulated industries (e.g., bank mergers) are classified in the four other merger categories.

Regulation-practice cases refer to all other matters argued by the Antitrust Division before the regulatory commissions.

Table 3-1 attempts to estimate the gain to consumers from a successful strong case in each of these categories. At this stage the estimates are expressed as

Table 3-1
Estimated Gains to Consumers from Successful Antitrust Cases

Type of Case	(1) Direct Gain to Consumers as a Share of Annual Sales	(2) Estimated Duration of Effect (Years)	(3) Present Value of Estimated Direct Gain as Share of One Year's Sales	(4) Number of Cases of the Same Size Prevented by a Success (Inc. Case)	(5) Estimated Total Present Value to Consumers of a Successful Case (as Share of This Case Sales)
a) Criminal Collusion	0.025	2	0.048	5	0.240
b) Civil Collusion	0.015	10	0.101	10	1.012
c) Horizontal Mergers	0.072[a]	10	0.486[a]	7	3.402[a]
d) Vertical Mergers	0.036[a]	10	0.243[a]	7	1.701[a]
e) Potential Entry Mergers	0.018[a]	10	0.122[a]	5	0.610[a]
f) Pure Conglomerate Mergers	0.009[a]	10	0.061[a]	5	0.305[a]
g) Structural Monopoly Cases	0.035	10	0.236	0.8	0.189
h) Leverage Cases	0.005	10	0.034	10	0.340
i) Regulation-Mergers	0.072[a]	10	0.486[a]	2	0.972
j) Regulation-Practices	0.025	10	0.169	1	0.169

[a]Proportion of annual sales of acquired firms.

proportions of the annual sales of the markets or firms involved. Some absolute values will be introduced later. Column (1) contains some very rough estimates of the direct gains to consumers from a success. The proportions shown are a little short of being completely arbitrary, but perhaps their relative values can be justified.

Criminal collusion provides a bench mark with some mild empirical basis. The *single* damages collected by the government in the electrical equipment cases ranged from 2 to 11 percent of affected sales with a mean of 8.8 percent.[4] Again, the FTC seemed to show that the Seattle bread conspiracy resulted in the elevation of bread prices by an average of about 12 percent relative to bread prices in other cities in 1956-64.[5] The bleachers conspiracy may have raised prices by 30 percent.[6] These were probably among the more successful conspiracies.[7] Triple damage suits or published FTC studies of collusive pricing are unlikely in cases where collusion is unsuccessful. At any rate, the majority of collusion cases involve small firms in small markets. An estimate of 5 percent of sales will be used for the average collusion case. Antitrust successes that reduce profits will reduce corporate income tax payments as well. Allowing a 50 percent tax rate, the gain to consumer-taxpayers would then be about 2.5 percent of sales during the period of conspiracy as shown in column (1).

The effect of horizontal mergers also has some mild empirical basis. There are numerous studies showing a positive relation between profit and concentration.[8] The most convenient are those where price-cost margins are dependent. They involve regressions of the form:

$$\frac{VS - MC}{VS} = a + bCR_n$$

where VS is value of shipments, MC is marginal cost, and CR_n is the n firm concentration ratio. It follows from this expression that:

$$\Delta \frac{VS - MC}{VS} = b \Delta CR_n$$

Letting VS_a be the shipments of the acquired firm (the smaller of the merger partners), then a horizontal merger where the acquiring firm is among the n largest firms usually increases concentration by[9]

$$\Delta CR_n = \frac{VS_a}{VS}$$

so that

$$\Delta \frac{VS - MC}{VS} = b \Delta CR_n = b \frac{VS_a}{VS}$$

Multiplying through by *VS* gives

$$VS \cdot \Delta \frac{VS - MC}{VS} = bVS_a = \Delta(VS - MC)$$

The gain to consumers from preventing the merger would be approximated by bVS_a.

Preston and Collins, using $n = 4$, find a value for b of 0.144 for all industries selling on broad geographic markets.[10] This figure is used in evaluating horizontal mergers. In column (1) of Table 3-1, it has been halved (0.072) to allow for corporate taxes. This is three times the figure used for criminal collusion, but it should be remembered that the collusion ratio is to be multiplied by the entire sales affected by the agreements while the merger figure is multiplied by the sales of the acquired (i.e., smaller) firms only. To have the same effect on industry margins as that assumed for collusion, a merger would have to increase concentration by 35 points (0.072 x 0.35 = 0.025) or, say, from 30 to 65. It seems plausible that such a drastic change in concentration could make the difference between competitive pricing and effective collusion.[11]

The direct gain to consumers from other types of cases are guesses based largely on the writer's judgment about the economic effect of the practice involved relative to those of collusion and horizontal merger. Civil collusion cases vary widely in effect, some patent cases probably saving the consumer more, and many exclusive territory cases probably saving the consumer less per year than a standard criminal collusion case of the same size. Patent cases represent a minority of the cases in this category, so a figure below 2.5 percent of affected sales was chosen.

The effect of vertical mergers on competition is controversial. Integration between two competitive markets (shoes and shoe stores?) seems unlikely to be harmful. Vertical merger seems more likely to carry anticompetitive effects if at least one of the two markets is concentrated and if nonintegrated producers would be at a serious disadvantage once a large part of output came from integrated producers. Occasional vertical merger races such as those in cement and ready mix or linerboard and cartons suggest that such disadvantages are sometimes compelling. Even then some argue that integration adds nothing to market power though it may hurt individual firms. A number of anticompetitive effects of widespread vertical mergers seem likely in such circumstances, however, Barriers to entry are apt to be increased because of higher capital requirements, because optimal scale for an integrated firm will commonly exceed optimal scale in one of the two markets, and because any special advantages of insiders in either market (patents, ore reserves, consumer loyalties) will thereafter impede entry into both markets. Moreover, large firms in one industry are often the most likely entrants into vertically related industries, so their merger may reduce the threat of entry further. Concentration in at least one of the two markets is apt to increase to accommodate optimal scales in the other market, and it may increase in both markets if some firms are forced out due to their failure to integrate effectively. In some cases, vertical integration permits price discrimination that was less feasible for the nonintegrated firm. Or vertical merger may sometimes enhance market power by transferring oligopoly from a market where experts buy in large lots to a final consumer market with less informed customers who buy in driblets. Most of these concerns apply to mergers combining firms in two concentrated industries as well, but it is often argued that under such circumstances, mergers can reduce cost by eliminating distortions due to bilateral monopoly.[12] This argument seems much less plausible when applied to the more common case of bilateral oligopoly where several large, informed buyers can often frustrate the attempts of sellers to collude.

Altogether, strong vertical merger cases will be less common and their competitive effects will be less direct than strong horizontal merger cases, but they are still judged to offer a substantial, positive gain when the specified conditions occur. Consumers are assigned a gain half as great as in a horizontal merger case of the same size.

Potential entry merger cases are judged to have less effect than vertical merger cases, and pure conglomerate cases must have even less effect on consumers. In Table 3-1, the consumer gain from a potential entry merger case is one quarter, and that from a pure conglomerate case is one-eighth of the expected gain from horizontal mergers of the same size. Many economists would probably conclude that pure conglomerate merger cases have no effect at all, but such cases are assigned a consumer gain of 1.8 percent of the sales of the acquired firm in Table 3-1 because of the reduced possibility of general deconcentration by *de novo* merger or foothold acquisition if large diversifying firms are prevented from acquiring leaders in concentrated industries.

Structural monopoly cases are given a somewhat higher value per dollar of sales in Table 4-1 to reflect an old prejudice of at least some economists. To be strictly consistent with the treatment of collusion and merger, the gain to consumers should be 2.5 percent of the monopolist's total sales or 7.2 percent of the sales of any divestiture. In fact, somewhat more than 2.5 percent of sales (and certainly much more than 7.2 percent of any likely divestiture was used). There is some justification for giving greater weight to structural monopoly cases. First, strong cases always involve very high market shares, and there is some evidence that margins are an increasing function of concentration.[13] Second, persistent monopoly in general and structural monopoly cases in particular can be expected to involve high barriers to entry, and relief generally affects entry conditions as well as (often instead of) concentration.

Leverage cases are expected to have only mild value to the consumer. Indeed, some economists argue that reciprocity agreements are harmless or even of positive value to consumers as a result of the effectively greater price flexibility they can introduce in oligopolistic industries.[14] On the other hand, such practices do protect substantial markets for the firms using them in some cases. It is difficult to imagine that block booking or the effective tie of tin cans to can closing machines did not create barriers to entry in the motion picture and tin can industries. The writer judges that on balance such practices do elevate margins but that the anticompetitive effect is small compared with the other practices subject to antitrust prosecution.

The effect of mergers among viable firms in regulated industries seems to this writer to be as likely to be anticompetitive as in unregulated lines because of important elements of price competition (electric power, gas pipelines), or nonprice competition (airlines) or because of their effects on the competitive alternative to regulation (rails, airlines, electric power).

The attempts of the Antitrust Division to weaken restraints on rail-freight rate reductions, to prevent the collusive setting of brokerage fees by the stock exchange, and to permit entry into the microwave communications industry are judged at least as useful to consumers as criminal collusion cases of the same size because the agreements in regulated industries are enforced.

The value to consumers from a successful case depends on the duration of the practice prevented. Most observers would probably agree that criminal collusion is likely to be effective for a much shorter period than structural changes or enforceable contractual arrangements. Column (2) of Table 3-1 assigns an effective life of two years to criminal collusion and ten years to all other causes of antitrust action. Obviously these numbers are guesses. Two years is much less than the duration mentioned by the government in most of its criminal collusion complaints,[15] but it is questionable whether most unenforceable agreements are effective over the entire periods cited. The electrical equipment conspiracy was interrupted by a two-year price war[16] and followed by another. Since most collusion cases involve less concentrated markets than electrical equipment, one might expect the typical conspiracy to be even more fragile than that one.

The ten-year duration of effects of contractual restraints and mergers was meant to be much longer than criminal collusion but economically less than forever.[17] The present value to the consumers of the expected stream of gains from each type of antitrust action is computed in column (3) using a discount rate of 10 percent.

Finally, a successful antitrust action can bring gains for consumers in other markets because of its deterrent effect. Column (4) contains some rough guesses of this effect. It shows the estimated number of violations prevented by a successful action. For instance, the figure 5 for criminal collusion means that each successful case is expected to prevent four other collusive agreements of the same magnitude in addition to ending the conspiracy in question. Column (5) then shows the product of column (3) and (4) or the estimated total gain to consumers per annual dollar of directly affected sales in successful conspiracy suits. It should be noticed that this procedure assumes that the deterrent effect of a case is proportional to its sales size—that is, that a $10 million collusion case deters twice as much collusion as a $5 million case measured in sales volume covered. This assumption seems roughly plausible because publicity for ordinary enforcement cases (as opposed to test cases) is probably roughly proportional to the size of the case.

The deterrent effect of criminal collusion cases is set lower than for civil collusion and leverage cases because the violations in the last two cases are open and easily attacked. The deterrent effect of horizontal and vertical merger cases is set between those for criminal and for civil collusion. Such mergers are easily detected, but participants may still attempt mergers since they may win, and there is no stigma attached to a defeat. The deterrent effects of potential entry and conglomerate merger cases are set lower than for horizontals because the law is less certain, so that a merger seems more likely to get by. Merger cases before regulatory bodies are given much less deterrent effect because of the high probability that the Justice Department will be overruled.

Structural monopoly cases are shown as having mildly negative side effects because other dominant firms will be induced to compete less hard, if anything, if the Justice Department wins such a case. Certainly few can be expected to spin off subsidiaries as a result of a Justice Department win. The total effect of a structural monopoly case is therefore something less than 1.0 times the expected value of direct gain. It should be pointed out that the conduct-oriented Section 2 cases that are excluded from Table 3-1 definitely can have a substantial deterrent effect.

The expected gain from regulatory practice cases—in column (1)—was expressed as a percentage of industry sales, so no side effects are expected here, either.

The estimated gains from successes per dollar of annual sales in column (5) are not comparable among types of action because they are to be multiplied by total sales affected in some cases and acquired sales in others. Interactivity comparisons will be easier at a later stage in the argument (see Table 3-4).

These estimates are all averages applying to broad classes of antitrust activities. There is a wide variance within each class. Some cases may actually lessen competition or impose suboptimal processes either directly or via their deterrent effects. Others may offer much more gain for consumers than indicated because they set precedents that yield far more deterrent effect than shown in column (4). Between these extremes, cases in each class can at least conceptually be ordered by their probable payoff—collusion would probably be more harmful the more concentrated the market involved, merger would be more harmful the higher the concentration and the higher the market share of the acquiring firm, and so forth. At any one time, the possible cases in each class would show diminishing returns. A rational allocation of antitrust resources would call for evaluation of individual cases rather than of the broad classes used here.

The probability of a success also varies among activities. Column (2) of Table 3-2 contains estimates of these probabilities. These are averages of estimates made by administrators responsible for the enforcement activities of the Antitrust Division in interviews by the author in 1970. All were persons with long and broad experience in the Division. Four persons were interviewed but they were not all asked the same questions. One of them was asked about regulatory cases only. For each of the nonregulatory actions, two persons were asked for their estimates of the probability of a good case being settled short of a trial in various ways and of its going to trial. These estimates were quite consistent for all categories except potential entry mergers. Three persons were asked for estimates of the probability of success if a case in each category went to trial. The probabilities of success in trial were less consistent than the probabilities of going to trial, especially in potential entry mergers, conglomerate mergers, and leverage cases.[18]

The overall probability of success shown in column (2) of Table 3-2 is the probability of going to trial times the probability of a win plus the probability of

Table 3-2
Probability of Success

Type of Case	(1) Gain from a Success (Col. 5 of Table 3-1)	(2) Estimated Probability of Success	(3) Expected Value of Estimated Consumer Gain per Dollar (1) x (2)
a) Criminal Collusion	0.240	0.98	0.235
b) Civil Collusion	1.012	0.96	0.971
c) Horizontal Mergers	3.402[a]	0.95	3.232[a]
d) Vertical Mergers	1.701[a]	0.95	1.616[a]
e) Potential Entry Mergers	0.610[a]	0.68	0.414[a]
f) Pure Conglomerate Mergers	0.305[a]	0.38	0.116[a]
g) Structural Monopoly Cases	0.189	0.77	0.146
h) Leverage Cases	0.340	0.91	0.309
i) Regulation-Mergers	0.972[a]	0.30	0.292[a]
j) Regulation-Practices	0.169	0.52	0.088

[a]Proportion of annual sales of acquired firms.

a settlement. In effect all settlements were counted as successes. Certainly not all consent decrees are successes—especially in structural monopoly cases. The probabilities of success sought in the interviews were supposed to exclude precedent cases, but it seems certain that estimates for potential entry and conglomerate merger cases did envision precedent cases. These probabilities may be too low as a result. On the other hand, a change in the orientation of the courts could change these probabilities sharply.

The probabilities of success in column (2) are multiplied by the estimated value to consumers from a success in each category from Table 3-1 to arrive at the expected value per dollar of sales from a Justice Department complaint of each type. These appear in column (3).

The persons interviewed were also asked to estimate the number of Antitrust Division full-time lawyer-years expended on an average case in each category. Separate estimates were made for pretrial settlements and for completed trials, and weighted averages of these were computed using the estimated probabilities of each event. These averages appear in column (1) of Table 3-3. The estimates were supposed to be for full-time man-years, so two men working half time for a year counted as one man-year. Appeals were not included except in the regulatory cases, but the average cost of appeals seems to be quite low relative to investigation and trial costs. No estimates of other Division costs were received.

Column (2) shows the total number of complaints filed by the Justice Department in each category in the three years 1968 through 1970.[19] These numbers are multiplied by the estimated lawyer-years per case to yield a total estimate of Division attorney time used in column (3). These add up to 239 lawyer-years over the three-year period or about 80 per year. The Division actually employed about 280 attorneys over this period.[20] Omissions in our list of cases may account for part of our understatement, but a corrected figure would probably be less than 100.[21]

Another part of the difference can be attributed to activities not covered in this analysis, such as legislation, appeals, consultation with other agencies, administration of decrees, and internal administration. Some of the discrepancy may be partially attributable to systematic underestimates by the interviewers. However, it seems likely that most of the attorney time not accounted for is devoted to investigations that never result in complaints. Column (4) attempts to allow for such "overhead" by tripling the estimated direct lawyer-years per case. This may exaggerate the cost of potential entry and conglomerate merger cases, since the complexity of these cases need not imply comparably large amount of prefiling investigation.

Table 3-3 provides some estimate of the cost in Justice Department lawyer-years of average "strong" cases in each category. If this analysis were applied to individual cases, it might be possible to allow for a probable tendency for attorney costs to increase with the size of the case.

Only Justice Department costs are considered in column (5) Private legal

Table 3-3
Estimated Antitrust Division Lawyer-Years

Type of Case	(1) Estimated Direct Full-Time Justice Department Lawyer-Years per Case	(2) Number of Complaints, 1968-70	(3) Estimated Total Justice Department Lawyer-Years, 1968-70 (1) x (2)	(4) Estimated Direct and Indirect Full-Time Lawyer-Years per Case (1) x 3.0	(5) Estimated Total Direct and Indirect Lawyer-Years 1968-70 (4) x (2)
a) Criminal Collusion	1.6	27	43	4.8	130
b) Civil Collusion	1.2	32	38	3.6	115
c) Horizontal Merger	1.1	31	34	3.3	102
d) Vertical Merger	1.1	5	6	3.3	17
e) Potential Entry Merger	2.6	17	44	7.8[b]	133[b]
f) Pure Conglomerate Merger	6.5	5	32	19.5[b]	98[b]
g) Structural Monopoly Cases	9.6	2	19	28.6[b]	57[b]
h) Leverage Cases	1.4	8[a]	11[a]	4.2	34[a]
i) Regulation-Merger	1.6	5	8	4.8	24
j) Regulation-Practices	0.33	12	4	1.0	12
		144	239		722

[a]Inflated by five major steel company reciprocity consent decrees.
[b]Probably inflated by exaggeration of indirect lawyer years (attributable to investigations which do not result in a complaint).

costs in a typical case probably exceed those of the Antitrust Division. The Section of Antitrust of the American Bar Association had 7,485 nonstudent members in 1971. This may understate the number of active antitrust lawyers since ABA membership represents only about 70 percent of attorneys who have been admitted to the bar.[22] On the other hand, it tends to overstate total membership resources devoted to antitrust because some members of the Section of Antitrust do not work full time in the field. Moreover, many who have passed bar exams do not practice. Perhaps these biases are approximately offsetting.

The Section of Antitrust does not have a breakdown of its membership into government employees and private bar, but some estimates of the government portion is possible. The Antitrust Division employed about 280 attorneys in 1968-70, and the FTC employed about 115 in its Division of Restraint of Trade and in its successor, the Bureau of Competition, during the same period.[23] Perhaps another 100 federal lawyer-years are devoted to antitrust matters in the Solicitor General's Office at the Justice Department, the Offices of General Counsel and of Policy Planning at the FTC, and the various regulatory agencies. Finally, the various states maintain some antitrust staff. Altogether, various public employments may account for about 600 full-time attorney-years. Since some of these represent part-time activities of appellate, regulatory, and state staffs, something more like 700 government attorneys are involved. The private antitrust bar would then consist of about 6800 attorneys.

Not all antitrust activity is attributable to government actions. According to Posner, the Department of Justice filed 195 antitrust cases and the FTC initiated 178 Restraint of Trade and Robinson Patman Act cases during 1965-69, while 3136 private federal cases were initiated during the period. In addition, state antitrust law enforcement involved 25 cases filed by state agencies and 81 private state cases where decisions were reported during the period. Presumably, many other state cases were filed but not reported.[24]

If all cases involved equal private legal costs, private cases would account for about eight-ninths of the private bar, leaving about one private attorney for each public attorney associated with government cases. This seems quite unrealistic, however, since a large proportion of private suits derive directly from government actions. Moreover, Posner does not include cases before regulatory commissions. If half of the private bar are arbitrarily assigned to government cases, the ratio of private to public antitrust attorneys associated with such government actions would be about 3400/700 or roughly five private lawyers for each government lawyer. This would imply that the figures in columns (4) and (5) should be multiplied by about six to arrive at total legal staffs employed as a result of Justice Department antitrust activities.

The implicit assumption that private costs of various types of cases are proportional to Justice Department costs is undoubtedly incorrect, but it is difficult to find any basis for adjusting the private-public cost ratio by type of case. Horizontal and vertical merger cases are probably relatively easy for the government to bring and hard to defend, while criminal collusion cases may involve a good deal of government investigation cost for which there is little private counterpart. On the other hand, collusion cases may generate damage suits that involve large private legal expenses.

Much of the private antitrust bar expense is associated with advice rather than litigation. The use of a single multiplier for all fields of antitrust involves the assumption that such advisory costs are proportional to litigation costs. It may be plausible that the overall costs of private advice are roughly proportional over time to the cost of Division investigations that do not end in complaints, but the relation between the two would probably differ from field to field. It does not seem profitable to speculate about systematic differences in advisory and noncomplaint investigation costs in the absence of information on the subject.

The costs external to the division are especially high in the regulation-practices field where the bulk of the record is generally developed by the staffs of the regulatory commissions rather than by Antitrust Division attorneys. Perhaps Division costs should be multiplied by fifteen or twenty in the regulation-practices cases to allow for the regulatory staff and private bar costs resulting from Division participation in such cases.

Only lawyer-years have been considered explicitly in this analysis. Other costs must be assumed proportional to legal staff. The Antitrust Division's outlays averaged $9 million in fiscal 1968-71 or about $32,000 per lawyer-year.[25] The cost of the private bar per lawyer-year is probably at least as high. The total private and public cost of Antitrust Division activities might be around $60 million per year.

In order to estimate the social gain from these antitrust actions, the size of market (or the size of the acquired firm in mergers) must be taken into account. Of course size varies greatly from one case to the next, and if the proposed method of analysis were applied in practice, the sales involved in particular cases should be examined individually. For the purposes of this chapter, however, the method is illustrated using the mean sales sizes cited in Justice Department complaints issued in 1968-70 in the CCH *Trade Regulation Reporter.*[26]

The mean sizes appear in column (2) of Table 3-4. They are multiplied by the expected consumer gain per dollar of annual sales (from column (3) of Table 3-2) to yield the expected dollar gain to consumers per case shown in column (3) of Table 3-4. The gain per Antitrust Division lawyer-year is estimated in column (4). These gains per lawyer-year are strikingly large, but they vary widely by type of case, and they are subject to many qualifications. A number of the most likely distortions in these estimates are tested in the recalculations of gain per Justice Department lawyer-year shown in Table 3-5.

The estimate that criminal collusion raises price by 5 percent on the average may appear low in view of the 8.8 percent, 12 percent, and 30 percent price effects in the three major criminal collusion cases cited. Line a)(ii) revises the

Table 3-4
Mean Size of Case (1968-70) and Expected Gain per Lawyer-Year

	Type of Case	(1) Basis of Size Measure	(2) Mean Annual Sales ($ millions)	(3) Expected Value to Consumers of a Successful Case [(2) x col. (3) of Table 3-2] ($ millions)	(4) Expected Gain per Division Lawyer-Year [(3) col. (4) of Table 3-2] ($ millions)
a)	Criminal Collusion	Covered Sales	19	4	0.9
b)	Civil Collusion	Covered Sales	173	168	46.7
c)	Horizontal Merger	Sales of Acquired Firms	18[a]	58	17.6
d)	Vertical Merger	Sales of Acquired Firms	59[a]	95	28.9
e)	Potential Entry Merger	Sales of Acquired Firms	90[a]	37	4.8
f)	Pure Conglomerate Merger	Sales of Acquired Firms	665[a]	77	4.0
g)	Structural Monopoly Cases	Sales of Firm	2680[b]	392[b]	13.7[b]
h)	Leverage Cases	Covered Sales	1657[c]	512[c]	122.0[c]
i)	Regulation-Merger	Sales of Acquired Firms	215[a]	63	13.1
j)	Regulation-Practices	Sales of Industry	600	53	52.8

[a]Sales of acquired firms.
[b]Inflated by the IBM case.
[c]Inflated by five large steel reciprocity cases.

estimated gain per lawyer-year using a 10 percent increase instead. Similarly, we ignored the average reported duration of 7.5 years from the 1968-70 complaints and used 2 years instead. Line a)(iii) uses 7 years instead of 2.

The mean case sizes are probably not representative in the leverage cases, which were dominated by six very large reciprocity complaints, five of them in the steel industry. Not only were the sizes of these cases probably unrepresentative of the usual leverage case, but the total sales of the firms involved must grossly overstate the extent of sales affected by leverage. Moreover, the consumer gain from such cases is still a matter of dispute. The estimated gain per lawyer-year from leverage cases in Table 3-5 is based on the estimated size of two nonreciprocity leverage complaints filed in 1968-70.

The gain per lawyer-year in structural monopoly cases is also atypically large.

Table 3-5
Possible Adjustments in Expected Gain per Division Lawyer-Year ($ Millions)

Type of Case	(1) Excluding Reciprocity Cases	(2) Also Assigning 5-Year Lives for All Offenses Except 2 Years for a),(i) and a),(ii)	Halving the Deterrent Effect (3) Excluding Reciprocity Cases	(4) Also Assigning 5-Year Lives to All Offenses Except a),(i) and a),(ii)
a) Criminal Collusion				
(i) Using 5% price effect and 2-year duration	0.9	0.9	0.6	0.6
(ii) Using 10% price effect and 2-year duration	1.8	1.8	1.2	1.2
(iii) Using 10% price effect and 7-year duration in columns (1) and (3) and 5 years in columns (2) and (4)	5.2	4.3	3.1	2.7
b) Civil Collusion	46.7	28.8	25.7	15.9
c) Horizontal Merger	17.6	10.7	10.1	6.2
d) Vertical Merger	28.9	17.8	16.5	10.2
e) Potential Entry Merger	4.8	3.0	2.9	1.7
f) Pure Conglomerate Merger	4.0	2.5	2.4	1.5
g) Structural Monopoly Cases	13.7[a]	8.5[a]	13.7[a]	8.5[a]
h) Leverage Cases	2.8	1.7	1.5	0.9
i) Regulation-Merger	13.1	8.1	9.8	6.1
j) Regulation-Practices	52.8	32.6	52.8	32.6

[a]Inflated by the IBM case.

It is based on a simple average of the sales of IBM and of Grinnell. No structural monopoly case except for IBM itself has ever involved a firm with as much as $2,680 million sales at the time of the suit (though some of the firms affected in past cases have attained sales that large since the suits). No adjustment in the size of structural monopoly cases was attempted in Table 3-5.

One of the most arbitrary estimates in this analysis was the assignment of ten-year lives to all offenses other than criminal collusion. Column (2) of Table 3-5 retains the leverage case adjustment in column (1) but reduces the average duration of all offenses to five years except for criminal collusion in rows a)(i) and a)(ii). It is difficult to imagine any shorter life for the effect of contractual collusion, merger, or structural monopoly.

Another set of relatively arbitrary estimates were the guesses as to deterrent effects. Column (3) shows estimates of gain per lawyer-year when deterrent effect is halved (so that a criminal collusion case prevents three conspiracies including the directly affected one instead of five, and so forth). The effects of structural monopoly and regulatory practices cases are unchanged from column (1) because no positive deterrents are expected. Finally, column (4) both allows for no more than a five-year life for any offense *and* halves the deterrent effects.

Other adjustments could of course change the relative values in Table 3-5 substantially. If estimates of the probability of success and the lawyer-years required for potential entry and conglomerate mergers could be made for (presently hypothetical) nonprecedent cases, the estimated consumer gain per lawyer-year in such cases would be greater. And various observers would probably want to adjust at least the more fanciful estimates of direct gains, perhaps reducing the effect of structural monopoly cases (because *substantial* structural relief is so rare) or vertical, potential entry, or conglomerate merger or leverage cases (because many doubt the procompetitive effect of these). While some justification can doubtless be found for any of the sets of estimates in Table 3-5, those in column (1)—including a)(i)—represent the best estimate of gain per lawyer-year in the eyes of the writer and will be used throughout the rest of this chapter.

The analysis to this point has been based entirely on the distributive effects of antitrust. Estimates of the traditional allocative losses due to various antitrust offenses are attempted here, although it was argued earlier that they are not the primary historic concern of antitrust and that conventional estimates probably understate the efficiency gain.

The estimates use Harberger's approach.[27] The allocative gain from a successful antitrust suit that reduces margins by M percent of the price would be approximated by:

$$1/2M^2 \cdot VS \cdot e$$

where e represents the elasticity of demand and VS is the value of sales in the market in question. The values of M used in the collusion, structural monopoly, leverage, and regulation-practices cases are twice the direct distributional effects per dollar of sale shown in column (1) of Table 3-1. The Table 3-1 values are doubled to include the effect of corporate taxes. Margin increases due to corporate taxes yield allocative effects of the same sort as those due to after-tax profits. The expected gain from the average strong case in each of these classes is estimated using an elasticity of one and the average values of VS from column (2) of Table 3-4.

In merger cases, the value of M depends on the market share of the acquired firm. For horizontal mergers:

$$M = \Delta \frac{VS - MC}{VS} = b\Delta CR = b\frac{VS_a}{VS}$$

The allocative gain from a successful merger case would then be:

$$1/2\,(b\frac{VS_a}{VS})^2 \cdot VS \cdot e = 1/2\,b^2\,\frac{VS_a}{VS}\,VS_a \cdot e$$

For this purpose b is estimated at the value found by Collins and Preston (0.144—double the value in Table 3-1). The sales of the acquired firm (VS_a) is taken from column (2) of Table 3-4. The average market share (VS_a/VS) reported or directly derivable in eighteen of the thirty-one horizontal merger complaints in 1968-70 was 0.14.[28]

The allocative effects of vertical, potential entry, and conglomerate merger cases are probably also dependent on the shares of the acquired firms in their own markets, but it is less clear what the relationship should be. It is again assumed that vertical mergers have half the effect, that potential entry mergers have one quarter the effect, and that pure conglomerate mergers have one eighth the effect on margins of a horizontal merger for an acquired firm of a given market share. The mean market share reported or derivable in nine of the seventeen potential entry merger complaints in 1968-70 was 0.28.[29] No market shares for acquired firms were reported in the complaints issued in other types of mergers. An average market share of 0.10 is assumed in vertical and pure conglomerate mergers and of 0.20 in regulation mergers. The 0.10 figure seems to be fairly close to the average market share of the acquired firms in their main markets in the five conglomerate cases brought in 1969, but it is a pure guess in the vertical cases. The market share in the regulation-merger cases is set higher because many of these were horizontals in highly concentrated markets (the rail mergers).

The average estimated allocative gains from various types of strong antitrust cases are shown in Table 3-6. Column (1) shows estimates of the direct allocative gain in one year per dollar of annual sales from a successful case—$1/2\,M^2$ or $1/2$ b^2 (VS_a/VS). Column (2) shows expected values of allocative gain per dollar of annual sales taking future effects, deterrent effects, and the probability of success into account. Column (3) estimates the expected present values of allocative gain for the average case on the basis of market or acquired firm sales reported in Table 3-4. Allocative gain per Justice Department lawyer-year appears in column (4). It corresponds to column (1) of Table 3-5.

The allocative gains are much smaller than the distributive gains, but they probably understate the efficiency gains for strong antitrust cases. They ignore such effects of monopoly as its protection of high-cost production or distribution methods and any possible impediment to technological progress. Of course, poor cases may offer no efficiency gains at all or may actually lessen economic efficiency where they lessen competition or serve to protect high-cost processes.

Structural monopoly cases look more impressive relative to other cases when

Table 3-6
Estimated Allocative Gain per Antitrust Division Lawyer-Year

Type of Case	(1) Estimated Direct Gain per Dollar of Annual Market Sales $(1/2\ M^2$ or $1/2\ b^2\ (\frac{VS_a}{VS}))$	(2) Expected Present Value of Gain per Current Dollar of Sales (Corresponds to Col. (3) of Table 3-2)	(3) Expected Value of Gain from Average "Strong" Case (in $ Millions) (Col. (2) x Col. (2) of Table 3-4)	(4) Expected Value per Division Lawyer-Year (in Dollars) (Corresponds to Col. (1) of Table 3-5)
a) Criminal Collusion	0.00125	0.0118	0.22	$ 46,000
b) Civil Collusion	0.00045	0.0291	5.03	1,398,000
c) Horizontal Merger	0.01037(.14) = 0.00145	0.0651[a]	1.17	355,000
d) Vertical Merger	0.00518(.10) = 0.00052	0.0235[a]	1.39	420,000
e) Potential Entry Merger	0.00259(.28) = 0.00073	0.0167[a]	1.50	192,000
f) Pure Conglomerate Merger	0.00130(.10) = 0.00013	0.0017[a]	1.13	58,000
g) Structural Monopoly	0.00245	0.0102	27.34[b]	958,000[b]
h) Leverage	0.00005	0.0015	0.06[c]	14,000[c]
i) Regulation-Merger	0.01037(.20) = 0.00207	0.0084[a]	1.81	377,000
j) Regulation-Practices	0.00125	0.0044	2.64	2,640,000

[a]Per dollar of sales of acquired firm.
[b]Inflated by the IBM case.
[c]Excluding reciprocity cases—if they were included as in Table 3-4, column (3) would read 2.85, and column (5) would read $592,000.

evaluated in terms of allocative efficiency because of the large effect on margins assumed. This may account for the widespread support for structural monopoly cases among economists, but it should be recalled that the direct effect on margins was deliberately set high in this field. The allocative effects of leverage cases are very small because of the low margin effects expected here. The merger cases look relatively less impressive in allocative than in distribution terms because the market shares involved are seldom large enough in any given merger to create effective monopoly. However, Table 3-6 understates the effect of merger cases to the extent that the actual deterrent effect falls within the same market. Deterring a merger of the same size and market share in another market will simply double the direct allocative effect case, but deterring a merger of the same size in the same market will quadruple it because M rises with VS_a/VS and the allocative effect rises with M^2.

The effect or duration of collusion may be understated. If M is raised from 0.05 to 0.10, the gain per lawyer-year rises to $184,000. If in addition, the duration of collusion is increased to seven years, the gain per lawyer becomes $519,000.

Even with the probable understatement of efficiency effects, the estimated allocative gain per lawyer-year exceeds the cost per Antitrust Division lawyer in all lines except leverage. If private bar and regulatory staff costs are taken into account, the average criminal collusion, conglomerate merger, or leverage case would have estimated benefit-cost ratios under one and the average potential entry case would be marginal. The same might be true of the typical structural monopoly case if IBM is excluded. Even limiting the analysis to these probably understated allocative effects, however, the gain from strong civil collusion, horizontal and vertical merger, and regulatory cases of average size would be worth all the costs.

It was argued earlier that the legislative purpose was more likely to have been to benefit consumers, even at the expense of monopolists, rather than merely to attain allocative efficiency. The consumer gain from this point of view would be the sum of the distributive and allocative gains—that is, the sums of column (1) from Table 3-5 and column (4) from Table 3-6. The relative rankings of various types of cases would then be the same as in Table 3-5 because the allocative effects add relatively little.

The figures in Tables 3-5 and 3-6 must be taken as only rough orders of magnitude. They are obviously open to substantial change where judgments of any of the relevant variables differ. And they should definitely be adjusted for specific cases of varying size, economic impact, and cost. Some tentative conclusions are possible on the basis of even these rough results, however.

First, the distributive gains per lawyer-year are much greater than costs in every line of antitrust considered. This leaves the value judgment of how much a dollar redistributed is worth in terms of real resources expended. Earlier arguments contend that redistribution was a major purpose of the antitrust laws.

It would seem to follow that a dollar redistributed has a positive real value, but it is probably not worth a dollar of real costs. The reader must decide for himself whether the millions of dollars redistributed per lawyer-year is worth the $32,000 that the government spends per lawyer-year, or the $192,000 of government plus private legal costs per Justice Department lawyer-year.

The allocative effect of antitrust *is* directly comparable with the real costs of antitrust activities, but the estimates of allocative effects clearly understate the real gains from antitrust, (1) because the distributive effects are worth something, and (2) because the high production costs induced by monopoly are ignored. Even when only the estimated allocative gains are considered, strong Justice Department antitrust cases in all fields except the leverage cases are worth their cost to the government, and all but criminal collusion, pure conglomerate merger, and leverage cases are worth their private plus government costs. Using higher direct costs or longer lives for criminal collusion, even these cases would be worth their public plus private costs.

It does not follow that all cases brought in 1968-70 were worthwhile. Very small cases may not be worthwhile and "weak" cases may not be, regardless of their size. Nor does it follow from the apparently high benefit-cost ratios for many types of action that a great increase in antitrust activity is warranted since diminishing returns can undoubtedly be expected in these endeavors. One would expect that diminishing returns would be less severe in collusion cases, where a large number of undetected offenses undoubtedly exist, and more severe in mergers where most cases are easily detected. It seems probable that the public might stand to gain from an expansion of activity in the fields where the benefit-cost ratios are high so long as the additional cases undertaken are strong cases, but such cases may be exhausted quite early in such lines as merger.

No attempt has been made to evaluate precedent cases. These should surely be examined individually. Their value to consumers would depend on estimated direct gains and costs and the range of economic activity over which the affected practices apply. One would expect their high deterrent value to justify them in many instances where they might not pass muster using the figures applied in this chapter. Finally, no analysis has been attempted for monopolistic practices cases, for any FTC cases, or for private antitrust cases. These could probably be evaluated following a format similar to the one used here.

Perhaps it is unrealistic to anticipate a large increase in Antitrust Division resources in any event. If so, the analysis might best be used in evaluating the allocation of present antitrust resources. The private bar and regulatory agency costs involved in antitrust should probably be ignored, and the distributive effect per lawyer-year seems the most appropriate basis for judging the allocation of Division resources. It would follow that the Division would do well to emphasize civil collusion cases (especially the strongest ones—e.g., patent cases), horizontal and possibly vertical merger cases, and regulatory practice cases, and minimize its smaller collusion, structural monopoly, and leverage cases.

The fairly high gain per lawyer-year in structural monopoly cases in Table 3-5 is due to the size of IBM. The gain per lawyer-year in a Grinnell, DuPont Cellophane, United Fruit, or United Shoe Machinery cases would be much less than those shown in Tables 3-4, 3-5, and 3-6. The small amount of these gains is due to the high cost of structural cases, their low probability of success, and the lack of any positive deterrent effect. This low payoff from typical structural monopoly cases is particularly striking in view of widespread support among economists for such cases. This result would be reenforced in view of the questionable distributive effect of such cases. Whereas successful collusion, merger, and regulatory practice cases have the effect of preventing a redistribution in favor of the persons who participated in these actions, a structural monopoly case redistributes wealth at the expense of "innocent bystanders" in many cases. The advantages of such market power has often been capitalized, the present owners of the monopolistic firms having acquired their shares at market prices that reflect the expected streams of monopoly profits. A successful case will often have little or no effect on those who actually created the monopolies involved. In addition, the direct gain from such cases was intentionally set high in Table 3-1 in order to reflect the common prejudice. Moreover, the disruptive effect of dissolution is probably greater than in collusion and merger cases. The general conclusion should probably be that only the strongest and largest structural cases are worthwhile. An IBM or a GM case would probably still pass muster, but many in history would not.

The actual allocation of Division resources comes out reasonably well by this analysis, but some criticisms may be appropriate. Columns (3) and (5) of Table 3-3 show some estimates of that allocation. The large emphasis on civil collusion and horizontal merger cases seems well justified. The heavy resource use in the potential entry merger, pure conglomerate merger and leverage cases is more questionable, but Table 3-3 may exaggerate the Division's resources used in those fields because these were exceptionally large in 1968-70. It does seem probable that, so long as its resources are limited, the Division could enhance its output by reducing effort in the smaller criminal collusion cases and expanding its regulatory practices activities.

The entire analysis here has ignored the general effect of the antitrust program. It may be that its most important effect has been to limit the development of publically enforced protectionist and cartel programs. The widely held antitrust philosophy and the concrete influence of antitrust officials on a wide range of policy formation within government both work in that direction. The distributive and efficiency effects of an active, procompetitive antitrust policy may be much greater than the limited estimates of this study indicate.

Comment

Richard J. Arnould

Weiss provides a basic cost-benefit framework for analyzing the gain per Antitrust Division lawyer-year expended on ten broad categories on antitrust activities. His analysis is divided into two parts: (1) estimating the redistribution effects of monopoly power, or estimating the gains to consumers from antitrust in terms of "excess profits" avoided, and (2) estimating the deadweight losses due to allocative inefficiency in the presence of monopoly power. The comment will be directed mainly toward the redistribution effects since they are the central focus of Professor Weiss' study. The following discussion is divided into two parts, the first focusing on the analytical content of the framework presented and the second dealing with the empirical content.

Weiss states that "the distributive effects of monopolistic practices seem to be one of the major motives for the antitrust laws. . . ." This probably is a safe assumption on three grounds. First, it might be assumed that many members of Congress may have difficulty making a technical distinction between redistribution effects and allocative efficiency. Second, constituents are likely to respond to the prevention of excess profits and inflated prices caused by monopolistic practices. Third, it seems politically remote to expect the tax system to be altered to accommodate the income distribution problem, even though most economists would argue that it is the most efficient system for accomplishing such ends, and the antitrust laws are more efficient for purposes of achieving allocative efficiency.[1] Thus one should accept Weiss's willingness to consider distributive effects as vital gains from antitrust.

The analytical framework then becomes one of determining the extent to which prices and excess profits were elevated in cases brought by the Antitrust Division of the Justice Department between 1968 and 1970, netting out the resource costs included in prosecution, and coming up with the net gain to consumers for each of ten areas of antitrust enforcement over this period. The framework and methods proposed by Weiss seem very plausible for an ex post evaluation of the effectiveness of the allocation of Antitrust Division resources. Yet Weiss does not indicate how this information is to be implemented into future planning. The implication appears to be that resources are to be allocated among the ten areas discussed in some proportion to the ex post gains in these areas.

If the proportional distribution is to be used, it is necessary to examine carefully the nature of the cases presented in the past and the likelihood of reasonably homogeneous cases in the future. For example, as Weiss indicates, the gains from cases in the leverage area are significantly increased by reciprocity cases in the steel industry where a larger volume of sales was influenced. Are

57

cases that may be available in the future in this area likely to be as significant? Similarly, the area of structural monopoly was said to be significantly influenced by the IBM case. Thus there must be concern whether the parameters estimated by Weiss apply to the future, even if they are correct for the past.

A more feasible, and possibly intended, use of the Weiss technique might be to utilize his framework to determine gains from the prosecution of the available potential violations in each of the ten areas. These bundles of violations might come from at least two sources. They may emerge at a point in the planning horizon as a backlog to be dealt with in the future. Alternatively, an investigative group of economists could seek out markets where performance is particularly noncompetitive, determine whether this aberration is caused by structural or behavioral conditions, and proceed to evaluate potential gains from prosecution.

Cases then should be prosecuted in each area until the marginal gains per dollar expenditure are equalized as constrained by the available Antitrust Division budget. This system should yield a typical constrained optimization solution but is dependent upon the ability of the planners to establish the bundles of available cases and to estimate gains for each case.

This system has an additional advantage over the Weiss technique. In this system, structural conditions, which are important in any possible antitrust violation and particularly in areas such as criminal collusion cases where it has a strong influence on the probable duration of the violation,[2] are introduced in direct relation to the market in which the violation occurred. The Weiss system of averaging (in the case of criminal and civil collusion) and using linear-parameter estimates (in the case of mergers) loses the distinction between the conditions that existed in the markets where cases were brought as compared to markets where violations still exist.

The second point assumes the Weiss framework for analyzing the effectiveness of resource allocation to be appropriate. The types of cases excluded from his analysis, that is, precedent-setting cases and incipiency cases,[3] might be very significant. The most important would appear to be the areas involving precedent-setting cases. It can be assumed that these were left out of the Weiss analysis because of the difficulty of formulating standards to meet the uniqueness of each such case.

Precedent-setting cases probably are very costly to bring; they are heavy resource users, the probability of success is difficult to determine, and the direct gains to consumers from one such action may be relatively small. Yet it would seem that the deterrent effect of a successful case should be large relative to that of cases resting on established precedence. The deterrent effect of any action is difficult to determine and is certainly more so in new areas where rules of law are being formulated. It is difficult to find areas where precedents have been established in the absence of other major influences. However, the mere filing of suits by the Justice Department against certain conglomerates may have had a substantial effect on pending mergers. Similarly, action brought against county boards of realty had a definite and significant deterrent effect across the nation.

The problem of arresting structural changes at their incipiency might be similar to precedent-setting cases in many respects. The direct and immediate gains of any case might be outweighted by the direct costs of taking action because of the relatively small amount of the market involved in a single case. Again, the deterrent effects should be relatively large, and the duration could be lengthened if action is not taken early.

The extent to which each of these activities expends resources makes it imperative that they be a part of the cost-benefit calculus. In fact, one could imagine a theoretical legal system where the rule of law that emerges from these types of cases is so clear that the deterrent effect becomes complete, at which time precedent-setting cases would far outweigh routine cases in importance. Of course, this is an extreme, but it suggests that a framework for policy planning and resource allocation must include these instances.

Lastly, considering the analytical content of Weiss' study, one may question whether there is a secondary effect of mergers that extends beyond the immediate companies involved. Briefly, if a merger causes a substantial increase in concentration in an already highly concentrated industry, the merged companies might hold a price umbrella over the remaining companies, permitting the latter to raise their prices and therefore extract higher excess profits. A similar effect could be achieved if the merged companies can, through some form of "discipline," encourage the remaining companies to charge higher prices.

Weiss has adequately cautioned the reader of the weaknesses of his empirical estimates. The possibility of obtaining more adequate estimates probably is very real. It remains difficult to determine the appropriate manner in which to estimate the duration of the effect, particularly in the case of mergers, and even more perplexing to determine the deterrent effects.

It is appropriate to estimate the sensitivity of the solutions to changes in the estimated gains. This is done with two very naive systems. The first is simply to determine the effects of changes in the parameters on the ranking of antitrust activities considered by Weiss. The second is to assume that resources are allocated to a specific area in a manner strictly proportional to the share of total consumer gains per lawyer-year accounted for by that area. Lawyer-years per area and average number of cases per area are then calculated. This information is provided in Table 3C-1. Columns 1 through 3 indicate the ranking, lawyer-years, and average number of cases per year using Weiss's Table 3-4; columns 4, 5, and 6 show the same with reciprocity cases deleted from the leverage cases; columns 7, 8, and 9 have reciprocity cases deleted and criminal collusion increased to 5 percent of sales for seven years duration (all changes shown in columns 1 through 9 were made by Weiss); columns 10, 11, and 12 are the same as 7, 8, and 9 with gains from mergers arbitrarily increased to 10 percent of the sales of the acquired; columns 13, 14, and 15 are the same as columns 10, 11, and 12 with gains from horizontal mergers reduced to 4.4 percent.

Changes in the rankings (by percentage of total gains) of antitrust activities

Table 3C-1
Rankings by Percentage of Total Distributive Gains, Lawyer-Years Allocated, and Average Number of Cases per Year

	Original Weiss Results			Reciprocity Cases Removed			Reciprocity Removed, Criminal Collusion 5%, 7 Yrs. Duration		
	Ranking	Lawyer-Yrs. Allocated	Average No. Cases/Year	Ranking	Lawyer-Yrs. Allocated	Average No. Cases/Year	Ranking	Lawyer-Yrs. Allocated	Average No. Cases/Year
Criminal Collusion	10	0.7	0.15	10	1.2	0.25	7	0.7	1.5
Civil Collusion	3	36.7	10.2	2	60.5	16.8	2	59.0	16.4
Horizontal Merger	5	13.9	4.2	4	22.8	5.4	4	22.3	6.8
Vertical Merger	4	22.8	6.9	3	37.4	11.3	3	36.5	11.6
Potential Entry Merger	8	3.8	.49	7	6.2	0.79	8	6.0	0.77
Pure Conglomerate Merger	9	3.1	.16	8	5.3	0.27	9	5.0	0.26
Structural Monopoly	6	10.8	.38	5	17.8	0.62	5	17.3	0.60
Leverage	1	96.2	22.9	9	3.6	0.86	10	3.6	0.86
Regulation-Merger	7	10.3	2.15	6	17.0	3.5	6	16.6	3.5
Regulation-Practices	2	41.5	41.5	1	68.4	68.4	1	66.7	66.7

	Same as Columns 7-9, Horizontal Mergers Increased to 10%			Same as Columns 10-12, Horizontal Mergers Reduced to 4.4%		
	Ranking	Lawyer-Yrs. Allocated	Average No. Cases/Year	Ranking	Lawyer-Yrs. Allocated	Average No. Cases/Year
Criminal Collusion	7	6.7	1.4	7	6.7	1.4
Civil Collusion	2	56.9	15.8	2	56.1	15.8
Horizontal Merger	4	29.8	9.0	6	11.0	3.3
Vertical Merger	3	35.0	10.6	3	34.8	10.5
Potential Entry Merger	8	5.8	0.74	8	5.8	0.74
Pure Conglomerate Merger	9	4.8	0.25	9	4.8	0.25
Structural Monopoly	5	16.8	0.59	4	16.6	0.58
Leverage	10	3.4	0.81	10	3.4	0.81
Regulation-Merger	6	16.1	3.4	5	15.8	3.3
Regulation-Practices	1	64.3	64.3	1	63.6	63.6

were most severe when the parameters were changed as suggested by Weiss. For example, the elimination of reciprocity cases from the leverage category reduced its share of total gains from 40 percent to slightly over 1 percent. This decreased leverage cases from first place to tenth place in the ranking. Looked at in terms of resource allocation, lawyer-years expended in this area would be reduced from 96.2 to 3.6, and average number of cases from 22.9 to 0.86.

Increasing the gains in criminal collusion from 2.5 percent to 5 percent of sales and the duration from two to seven years increased the percentage gains accountable from 0.3 of a percent to 2.9 percent, lawyer-years expended from 0.7 to 7, and cases brought from 0.15 to 1.5. This increased the criminal collusion cases from tenth place to seventh place in the ranking.

Increasing the gains in horizontal mergers to 10 percent (which might still be low if there is an industry effect) increased the share of gains from 9.3 percent to 12.4 percent, lawyer-years from 22.3 to 29.8, and cases from 6.8 to 9.0. Decreasing the gains by a similar amount to 4.4 percent caused the share of gains to drop to 4.6 percent, lawyer-years to 11.0, and cases to 3.3 per year.

It is clear from this little experiment, naive as it may be, that certain categories are very sensitive to certain types of cases. Beyond such drastic changes, one might argue that the difference between three, seven, or nine merger cases in one year is also quite significant.

Finally, each area may be subject to sharply diminishing returns. This cannot be determined with the Weiss system. The existence of such a declining factor is subject to the availability of cases in each area. If there are enough cases available in industries with substantially similar structural conditions, returns may not diminish. But surely the deterrent effect will decline as the number of cases initiated in any area increases. This suggests the need for a system of resource allocation that accounts for the possibility of this declining factor. Similarly, the system of resource allocation applied to the Weiss results calls for an unrealistically large number of cases involving regulation practices.

In conclusion, it should be reiterated that the system developed by Weiss has strength as a means to evaluate the effectiveness of resource allocation ex post, but it appears to have at least three difficulties for planning purposes: (1) past conditions may not reflect future possibilities; (2) a process necessary to implement the framework developed by Weiss is difficult to develop and certainly must be much more complex than the one of direct proportional allocation used above; and (3) data adequate to make the necessary estimates may be difficult to find. The alternative provided earlier in this comment overcomes the first two difficulties. The data and parameter estimation problem remains.

4

Antitrust Cases as a Guide to Directions in Antitrust Research and Policy

Richard O. Zerbe

The study of antitrust is particularly attractive because the economist's microeconomic theory can be put to good use. Moreover, theory itself is primarily advanced in struggles toward concrete application. Thus, in the antitrust field, microeconomic theory can fulfill its promise of relevancy by setting out the basis for antitrust policy, and the theory will gain in the process.

Since opinions and cases are the end products of the antitrust process, it seems that this is the best place to look in order to determine the level of achievement attained through this supposed happy mix of economics and law. In addition, the opinions in the major antitrust cases seem the best sources for getting a substantial impression of the field as a whole in a short time. A reading of the opinions of the major cases vindicates the view that this is the place to begin the study of the economics of antitrust.

However, they do not bear out the picture of microeconomic theory, economic reality, and the law working together toward sound policy, rational law, and useful theory. The theory expressed in the opinions does not seem to fit the theory as it is normally understood. Most of the inferences central to the cases are based on implicit theory that seems quite erroneous. Furthermore, it is difficult to tell whether or not the opinions are correct since the information they contain generally does not permit one to judge or infer this. These are, of course, grave deficiencies. Why do they exist? The possibility that these deficiencies are due simply to substantial economic ignorance on the part of the judiciary indicates that an examination of the record of the cases is appropriate.

There the same phenomena exists. Crucial facts are missing; results and facts alleged to be true in the arguments are unsupported by the data; in short, no viable theory is developed or supported by attendant facts. No wonder the judges' opinions seem deficient. Indeed, it seems that the opinions, taking into account that the judges are lawyers, not economists, are often fairly good ones in light of the record before them. The economists' discussions are perhaps somewhat better, but these too are disappointing. The economists are unable to add a great deal, in part because their discussions are mainly based on opinions defective in their facts.

In writing this study, I have benefited from discussions with Ronald Coase, John S. McGee, and John Peterman. The usual caveat holds. The American Bar Foundation provided time for me as a Scholar in Residence.

These deficiencies in theory and facts exist not only for the older cases, but for the newer ones as well. However, there are important differences between the older and newer cases. The older cases seem concerned with real effects and express a willingness to determine what was actually going on. In this sense, the older cases were struggling, if weakly, toward systematic concepts of markets and competition. If many of their inferences are wrong, it is not because no systematic views were held or attempted, but rather because the views of some business practices such as predatory pricing were erroneous and, more fundamentally, because a fuller understanding of competition and of markets had yet to be gained.

It might not be thought that over time these deficiencies would be ameliorated and that experiences and especially improvements in economic theory would lead to a much sounder basis for antitrust policy. Such has not been the case. Rather, the deficiencies in fact and theory seem to have increased. Why is this? It is possible to speculate that the answer lies partly in the increased bureaucratization of antitrust activity, with the consequent use of a simple and inappropriate criterion for success—namely, winning cases. The deficiencies have also risen, in part, because of the growth in the pernicious tendency of courts generally to give great and perhaps undue weight to agency expertise. This has meant an increase in the importance of law relative to economics in antitrust.

It has also meant a very considerable increase in the government's ability to win cases. The diminution of the importance of sound economic criteria for deciding cases, coupled with the government's increased ability to win them, has seriously eroded the foundations and meaning of present antitrust activity. This is well illustrated by the deterioration and finally the perversion of the concept of competition in antitrust. Competitive efficiency is the thing that most harms rivals. By focusing on harm to rivals rather than market effects, the government has been lead to a subtle condemnation of efficiency. The impression created is that the government does not like competitive efficiency.

Indeed, it seems that the denouement of this process has been attained: there is no such thing as a legal contract: there is no such thing as a legal franchise; there is no such thing as a legal price. Every contract, as Justice White pointed out long ago, is in restraint of trade. A contract specifies certain trade obligations of parties, and thereby the ability of other parties to gain part of this trade is less than what it would be without the contract. On this basis, any contract is illegal under present law. The same thing is true of franchise operations. Similarly, every price is subject to attack. If the price is too high, it is illegal because it means monopoly power. If prices are the same, collusion exists. If one price is lower than others, there is price discrimination, predatory pricing, or monopolization. Now this view is undoubtedly exaggerated and oversimplified, yet not by much. It seems to be substantially accurate. It is a more detailed statement of the fact that the government has been moving toward a position in which it can win any case it cares to bring.

This does not mean, however, that present antitrust law and policy have substantial effects on the nature of business structure or behavior. The resources devoted to antitrust prosecution are scarcely sufficient to bring every conceivable case. Under the present arrangement, indeed, a very small percentage of possible cases can be brought. Normally, it is not necessary to bring many cases since the cases that are brought establish precedents. With illegal business behavior spelled out by these precedents, such behavior generally will be avoided by businesses, obviating much of the need to bring cases.

But with nearly all business behavior illegal, what are the incentives to avoid one particular kind of behavior? To be sure, some activities are, as it were, more illegal than others, and thus are avoided more than others. Nevertheless, the general unclarity about what is illegal, and the range of activity probably made illegal, tend to lessen any beneficial effects on business behavior that would otherwise be derived from the cases that are brought.

Of course, to determine the effects of antitrust, one must look beyond the definitions of illegality and the percentage of cases won to determine the remedies actually achieved. While the remedies are often inappropriate, they are, more than anything else, ineffectual, especially in the more modern cases. In the actual working out of the remedies, few changes of substance are made. In this sense, the government wins the battles over legality, but loses the wars concerning remedies. In sum, then, the conclusion is that under present antitrust law, everything is illegal, but it does not make much difference.

These are, of course, very general statements and their meaning can now be illustrated more explicitly by considering a few cases. These cases are in no sense unique. They are suggestive of what a broader investigation would uncover.

For a variety of reasons, perhaps the most frequently cited antitrust case of all is *Chicago Board of Trade* vs. *United States,*[1] 1918. An examination of this case strikingly shows, among other things, the advantages for antitrust policy of the government knowing what it is doing. In this case, the government attacked a rule of the Chicago Board of Trade known as the "Call Rule," a price-fixing rule adopted by the Chicago Board of Trade in 1906.[2] Its central feature was that it essentially pegged the price of cash grain for that part of the day in which the Board of Trade was closed. In spite of this blatant price-fixing aspect, the Call Rule was upheld by the Supreme Court. Subsequently, the case has become one of the more important antitrust cases, even if one of the more puzzling. Clearly, it is anomalous in the context of the doctrine of per se illegality of cartels, and while in the light of this doctrine it is easy to regard the decision as a bad one, the quandry of Justice Brandeis evokes a certain sympathy. This quandry existed because the government failed not only to delineate the economics of the case, but also to show any adverse effects arising from the Call Rule; apparently, they proceeded with confidence on the grounds of per se illegality. As Brandeis said:

It [the government] made no attempt to show that the rule was designed to, or that it had the effect of limiting the amount of grain shipped to Chicago; or retarding or accelerating shipment; or raising or depressing prices; or of discriminating against any part of the public; or that it resulted in hardship to anyone. The case was rested upon the bold proposition that a rule or agreement by which men occupying positions of strength in any branch of trade fixed prices at which they would buy or sell during the important part of the business day, is an illegal restraint of trade under the antitrust law.[3]

Brandeis found that the rule was of the type regulating business hours, that it applied "only to small part of the grain shipped from day-to-day to Chicago, and to an even smaller part of the day's sales."[4] Moreover, "it applied only to grain shipped to Chicago.... Country dealers and farms had available in practically every part of the territory called tributary to Chicago some other market for grain 'to arrive'."[5]

Brandeis found, in addition, the effects of the rule to be beneficial or at least innocuous. It had no material effect on prices nor the value of grain coming to Chicago. It increased market knowledge, the number of buyers and sellers, and reduced risks and the number of bids; it reduced risks for country dealers; it allowed Chicago grain merchants "who sell to millers and exporters to trade on a smaller margin and, [thereby] ... to make the Chicago market more attractive for both shoppers and buyers of grain";[6] it brought into the regular market hours "more of the trading in grain 'to arrive'."[7]

Having determined that every trade agreement restrains trade in some sense and degree and understandably impressed by the arguments of the defense as to the variety of beneficial effects, and the absence of harmful ones, it is perhaps not surprising that Brandeis and the Court failed to find the price agreement illegal. The record, indeed, supports Brandeis's statement of effects. This is, of course, very puzzling. If the Call Rule had no effect on grain prices, what was its purpose? This is the question the government should have asked itself; the answer is important.

The answer is that the purpose of the Call Rule was to allow policing of commissions on after hours trading. Without the Call Rule, it was impossible to determine cheating on commissions, since there was no established price for grain after regular market hours. However, with the Call Rule, it was relatively simple to determine if bids included full commission charges, since the Call Rule fixed the price and since freight rates to particular points were well known. The evidence for this is simple and direct; the Call Committee and its successor, the To Arrive Committee, the administrating agencies under the Call Rule, concerned themselves exclusively with policing commissions. In addition, present members of the Board of Trade who operated when the Call Rule was still in effect wholly regarded the rule as a commission rule. Insofar as the Call or To Arrive Committees were effective, they were able to direct competitors away from cheating on commissions to "tattling" on each other.

In addition, the Rule would divert trade from after business hours to normal business hours where the policing of commissions were easier. When the Call Rule price was such that the unrestricted price would be above the Call Rule price, the supply curve would limit the amount of the grain bought and this would vary from zero to something less than would be bought if prices were unrestricted by the Call Rule. When the Call Rule price was above the price that would prevail without restrictions, the demand curve would limit the amount bought, which again would vary from zero to something less than the amount that would be bought if prices were unrestricted. Accordingly, the amount bought during the period of the day when the Call Rule was in effect would be less because of the Call Rule, and additional business would tend to be forced into the normal hours of the exchange.

The mistakes of the government in the *Chicago Board of Trade* case were serious but explicable. The government failed to discover the real case, but the real case was perhaps difficult to discover. The government was basking, prematurely, in the strength of per se illegality. Moreover, they lost the case. Given the government's presentation, one cannot be sorry they lost. Hopefully, such a loss would have been an incentive to the government to learn the economics of the cases they bring. Instead, the government reacted by gaining more power to win cases, in part, through obscuring their economics.

The *Window Glass* case,[8] 1923, furnishes an example somewhat parallel to the *Chicago Board of Trade* case in the sense that economic theory should have suggested to the government that additional investigation was in order. In this case, all manufacturers of handblown glass were involved in an arrangement whereby one set of factories operated with the existing labor force for six months and the other set of factories for another six months. Holmes noted that "the defendants contend with a good deal of force, that it is absurd to speak of their arrangements as possibly having any effect upon commerce among states, when manufacturers of this kind obviously are not able to do more than struggle to survive a little longer before they disappear. . . ."[9] The Court held for the defendants. It is easy to understand why. Handblown glass manufacturing was a dying activity and only a part of total glass manufacturing.[10] The fact that the government began the labor allocation practice during the war predisposed the court to look favorably on the practice. However, this was probably a misguided attempt by the government to save resources by looking at average costs, rather than marginal costs.

Indeed, the arrangement in this case is peculiar and suggestive. The efficient allocation of workers among plants is one that minimizes variable costs. It does not appear that this arrangement did that. If a plant is to be operated at all, production is pushed to the point where $MR = MC$ and marginal costs are equal for all plants. Thus, in Figure 4-1, costs in this case are areas $a + b$, but costs in the case where each plant is operated for half time at capacity are $a + b + c$.

What was going on in the *Window Glass* case? The defendants labor-sharing arrangements did not minimize these costs. In what respect did they gain? A Patinkin cartel model shows that it is desirable to include in the cartel even dying members of the trade. It was said that at this time large pieces of window

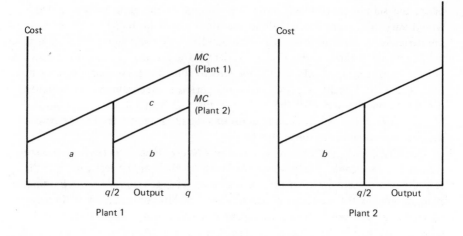

Figure 4-1. Multiplant Efficiency

glass cost more per square foot than smaller pieces per square foot that were cut from the larger pieces. Other peculiarities seem to have existed. All of this is very suggestive of a cartel embracing the window glass industry, not of a monopoly of just the handblown glass.[11] If this is correct, this is a situation similar to the *Chicago Board of Trade* case in that the government and the court failed to follow the lead of theory in discovering what was going on. Holmes said in this case, "To determine the legality of the agreement requires a consideration of the particular facts."[12] He then cited the *Chicago Board of Trade* case for support. Holmes suggestion is laudable, but the *Window Glass* and *Chicago Board of Trade* cases do not seem a very promising line of precedents for considering the particular facts.

A more recent case, *United States* vs. *Aluminum Company of America*, 1945, the *Alcoa* case,[13] is usually regarded as a high watermark of economic sophistication in legal opinion. If one were arguing that recent antitrust decisions had improved on old ones, it is probable that this case would be cited for support. It might be supposed that in the powerful formulation of Learned Hand, the mistakes of earlier years would be avoided. This does not seem to have been the case.

Two mistakes in economics were made that were fundamental to the decision. Essentially, the basis of the decision against Alcoa was Alcoa's market share. It was found that Alcoa had over 90 percent of the relevant market:

The [lower court] judge figured its [Alcoa's] share as only thirty-three percent; to do so he included 'secondary' and excluded that part of Alcoa's own production which it fabricated. ... If, on the other hand, Alcoa's total production fabricated and sold, be included and balanced against the sum of

imported 'virgin' and 'secondary' its share of the market was in the neighbor-
hood of sixty-four percent for that period. The percentage we have already
mentioned, over ninety, results only if we both include all Alcoa's production
and exclude secondary. That percentage is enough to constitute a monopoly; it
is doubtful whether sixty or sixty-four percent would be enough; and certainly
thirty-three percent is not. We conclude therefore that Alcoa's control over the
ingot market must be reckoned at over ninety percent. . . .[14]

Hand is to be commended for focusing on market share. His doctrine as to
what market share constitutes a monopoly, while perhaps reflecting the state of
the law, is unlikely to be echoed with such authority by economists. Indeed, it is
doubtful that the law was this clear.[15] However, the real problem is that Hand
got the wrong market share; the relevant market share is 64 percent. The
apposite question was what percentage of the market was furnished by Alcoa at
the time? It makes no difference that secondary aluminum was produced
originally by Alcoa sometime in the past. On the basis of his own definitions of
monopoly, Hand's decision was erroneous.

A second fundamental mistake may be discovered by referring to Coase's
recent article on product durability and monopoly.[16] Coase shows that in the
absence of certain types of contracts, the manufacturer of a durable product
must charge the competitive price regardless of market share. The monopolist
producer of a durable product, having sold to some demanders at a high price,
will then expand output and sell an additional quantity at a lower price, and so
on until marginal cost is reached. Yet each sale at a lower price harms the
previous purchasers. Hence no one would pay more than the competitive price.
A monopoly price can, however, be maintained through leasing arrangements
and contracts such as those allowing for resale to the manufacturer at a fixed
price. This analysis may explain in part the leasing arrangement by U.S. Shoe
Machinery and the character of contracts in the distribution of motion pictures.
No evidence of such contracts or leases are shown to have existed in the case of
Alcoa.

One cannot, of course, have expected Hand to develop this argument
unaided, but one could have expected him to get the right market share.
Moreover, Hand's view of competition is illustrative of the erroneous or
misleading analyses that are to be found in many decisions. The view is
particularly interesting because it presages modern governmental policy and
court decisions. In speaking to the question of whether Alcoa sought monopoly
or not, he says:

It was not inevitable that it should always anticipate increases in the demand for
ingot and be prepared to supply them. Nothing compelled it to keep doubling
and redoubling its capacity before others entered the field. It insists that it never
excluded competitors; but we can think of no more effective exclusion than
progressively to embrace each new opportunity as it opened, and to face every
newcomer with new capacity already geared into a great organization, having the
advantage of experience, trade connections and the elite of personnel.[17]

This unfortunate language and confusion of competition with monopoly sounds very modern.

The other case that would surely be mentioned as an example of a relatively sophisticated economic approach is the 1956 *Dupont Cellophane* case.[18] The essential question in this case as seen by the Court was the scope of the relevant market. In determining this, it found that "what is called for is an appraisal for the 'cross-elasticity' of demand in the trade."[19]

The dissenting opinion on the basis of a similar analysis stresses the similarities between cellophane and related products and comes to the opposite conclusion concerning monopolization. Stocking and Mueller also arrive at this same conclusion, in part, from the same type of consideration: "Rather, cellophane is so differentiated from other flexible wrapping materials that its cross elasticity of demand gives DuPont significant and continuing monopoly power."[20]

The bothersome element in all of these analyses is not so much that no cross-elasticities were calculated, but that there is and was a better measure of monopoly power available through calculating directly the demand elasticity for cellophane:

Since total revenue (*TR*) equals price times quantity (*PQ*) and since marginal revenue (*MR*) equals marginal cost (*MC*), then

$$TR = PQ$$

$$MR = MC = \frac{\alpha(TR)}{\alpha Q} = p + \frac{q\,dp}{dQ}$$

$$\text{or } MC = P(1 + \frac{q\,dp}{p\,dQ})$$

Then:

$$MC = P(1 + 1/e) \text{ where } e \text{ is demand elasticity.}$$

On this basis, the divergences between price and marginal cost could be calculated. If the demand elasticity were high at the point at which DuPont sold, this would have indicated little monopoly power. On the other hand, a relatively low demand elasticity would have given some support to an argument that DuPont had monopoly power. Indeed, one satisfactory measure of monopoly power is $P - MC/P$ which becomes simply $1/P_e$. This has a limited usefulness perhaps, but it has far more use than the vague discussion of cross-elasticities.

The government in this case made much of the fact that cellophane and its substitutes were not fungible. They were impressed that cellophane sold for a higher price than the substitutes, and this argument was accepted in the dissenting opinion. But this by itself shows nothing. Suppose that while cellophane had certain advantages over the other products, its production costs were higher. In this case, if it sold at cost, it might gain a share of the market and yet have a higher price than its substitutes. The wrong decision may have been made in this case, but neither the opinion, the dissent, nor even the analysis of Stocking and Mueller provide the data that seem most relevant.

The 1967 *Clorox* case[21] represents the first important proceedings against what might be called a conglomerate merger. Procter and Gamble, which did not manufacture bleach, purchased Clorox—a producer of liquid bleach. The government successfully challenged this merger on the general grounds that Procter's entry would lead over time to monopoly in the production of liquid bleach by Procter. The basic argument of the government was that Procter could purchase an important factor of production—advertising—much more cheaply than could other producers. An ancillary, though important, part of the argument was that the existence of Procter, prior to the merger, prevented the old Clorox Company from exercising whatever market power it might have had. That is, the threat of entry by Procter kept Clorox's prices lower than they otherwise would have been. The idea was that since Procter could produce bleach at lower cost than others, a given rise in the price of Clorox would be more likely to invoke the entry of Procter than other firms. Clearly, this case introduces with a vengeance the idea of potential competition which has become so important as a basis for antitrust policy. Although this idea will not be discussed here, it is interesting to determine the basis of the doctrine in this particular case.

The essence of the government's case, and the basis of the potential competition argument, was the unexercised advantage of Procter in producing bleach. The government assumed that since there were discounts in television advertising rates, these rates fell continuously with increases in the size of the advertisers' budget. The court accepted this assumption, something that earlier (postwar) courts may have been less likely to do. If this assumption were true, this would hardly limit potential competition to Procter. Lever Brothers and all large advertisers would serve as well or better as potential competitors. The merger of Procter could not have lowered competition at all with the massive potential competition that existed by the government's own definition. Clearly, the concept of potential competition was not well defined in this case.

Moreover, it seems extraordinary to bring a case against potential bleach producers when the basic difficulty was alleged to be in the structure of television rates. The effect of the rate discounts would be felt in many markets. The legal and economic question is if these differences in rates were based on differences in costs. The government did not and could not answer the question since it failed, indeed, to answer a much more basic question—did the alleged discounts on the basis of the size of the advertisers budget exist? John Peterman has shown that they did not.[22] Discounts were given, not on the basis of the advertiser's budget, but on the basis of the value of time. That is, rates varied according to audience size; prices per unit of audience were approximately equal. This was for network advertising. But Clorox and Procter never purchased network television for sales of bleach. They bought advertising in the national spot market where prices were essentially identical between Procter, Clorox, and other bleach producers. In sum, the government failed to define potential competition, and the existence of this competition was in any event based on the existence of size discounts that, in fact, did not exist.

This vagueness over the concept of potential competition shows up in the remedy. In fact, the decree in this case prevented Procter from entering the bleach business for five years. Of course, this is a ridiculous remedy. It obviated for five years the potential competition that the government sought to maintain. In this case, the government clearly had got itself into a box in the area of remedies. No remedy regarding the merger would prevent what they sought to avoid. This difficulty would have been avoided had the government focused on television rates, instead of bleach, and had they done this, and done it correctly, the problem they were concerned with would have vanished. It seems that the court in the Clorox case accepted arguments and assumptions of the government that earlier courts might not have accepted.

This type of difficulty over discounts exists in other cases. For example, in the 1948 *Morton Salt* case[23] discounts by Morton were found to be illegal. Not only was no evidence given about the character of costs in the distribution of salt that might explain the discounts, but the government argued that the evidence on costs was irrelevant and excluded that which was available from the record. The evidence seems vaguely suggestive of collusion in the industry. Moreover, there is evidence that transaction prices differed considerably from the list prices on which the court based its decision. Was this evidence of erosion of collusive prices, and if so, did the courts order to cease discounts make collusion easier? The *Clorox* and *Morton* cases are reasonable examples of the thesis that, while earlier antitrust opinions were not very good, the later ones were even worse.

However, both a more important and better example of this thesis is found in the famous 1962 and 1966 *Brown Shoe* cases.[24] Originally, Brown was attacked by the Department of Justice and, on the basis of the Supreme Court's ruling, certain other of Brown's practices which came to light were attacked by the Federal Trade Commission. The government won both cases.

The first case involved the merger of Brown Shoe, primarily a manufacturer, with Kinney, primarily a retailer.[25] This merger was thought to reduce competition in both the production and distribution of shoes. Brown produced about 4.5 percent of shoe output and Kinney less than 0.5 percent, so that together they produced less than 5 percent of output. However, the government argued that Brown's sales at wholesale were equivalent to retail. On this basis, they calculated the market share for each of 300 cities by adding the percentage of the wholesale sales controlled by Brown to the percentage of retail sales controlled by Kinney in that city. This procedure is clearly incorrect. A rise in wholesale prices by Brown to independent dealers would cause them to turn to other suppliers, and the ability of Kinney to raise retail prices in any city would not be affected by the fact that Brown sold wholesale in that city.

In addition, it appears that Kinney did not vary its prices according to its market share. That is, its price was the same in cities where its share of the market was large as in cities where its share was small. Moreover, in some markets where Kinney operated alone, its share exceeded the maximum combined market share in cities where Kinney and Brown operated together.

An important part of the argument by the Justice Department was that this merger culminated a trend in which manufacturers were buying retailers and forcing them to purchase the shoes produced by the manufacturer. This process was seen as increasing concentrations in shoe manufacturing. In actual fact, concentration had been falling in the shoe industry since mid-1930, and the proportion of output sold through manufacturing owned retail outlets has remained constant since 1929. If the alleged trend existed, it must have been on the basis of century long extrapolations.

The second *Brown* case dealt with Brown's distribution practices to those independent retailers that purchased the bulk of their shoes from Brown.[26] The commission argued that Brown's exclusive dealing contracts with these retailers precluded their purchase of shoes from others. Such contracts do, as all contracts do, generally preclude others. There is, however, nothing in this incompatible with competition. Moreover, foreclosure is perhaps not a helpful way to look at business activity. But the peculiar feature of this case is that no such contracts existed. The dealers were free to purchase at any time from others and hence must have bought primarily from Brown because of the advantages of doing this. The Commission, however, went on to argue that these firms bought from Brown because Brown sold to them below cost. That is, Brown was engaging in predatory pricing. If predatory pricing was the explanation, it was nearly as unsuccessful as in most other instances. Brown had been pricing this way since 1920, and by 1963 about 0.7 percent of domestic output was distributed to dealers receiving the supposed predatory pricing.

The remedy in this case was peculiarly undramatic, but not untypical. Brown was required to stop receiving a monthly report voluntarily submitted by about 40 percent of its dealers. The court in the first *Brown Shoe* case noted that "it is competition, not competitors that the (Clayton) Act protects."[27] Unfortunately, Brown Shoe helps disprove this very point.

The view of antitrust presented here is, of course, oversimplified. Much more needs to be known about the procedures by which cases are selected, what happens to them as they progress through the system and the courts, and the appropriateness of the remedies achieved in relation to the real problems. But the deficiencies noted here at the highest level of the process are not only interesting in themselves, they support a strong presumption that even with the present poor state of microeconomic theory, an examination of the supporting system could scarcely be expected to yield propitious results.

Comment

Charles G. Stalon

One can only agree with Zerbe's laments that: (1) history indicates many failures by prosecutors and judges in antitrust cases to pay attention to the best of economic theory, (2) there has been an increasing tendency since the early 1930s for the courts to develop a "perversion of the concept of competition," and to protect "competitors" rather than competition—the Robinson-Patman Act is, from the viewpoint of an advocate of a competitive system, an anomaly—and (3) the record does demonstrate that the courts are frequently unable to find a remedy even after they have awarded the government a victory in the antitrust trial. The fifteen-year dispute over how to rid El Paso of its subsidiary, Pacific Northwest Pipeline, is a classic example of how difficult it is to bring about even minor restructuring of the market.[1]

Narrow economic considerations—that is, considerations of price, cost, and quantity as those terms are used in textbooks—can never be the only ones in an antitrust suit and frequently are not even the important ones, so before unduly criticizing the courts and the prosecutors for failing to respond to economists' views of appropriate antitrust policy, an analysis of the reasons for their failures and the economists' responsibilities for them needs to be made. This comment addresses two considerations:

1. Democratic societies must be expected to pursue somewhat inconsistent objectives, and the severity of the inconsistencies can only be expected to increase as the pace of economic and social change accelerates.
2. Contemporary microeconomic theory—indispensable as it is to the rational organizations of society—is a feeble guide for the antitrust authorities and the courts.

The process of debate and action within a democratic society insures that some inconsistencies in social policy and action will develop. It is sometimes only by launching inconsistent policies that the legislature can clarify to the population and to itself the necessary tradeoffs.

The most important question today apparently is whether there is or is not a higher level of experimentation and inconsistency now than there was in the past. Indeed, it appears that the evidence of recent years, especially the "micro" programs designed to raise wages and provide employment that in turn prevent the attainment of full employment, is persuasive that this problem is worsening for the U.S. democracy. It does appear that in the 1930s, symbolized by the passage of the Robinson-Patman Act as well as by the legalization of fair trade laws, there was a nonsystematic retreat from "competition," that is, intense rivalry, as a vehicle for organizing the economic sphere of society. More important than these symbolic acts were the changes in public attitudes which supported (demanded?) this retreat in many areas, agriculture and labor being the most important. It may be easy for an economic theorist to denounce this retreat as shortsighted and perhaps even as impossible, since grossly inconsistent objectives were and are being sought, but it was not and it is not possible for the politicians and the courts to ignore the change in public attitude which compelled this inconsistency. Following the 1937 attempt by FDR to pack it, even the Supreme Court was forced to recognize that no matter how sacred their principles of interpretation of the interstate commerce clause and of the meaning of the antitrust acts, it was necessary to bow to a changed public opinion, if the continuity of the democratic order was to be maintained.

In the recent economic climate, a climate in which labor unions have broad exceptions from antitrust laws, agricultural prices are supported, and the government uses its power in innumerable ways to prevent painful price and/or wage declines, it is unrealistic to expect elected officials to pursue and judges to confirm market fragmentation policies designed to increase dramatically the flexibility of prices. Only after the federal Congress has changed many of its price support policies can the courts be expected to enforce with vigor similar policies on others.

Since the passage of the Clayton Act, the courts have been compelled to pay close attention to orthodox economic theory, that is, theory which is widely accepted as relevant and useful by a large proportion of the economics profession. This act, which prohibited a list of activities where the effect "may be substantially to lessen competition or tend to create a monopoly in any line of commerce," in effect made an act illegal or illegal according to its consequences. In short, an economic forecast was required before a court ' decision could be made.

Before criticizing the courts for their failure to listen to the lessons of economic theory, perhaps one should address the gross weaknesses which exist in contemporary microeconomic theory. It is fair to say that current theory does not provide guidelines for marginal improvements in most of the cases with which the courts deal. The courts are never faced with converting a monopoly into a perfectly competitive industry; they are faced with making marginal changes in a highly concentrated industry. And economic theory has provided very little guidance for such decisions.

It is said to note that to a large extent economists have paid much attention to some of the consequences that would exist if the society ever achieves the "dry rot" of perfection, but have paid surprisingly little attention to the reforms necessary to move in an orderly manner closer to that condition.

Economic theory today is so far from an acceptable theory of price behavior in many large segments of economic theory that it is of little value as a guide to the courts. When economists cease to differentiate, or do not bother to differentiate between General Motors and a local candy store in theory, the courts should not be expected to take them seriously.

The most important forms of business rivalry are those which determine simultaneously the components of the firm's "market basket" and the shape of its cost curve. This is especially true in the production and distribution of consumer goods. A theory which takes the product as a primitive concept can never be expected to provide badly needed guidance in an economy of such rivalry. The seeds of a theory which can provide guidance into many of the problems of antitrust and trade regulation can be found in a recent article by John A. Menge[2] and one by Bradford C. Snell.[3] The thrust of both articles is that the products offered by the automobile industry are largely determined by the large firms' desires to build effective barriers to entry and to create products which could be produced and distributed efficiently only by large firms.

Such a theory, after it is expanded to consider other techniques by which large firms create for themselves a comparative cost advantage, will offer an opportunity to separate economic activities according to whether they regulate, that is, facilitate competition or restrain it. Then, perhaps, one can make a better judgment on cases similar to the Chicago Board of Trade. Such a theory offers an opportunity to differentiate between promotional practices designed to create and/or maintain a noncompetitive structure from those constructively competitive in nature. Then, perhaps, one can make a better judgment in cases similar to the Clorox case. Such a theory can illustrate how an imperfection in one market (e.g., the money market) can be used to create a barrier to entry in another. Then, perhaps, economists can give better advice in cases similar to the Alcoa case, as well as direct the use of government antitrust resources more effectively. Such a theory should permit differentiating more clearly between predatory price competition and constructive price rivalry. Then, perhaps, the economics profession can provide the society with a meaningful escape from the paradox of Robinson-Patman.

One of the first casualties of a theory which drops the product as a primitive concept is likely to be the "structure, conduct, performance" paradigm; a paradigm which has not forced economists to face up to questions such as what is the optimum variety of products, what is the appropriate role of government in product standardization and simplification, and in what dimensions of rivalry should firms be permitted (or encouraged) to restrain other (uncooperative) firms?

Until economists can build on the seeds of current theory, they ought to sympathize with courts which must look to the economics profession for guidance. Until then, there are only the words of Milton Handler: "The history of the control of competition has been singularly disappointing. It is distinguished only by poverty of idea and mediocrity of craftsmanship."[4]

Part IV
Penalties and Remedies

5

The Role of the Economist in Developing Antitrust Remedies

Michael L. Glassman

Industrial organization economists and antitrust economists have not systematically approached the problem of attaining optimal or even "workable" remedies in antitrust cases.[1] Much descriptive work has been done with respect to both memorable and eminently forgettable antitrust cases. Upon occasion, economists have applied the tools of microeconomics to the analysis and evaluation of specific legal actions, and from time to time the same tools have been used to scrutinize the relief ordered in those actions.[2] Some industrial organization literature has been concerned with the deterrent impact of antitrust actions (and implicitly or explicitly relief) on further violations of the same sort.[3] However, even where particular ordered relief is evaluated by economists, little which has general applicability is learned about the efficient design of remedial measures. It is a strange state for the literature when one considers that if antitrust actions are to "pass" the benefit-cost tests of economists, they must produce benefits largely or entirely through relief. This chapter attempts to make a modest contribution to a field that has been neglected by economists.

Since economic benefits flow from adequate relief and since unsound relief can impose additional real costs upon society,[4] economists properly have a role in designing and evaluating relief provisions which are urged upon the courts. Yet, typically proposed antitrust orders are written by attorneys and evaluated, modified, and imposed by judges. Further, precedent seems to be an important factor in determining what relief is written by the attorney so that over time "traditional relief" has been developed to deal with specific types of offenses. If by chance "traditional relief" produces severe social costs by leading to higher consumer prices, for example, it is surely appropriate for economists to point out the consequences of the relief and to suggest alternatives. To the extent that remedial action is taken to promote welfare rather than for punitive purposes, economists may be best suited by virtue of training to design and measure the impact of antitrust remedies. Economists have judged that many antitrust triumphs have been "Pyrrhic Victories."[5] Might not that negative evaluation be altered by positive and productive policy recommendations?

There are three ways to approach the question of effective remedies. First, one might attempt to derive from economic theory some postulates of "optimal

The views herein are the personal ones of the author and do not necessarily reflect the official views of the Federal Trade Commission.

relief." One could state some marginal principles without much effort. For instance, if one considered the optimal amount of divestiture that should be applied to diminish deadweight loss in an industry, the principle that divestiture should continue until an incremental unit of divestiture produced benefits (reduction in deadweight loss) just equal to the marginal cost of divestiture appears sound. Such an approach may be of some use, but only if subjected to heavy qualification and modification. One obvious difficulty with the above stated principle on divestiture is indivisibility; incremental bundles of assets are rarely viable. Second, what properly are costs of divestiture? Are they transactions costs, government compliance costs, private compliance costs, foregone private profits (presumably monopoly rents), or all or some of the listed costs or perhaps other unnamed costs?[6] Third, should benefits be confined to allocative efficiency gains, or should one delve into the attempted measurement of redistributive gains or gains from the reduction of X-inefficiency? The mathematics can be written for a variety of marginal conditions, but given the present state of data, the translation of mathematics into useful rules for policy-making is doubtful. Though reasoning along these lines by policymakers would help to avoid serious errors, such a framework is not used in the discussion of the economics of remedial action.

A second approach to identifying principles of effective antitrust relief is empirical. In merger cases, Elzinga advises against partial divestitures because they have rarely created viable, independent business entities.[7] Many economists and lawyers have argued against the use of conduct remedies[8] because conduct remedies have very frequently been evaded and conduct remedies when effective have distorted resource allocation. This approach will not be adopted for two reasons. First, most of the empirical generalizations about antitrust remedies are wrong. Second, there is a methodological objection to arriving at an hypothesis by looking at a sample and using the same sample to test the hypothesis. This procedure is particularly uncomfortable when the hypothesis cannot be reached independently by appeal to economic theory.

The third approach, the one used in what follows, appeals to economic theory and an implicit evaluation of past order provisions in an attempt to derive some principles which might contribute to improved antitrust remedies. It is assumed that remedies are to be applied only in instances where a problem exists, the complaint issued by the antitrust authority addresses the problem, and an effective and enforceable remedy can be employed to solve the problem. Since so many economically "bad" cases have been filed by antitrust authorities, this assumption is for convenience rather than because it depicts reality. It is, however, beyond the scope of this chapter to engage in a prolonged discussion of what constitutes a "good" antitrust case. It is amusing to note that for bad cases, the optimal remedy may very well be no remedy.[9] Thus an important contribution of an economist who cannot dissuade authorities from filing a bad case may be to "minimize costs." That is the first principle in designing antitrust remedies. Other principles of remedial action will be discussed in the context of particular types of antitrust violations: (1) mergers, (2) monopoly, and (3) anti-competitive practices. No claim is made that the following discussion is exhaustive; it is quite preliminary.

In most antimerger actions, divestiture of the acquired assets is a primary goal. The case for such divestiture is particularly clear in the instance of horizontal mergers. Assuming that hypotheses that relate concentration posi-tively to profitability are correct, the horizontal acquisition of a competitor by a leading firm in a market will impose an added welfare loss upon consumers.[10] That loss can be hypothetically eliminated by restoring the market to its preacquisition position (i.e., by a total divestiture of the acquired assets to other than a horizontal competitor). If total divestiture orders were without cost (litigation, compliance, transactions, and time costs), then such orders would be preferred to lesser orders in all horizontal merger actions. But, total divestiture can be employed to produce more than a single new firm. Later it will be argued that the feasibility of creating more than one new firm should be studied in horizontal merger cases and that, in certain circumstances, such a remedy will be practical and effective.

The case for total divestiture in a conglomerate merger action is much weaker. For simplicity, it is assumed that all conglomerate mergers attacked are challenged on the "potential competition" theory and that all cases brought are defensible on economic grounds. Thus each case involves the acquisition of a leading firm in a concentrated market protected by high entry barriers by a firm which is one of a very few that qualify as potential entrants. Further, potential entrants are presumed to increase the elasticity of the long-run demand curve (relevant for price decisions) for actual competitors. The elimination of a substantial potential competitor would raise the profit-maximizing price charged within the market. The elimination of an actual competitor through a horizontal merger is assumed to have a larger impact upon price than the elimination of a potential competitor of equal size (where the size of the potential entrant is determined by measuring the size of that firm in the relevant market if it chose to enter *de novo*).

A total divestiture in the case of such a conglomerate merger has no direct impact upon the structure of the market. It provides the single benefit of increasing by one the number of potential entrants. The gains from adding one more potential entrant are inherently very difficult to measure and intuitively of considerably smaller significance than from adding a horizontal competitor. The impact of a potential competitor upon monopoly rents is likely to be much smaller than the impact of the emergence of a new actual competitor for several reasons. First, potential entrants require time to become actual competitors, so that they provide gains which must be discounted when measuring antitrust benefits. Second, the probability that a potential entrant will become an actual competitor is less than one and is a rising function of price within the market unless entry is unimpeded. Thus actual competitors will respond to virtually all price changes by rivals, while potential entrants will not. Third, the potential competitor (assumed to be one of few) may enter a market (assumed to be highly concentrated and protected by high entry barriers) and find that the profit-maximizing course of action is to join with other firms to establish a collusively agreed-upon price above the competitive level. Therefore the gains of new entry may be partly or largely offset by subsequent collusion if the market is appropriate for collusive behavior.[11]

Under the assumptions adopted in this discussion, therefore, partial divestiture may be superior to total divestiture as an antitrust remedy. If, for instance, Procter and Gamble had been ordered to divest one-half of Clorox, rather than the whole firm in the *Procter and Gamble-Clorox* case,[12] the bleach market would have had three substantial competitors (Procter and Gamble, Clorox, and Purex) rather than two. In addition, Clorox would no longer have possessed a dominant share of the market (50-60 percent) but would have had a more modest share (25-30 percent). Concentration would have been lower, assymetries in firm size would have been reduced, and the number of competitors would have been increased. In short, performance would surely have been improved at the modest cost of reducing the number of potential entrants by one. But there are many more advantages to this particular remedial approach. First, Procter and Gamble would have moved to a preferred position compared to its position with full divestiture since it would be permitted to keep half of what it acquired. Second, since Procter and Gamble would have preferred this remedy, it might well have litigated less or appealed decisions less often. Procter and Gamble might well have entered into a consent agreement. Thus both private and public resources would have been conserved. Third, with a lower total cost of action, net benefits would have been larger. As indicated, the partial divestiture remedy would have yielded greater benefits than a total divestiture remedy by reducing concentration, reducing firm size inequality, and adding a substantial new competitor to the bleach market. In addition, benefits would be larger because the partial divestiture remedy might have been consented to or been finalized with fewer appeals. Thus benefits would have begun to flow to society at an earlier date and from that factor alone, the present value of a stream of welfare benefits would have been larger.

A crucial question at this point is whether the divested firms would have been viable. Elzinga argues that on the basis of past experience with partial divestitures, one can be only pessimistic.[13] If Clorox could have been split into two firms without difficulty, and if multiple plants existed and no problem arose with respect to plants designed to produce joint or multiple products, might not Procter and Gamble have complied with a divestiture order by conferring the least desirable assets (those generating the highest costs) upon the new Clorox? Or might not Procter and Gamble have divested to a firm not well-equipped to compete effectively in the bleach market? How could the divestiture of a nonviable or inefficient firm be avoided? Presumably, the viability of new Clorox would have been enhanced if the divestiture order conferred the trade-name "Clorox" upon the new firm.[14] But the problem of nonviability of partial divestitures can be dealt with more generally. It is clear that certain technical requirements must be met in order to write effective partial divestiture relief. Economists and/or lawyers can, however, determine whether a firm has multiple plants and whether those plants produce single or multiple products. It should also be possible for those writing relief to make some determination about plant efficiency in order to avoid the divestiture of a "high-cost" plant. A thorough investigation should enable one to determine which nonplant assets such as patents or trademarks would be essential to the creation of a viable competitive entity.

Yet there is an analytically sounder approach to the question of viability. One of the basic problems with specifying detailed relief is that the antitrust authority has limited expertise in the industry and does not and cannot respond quickly and accurately in a profit-maximizing fashion to the imperatives of the market. It is the participants in the industry who are best qualified to write efficient relief and carry out relief imposed upon them in a successful fashion. Thus, in theory, one should create incentives to the provision of optimal relief and then say to the respondent, "Here are the ground rules; implement the relief in the manner that is best for you." If the antitrust agency determines that ideal relief to combat the impact of a product extension merger is to create three viable competitors, leaving the respondent with one-third of the acquired assets, then the agency should provide an incentive to the respondent to create two additional viable entities; other things being equal, the success of relief will be positively related to the incentives provided to implement successful remedies. The single best incentive that seems to work in the direction of creating viable partial divestitures is the utilization of spin-offs rather than sale of assets.[15] The respondent firm is told what assets must be divested and approximately what volume of sales the divested firm should be able to realize, and the respondent is told to create a new firm including those assets by issuing stock in the spin-off entity to respondent's shareholders. If the firm created is not viable, then respondent's stockholders suffer. A strong incentive is thereby provided for accomplishing a successful divestiture in a profit-maximizing (i.e., least cost) fashion. In order to avoid having the spin-off corporation fall under the control of its parent, a provision requiring large holders of respondent's shares to sell stock in either the parent or the offspring is desirable. Such a provision adds a second incentive to successful divestiture. If holders of large blocks of respondent's stock are forced to sell their holdings in the spin-off, the size of their losses will be a function of the viability of the new firm. To the extent that major shareholders are represented in management and by directors, there will be pressure exerted to minimize capital losses by creating a viable entity.[16]

A more abstract but interesting question is whether the firm found in violation of the law should be required to spin off monopoly rents earned during the possession of the assets required to be divested.[17] Such a provision might provide greater assurance of viability and might deter many actionable mergers. However, measuring incremental monopoly rents directly attributable to a merger, given the present state of the arts, seems to be extraordinarily difficult.

Creating new firms by a spin-off technique enhances the potential viability of partial divestitures while reducing the costs of antimerger litigation. In the area of conglomerate merger relief, partial divestitures promise greater immediate benefit than total divestiture. How many new firms should be created in any particular instance is a matter which could be determined by careful investigation. Practically, however, as spin-offs become smaller, chances for nonviability rise, so that those writing relief might well be wise to err in a conservative direction when dictating the number of new firms to be initiated as a result of an anticompetitive merger.

Some of the principles discussed also apply to horizontal mergers. It seems evident that, other things equal, competition would be promoted more by the creation of several new firms rather than by a single-firm divestiture. However, in the case of a horizontal acquisition, one would presumably be reluctant to permit the acquiring firm to retain ownership of a portion of the acquired firm. Thus employing partial divestiture orders to horizontal mergers would not reduce the cost of action by inducing the respondent firm to settle or to litigate or appeal less. This being the case, benefits would be deferred until the adjudicative process had been exhausted by the respondent. Further, costs would be increased if two or more divestitures involve greater transactions costs than a single divestiture. Net benefits might be increased, however, if the spin-off includes monopoly rents, for then the firm has less to gain by delaying the ultimate decision. On balance, the case can be made—albeit with less strength than for conglomerate mergers—that partial divestitures are superior to full divestitures in those horizontal merger cases where that remedy is technically feasible. Again, the use of spin-offs is essential to attaining a maximum likelihood of viability.

Another instance where partial divestitures seem appropriate is in the case where a single firm has made a large number of acquisitions with anticompetitive results in many different geographical markets. If the government is required to show an anticompetitive impact in each and every market, then it seems obvious that attention should be directed to those markets where welfare losses are largest, and the government attorneys should proceed down the list of markets until the marginal cost of an additional divestiture is equal to the marginal benefits of an additional divestiture. To go beyond that point would imply too much enforcement in terms of social welfare. In this situation the problem of viability is not so serious, for each of the many acquired firms was once a separate entity and can presumably stand alone in the future. However, it might be beneficial to employ the spin-off technique in order to discourage the divestiture of a concealed nonviable firm.

The use of merger bans as a remedy may very well be appropriate in this latter class of cases. A ban on future acquisitions is frequently employed in instances where concentration has risen rapidly in preceding years. Sometimes a ban is substituted for structural relief, but often a ban supplements other relief. Under a ban the antitrust authority must approve or reject future acquisitions of a particular variety. In practice the standards applied to evaluating these proposed mergers are more stringent than the standards applied in litigated merger cases. Merger bans, like other "preventive" antitrust measures, have the advantage of costing less than remedies designed to undo a particular structure after the fact. Costs of litigation, transactions, and enforcement are reduced or eliminated, and the cost of having welfare losses generated during the time from acquisition to final divestiture is avoided. Of course, an additional cost may be borne by virtue of the fact that the probability of stopping a merger, one which has no anticompetitive impact but simply results in real cost savings, is increased because presumably the government will often disapprove mergers on the basis of less evidence than would be required to find an acquisition in violation of Section 7 of the Clayton Act. In the case of a firm acquiring many firms in many geographical markets, the government faces two problems. First, it may find it too costly to challenge all of the acquisitions, and second, the acquisitive firm may continue its merger activities after a final order is reached, necessitating acquiescence or new suits by the authorities. In such an instance, a ban on future acquisitions may produce greater net benefits than no relief at all or than a series of antitrust actions against some or all future acquisitions.

To sum up the discussion of merger relief, certain conclusions based upon economic theory can be stated. They are as follows:

1. Partial divestitures which create viable firms will often be preferable to full divestitures in conglomerate and horizontal merger cases.
2. The case for partial divestitures over total divestitures is stronger for conglomerate mergers than for horizontal mergers.
3. Viability of divested entities should be encouraged by providing positive incentives to the divesting firms. One such incentive is the utilization of spin-off divestitures where the spin-off of monopoly rents may or may not be included.
4. Bans on future acquisitions may be a useful supplementary remedial tool where the cost of litigation may not justify a series of suits. In particular, in industries where many acquisitions are taking place and where concentration is rising rapidly in many geographical markets, a merger ban may contribute to maximizing antitrust benefits.

In this section, a few sensible principles of antitrust relief have been derived for merger cases. It seems that the conclusions follow rather directly from elementary principles of economic theory (and, of course, from the assumptions herein). The fact that economic theory can be of considerable help in avoiding pitfalls of antitrust relief suggests that the economist is in a very advantageous position to evaluate and to construct antitrust orders. The economist is also well-qualified to tell judges and lawyers why certain types of relief will not be adequate and why particular remedies are essential to obtaining the relief that the government seeks. In short, it seems that the economist has a role in designing and evaluating merger relief and that it makes sense to use economists' talents in performing those functions which are critical to successful antimerger activity. Not surprisingly, the same proposition holds for monopoly relief.

Some of the problems in designing monopoly relief are similar to those confronted in merger cases, but additional unique problems arise as well. There are three areas of monopoly relief that deserve some attention. They are (1) a discussion of the general approach to monopoly relief, (2) a comment on the special remedial problems posed in cases involving discriminating monopolists, and (3) the possible interaction of economics and politics in designing monopoly relief. The term *monopoly* in this discussion shall be employed as shorthand for traditional single-firm monopolies and those tight oligopolies[18] where behavior is sufficiently cartelized to approximate monopoly behavior. The analysis will deal with those types of cases that have been brought as violations of the Sherman Act or of Section 5 of the Federal Trade Commission Act. Again, no attempt is made to provide an exhaustive treatment of this complex subject.

If, as before, industry performance is related to concentration, the accepted wisdom about monopoly relief is that remedial action should be fashioned to deconcentrate the subject industry. It is also generally accepted that the efficient way to obtain deconcentration is through structural relief, usually through divestiture. Great skepticism is voiced about the efficacy of conduct remedies in dealing with monopoly, although certain behavioral orders are viewed as being more productive than others.[19]

If, as assumed, deconcentration is the appropriate goal of monopoly antitrust action, then theoretically there exists a set of possible remedies that will achieve the desired level of deconcentration. The remedies differ with respect to costs imposed upon society, where costs include foregone welfare benefits incurred because some remedies take longer to attain the desired deconcentration than others. Presumably, the economists often object to conduct remedies because they may not be least cost remedies or they may never achieve the desired deconcentration (i.e., they are infinitely costly relative to other remedies). One of the "remedies" that can be employed to achieve deconcentration is to allow the market to do it naturally. This might be termed the "Yale Brozen Remedy."[20] If it is the least cost remedy, then no explicit antitrust action is warranted. Another possible remedy has been explored only in the area of regulated utilities.[21] Perhaps the government should sell monopoly rights into all perpetuity for each and every market to the highest bidder and distribute the proceeds to society. A similar type of remedy is to levy fines against monopolists and to distribute the proceeds to the public. Both approaches open the gates to new sets of problems having to do with neutral and optimal ways of distributing proceeds to the public. The sale of monopoly rights creates the additional problem of defining markets within which rights can be exercised. Some of these new approaches to monopoly may be practically feasible, and they are certainly theoretically interesting. However, the analysis will be confined to two rather traditional methods of attaining relief.[22]

Within the set of possible deconcentrating remedies, divestitures and the reduction or elimination of entry barriers are remedies that have been employed by antitrust authorities and discussed by economists. Successful divestiture remedies have an immediate impact upon the market but are subject to several shortcomings. As a practical matter, antitrust authorities cannot and probably would not consider drastic structural change sufficient to transform an industry from monopoly or oligopoly to competition—much less atomistic competition. Further, in creating new firms, the author of relief must be concerned with economies of scale, viability, and a host of other ominously practical problems. Still it seems likely that serious attacks on monopolies and oligopolies in the future will include some horizontal divestiture as a remedial ingredient. Certainly, with problems like economies of scale and viability, the case for providing respondent firms with an incentive to successfully divest is a strong one. As in the case of merger relief, divestitures probably stand a better chance of being viable if spin-offs are employed. Again, spin-offs tend to reduce the real costs of divestiture while increasing societal benefits.

If divestiture is impractical, then deconcentration may be accomplished by encouraging future entry. In order to promote entry, the antitrust authorities must identify the relevant barriers to entry and lower or eliminate them. This type of relief is best exemplified by orders that call for the licensing, dedication, or divestiture of patents and trademarks. With these remedies, an attempt is made to create a favorable environment for entry for firms attracted by higher than competitive profits. The success of such a measure depends upon the adequacy of the order, the proper identification of barriers, the existence of "economic profits," and the rate at which new entrants can and will take advantage of the reduced barriers. Obviously, if entry is at a very slow rate, the present value of benefits from such relief will be small. Sometimes it is more efficient to combine licensing provisions with some divestiture (i.e., the authority creates one or more licensees to accelerate the timing of benefits).

Entry barrier-reducing remedies have not been extended beyond barriers associated with patents and trademarks in any systematic fashion, although one gets the impression that some of the conduct orders adopted have been at least directed toward that end, albeit in a fuzzy manner. There are two reasons for the failure to utilize entry encouraging remedies more generally. First, it is clear that for traditional microeconomic models that include perfect capital markets and perfect information, economists have been unable to identify barriers to entry once they leave the realm of economies of scale (an indivisibility), government imposed barriers (licenses, patents, etc.), or vertical supply curves. No business practice or strategy has been rigorously shown to create a true asymmetry between firms within and without the industry. Indeed, some claim that none can be found. It is true that asymmetries can be generated by relaxing assumptions about perfect capital markets and perfect information, but several problems arise. How does one realistically specify an "imperfect capital market" for example (by how much and in what direction is it imperfect)?[23] If one assumes an imperfect capital market, how does one explain how entry by General Motors, General Foods, or Procter and Gamble is inhibited without resort to ad hoc reasoning? What does one do about reaching policy prescriptions in the "second best" world that relaxed assumptions imply?[24] It appears that the state of the barriers to entry literature is in such disrepair that little can be said about barrier-reducing remedies except for those involving patents, trademarks, licenses, and the like. Research in this area, starting with a rigorous definition of entry barriers, is sorely needed before barrier reducing remedies can be sensibly employed at the policy level.

The second reason that barrier-reducing remedies may not have been employed more extensively is that such remedies may be equivalent to unenforceable, evadable, or unproductive conduct measures. For example, suppose it is argued that heavy advertising or high advertising to sales ratios constitutes a barrier to entry.[25] Presumably, the entry-encouraging remedy is to ban or limit advertising. The decision to ban cigarette ads on television has certainly not attracted a drove of new entrants, whatever other impact it has had. In fact, some case can be made that entry has been made more difficult since entry may be facilitated by heavy advertising.[26] Other difficulties with limiting advertising include determining the extent of the limit, defining the units of limitation (by media, by dollar value, by minutes, by type of audience, or by some other standard), evaluating the welfare loss created by forcing a nonprofit maximizing level of advertising, and evaluating the impact upon the media of imposing a leftward shift in the demand for their services. As can be seen, there are serious problems in imposing barrier-reducing remedies beyond rigorously defining the barrier. Still, such forms of relief deserve further attention, and effective monopoly relief will often involve some combination of barrier reduction and divestiture.

Should a remedy that created new competition and induced new entry be imposed, it might be sensible to also employ a merger ban to avoid the acquisition of new entrants or spin-off entities by existing established firms and to avoid the acquisition by spin-off firms of new entrants. In short, one might argue that behavior which might undo the salutary impact of the remedy should be constrained. A merger ban might accomplish that goal cheaply.

Special remedial problems arise in dealing with a discriminating monopolist. As is well known, a perfectly discriminating monopolist produces the competitive output and imposes no welfare losses upon society.[27] One can assume, however, that real world discriminating monopolists like IBM and United Shoe Machinery discriminate imperfectly and therefore generate deadweight losses. In cases involving such firms, discriminatory pricing is often attacked directly. For example, provisions which break the tie between the product and the metering device (e.g., computers and computer cards) or which require that the product be sold and leased on "equally advantageous" terms are written into the orders. But surely this is the wrong way to combat a discriminating monopolist. To attack the discriminatory pricing rather than the market power of a discriminating monopolist may impose serious losses upon society. If order provisions effectively end discrimination so that in the place of a discriminating monopolist there is a "single price" monopolist, then output may very well fall and the remedy may have brought about a larger deadweight loss than existed before.

Further, one can make the argument that such a remedy will, in fact, deter entry. Entry presumably is triggered by expected high profits, and profits are highest from sales to users of the discriminating monopolist's products with the most inelastic demand. If entry barriers were lowered, then new entrants would be attracted to these high profit segments of the market. In the process, these prices would be reduced and ultimately the discriminatory price structure would be collapsed toward a single competitive price. If entry does occur in the higher profit segments, then the remedial benefits are large and the improvement in performance is relatively great. Suppose, however, that the remedy successfully eliminates price discrimination before dealing with market power. If government relief leads to the charging of a single price, then it appears that the market will not be able adequately to send signals (through price differentials) to prospective entrants, informing them of the most profitable segments and guiding them to efficient, profit-maximizing entry. Thus the conclusion is that in dealing with a discriminating monopolist, the relief writer should attack the monopoly and not the discriminatory pricing which is merely symptomatic of market power; ending the monopoly will inevitably end discriminatory pricing.

Finally, one of the most difficult questions to consider in writing antitrust remedies is the interaction between economic and political forces and to what extent economists ought to get involved in designing relief which works in part through political channels. An example of this sort of situation ought to make the problem, if not the solution, clear. In an industry that is vertically integrated and is protected by an import quota on its raw material, the import quota was supported actively by industry participants through lobbying and other techniques. Thus the quota apparently enhances profitability of domestic concerns. The increased profitability may be of long duration if the industry is concentrated and is protected by substantial barriers to entry. Suppose the antitrust authority sought to improve industry performance. Might not vertical dissolution of the raw material stage of production (e.g., mining) be effective? Now major firms would become purchasers of the raw material rather than sellers. These firms would be interested in low input prices. Might they not be expected to lobby for relaxed import restrictions, which would lead to increased foreign supplies, lower prices, and improved industry performance? Such an antitrust remedy would change optimum price-quantity configurations for major companies, who would probably make their wishes known to appropriate governmental agencies.

But the economist/relief designer who proposes this approach has wandered into relatively uncharted waters. What he is doing is arguing for the efficacy of his remedy on the basis of a rather speculative understanding of interactions within political institutions. It may be inappropriate for the economist to venture into this arena, admittedly beyond his area of primary competence. On the other hand, so many industries are subject to governmental intervention that declaring these fields beyond the scope of antitrust activity severely limits the possible impact of antitrust enforcement.

Certainly, similar problems arise with antitrust treatment of rate-regulated utilities and quasi utilities. They arise in certain instances where the government is the chief customer of an industry and where government purchasing habits may facilitate monopolization, collusion, or both. The role of antitrust in these areas has yet to be defined and the usefulness of economic expertise in writing effective relief is at least open to doubt.

As with merger relief, the case is clear that for traditional monopoly cases the economist can play a significant role in designing effective remedial measures. Principles of economic theory frequently imply what relief is appropriate in a particular case and very often suggest what relief will be ineffective or counterproductive. Who other than an economist is best able to analyze the nature and importance of barriers to entry, the relationship between structure and performance, or the relative costs of alternative remedial actions? A more difficult question, however, is whether the economist ought to attempt to fashion relief in industries where political institutions are intricately interwoven with the more familiar economic forces which affect industry behavior and structure. Further, should the economist attempt to write relief which depends upon forces impinging upon political institutions in order to succeed?

These familiar examples illustrate why the economist is well qualified to write antitrust relief in merger and monopoly cases. I have suggested that the pyrrhic victories of past antitrust action can be avoided in part by the application of remedies which logically should lead to improved performance. Effective remedies flow inexorably from appeal to underlying economic theory, and economists are in a particularly advantageous position to understand the implications of the underlying theoretical principles.

Antitrust authorities frequently file so-called practices cases. Anticompetitive practices include, but are not limited to, price fixing, vertical price fixing,[28] price discrimination of all sorts, reciprocity, refusals to deal, customer allocations, dividing territories, establishing joint selling agents, price squeezes, and exchange of information through trade associations for collusive purposes. In antitrust law, there seems to be a tradition that forecloses the application of structural remedies to these types of cases. Apparently, structural relief is usually only available in cases involving mergers, monopolization, or acts which directly and overtly impinge upon industry structure. In a very special sense the penalty must fit the crime. Thus practices cases are usually dealt with by employing one or more measures of conduct relief.

Most, if not all, of the practices attacked by antitrust agencies are not anticompetitive unless they are employed by firms that enjoy market power. However, the practices, when utilized by firms with discretionary power, seem in general to be mere symptoms of monopoly power. Thus, as in the case of the discriminating monopolist, it seems preferable to attack the underlying cause of poor performance rather than the symptoms associated with that cause. In many instances that implies structural relief, but such relief, as has been pointed out, is not available. Perhaps the dilemma can be resolved by imposing entry barrier-reducing measures in practices cases. If so, the case for directing additional resources to the definition and economic theory of entry barriers is further strengthened. Perhaps, however, the implication of this analysis is simply that practices cases ought not to be filed in most instances.

Despite these conclusions, some reservations must be stated. Practices cases are currently being attacked with conduct remedies, and economists have generally been critical of these measures. Apparently, however, some conduct relief is significantly better than other conduct relief. For example, little good has been said about the efficacy of cease and desist orders with the possible exception of their use in overt price fixing cases. The "sin no more" type of order, it is believed, is easily evadable. Other conduct remedies seem to be highly regulatory in nature so that they are both evadable and difficult to enforce. Still others are deficient because they generate serious welfare losses through an enforced misallocation of resources. Yet some conduct remedies appear not to be flawed so seriously. An order requiring respondents to stop selling through a joint selling agent would probably win approval from economists because it is neither evadable nor expensive to enforce and apparently does not lead to serious distortions of resource allocation. An order which terminates a trade association may be effective as well. Perhaps other examples could be listed.

The point is that some conduct remedies may, in fact, effectively reduce market power and improve industry performance while being less costly than more drastic structural remedies. Since it is apparent that some conduct remedies are better than others, it may be worthwhile for economists to examine more carefully possible behavioral remedies which will reduce entry barriers or have an indirect impact upon industry structure. If such remedies were also nonevadable, enforceable, and without adverse influence on resource allocation, then the range of possible antitrust relief would be greatly expanded.

This chapter has urged that economists be given major responsibility for designing antitrust relief, particularly in merger and monopoly cases. The reason for displacing the attorney from his traditional role is simple. The effectiveness of antitrust relief depends upon adopting remedies which will generate benefits to consumers, and the economist by the nature of his discipline and by his training is especially well suited to prescribe remedies which will be both beneficial and relatively inexpensive. This position has been supported largely by showing the connection between principles of economic theory and effective relief in a series of examples. A further argument is that economic research efforts in the direction of studying barriers to entry and conduct relief could greatly enrich the art of writing antitrust remedies.

If, as is usually the case, economists are wary about providing answers to questions of policy, they can receive consolation from looking at the record of antitrust performance. There can be little doubt that economists could have done no worse and might have done significantly better than attorneys had they accepted the responsibility of designing antitrust remedies. With the cost so small and the potential benefits so great, much is to be lost if economists withhold their policy prescriptions in the field of antitrust relief.

Comment

Stanley E. Boyle

Glassman makes two important points often overlooked by students of antitrust economics.[1] First, he points out that efforts devoted to the planning for the remedy, ex ante, are as essential as those directed to the form of the decision, ex post. Therefore both planning, ex ante, and shaping the remedy, ex post, are of crucial importance if the prosecution of the case is to be successful in the marketplace. Unless reasonable results are obtained in these two aspects, the act of simply "winning" the case in the district, circuit, or Supreme Court may prove to be inconsequential.

Second, Glassman points out that economists not only should, but must, play as crucial a role in fashioning remedies as they do in selecting cases. Moreover, their role should expand in both areas. The reasons for this are twofold. First, the goals sought by the antitrust laws are essentially economic ones, that is, Congress apparently hoped that the enforcement of these laws would improve, or at the very least maintain, the quality of competition existing in the marketplace. This was, after all, the ostensible purpose of passing the Sherman Act, the Clayton Act, and the FTC Act. Second, the cases that are litigated involve complex economic interrelationships, many of which are beyond the economic capability of most lawyers. All one has to do to verify this statement is to look at the many and complex economic issues raised, but ignored, in a case such as *U.S.* vs. *I.T.T.*[2] Thus the analysis of these complex economic issues and solutions is the proper purview of well-trained and knowledgeable economists and should not be viewed as a playground for budding lawyers.

Despite these positive aspects, there are parts of Glassman's analysis which raise substantial problems. The first is concerned with the nature of the impediments facing economists in the area of devising remedies. He appears to view the restrictions on the role of economists as ones imposed upon them by others. While there is an element of truth to this allegation, it represents for the most part a considerable oversimplification of the issue. The major restrictions that exist have been self-imposed. In recent years economists have become primarily interested and involved in developing models of market behavior that contain a growing degree of elegance and sophistication. And, while engaging in this delightful pastime, the real world has passed them by. Economists have tended to retreat from the role of policymaker, forgetting that few if any important decisions have ever been made on the basis of full-information models.

Much of Glassman's discussion with respect to the role of the economist suffers from the fact that the author is unclear as to the real roles of the "inside" vs. "outside" economist.[3] He states, for example, that "economists have not *systematically* approached the problem of attaining optimal or even 'workable' remedies in antitrust cases."[4] Unless memory serves this writer badly, having worked for both the Antitrust Division and the Federal Trade Commission, economists, particularly at the FTC, play a substantial role in selecting and organizing cases as well as in fashioning the remedy which is to be applied. It is true, unfortunately, that the Commission itself tends not to follow the remedial advice given it in many cases.

Nongovernmental economists attempting to provide inputs into the process of developing remedies are faced with a more substantial impediment, that is, they do not have any accessible outlet through which they can make their views known. Most government economists are less than totally receptive to the inputs of "outside" economists who offer to share their insights into these problems. Most of the existing journals are not particularly interested in the publication of articles or notes dealing with antitrust matters. The fact remains, however, that the existing restraints tend to be self-imposed.

In the remainder of his analysis, Glassman attempts to analyze the past and present role of the economist in fashioning remedies through "appeals to economic theory and an implicit evaluation of past order provisions."[5] As a prelude to this analysis, he notes "that remedies are to be applied only in instances where a problem exists, the complaint issued by the antitrust authority addresses the problem, and an effective and enforceable remedy can be employed to solve the problem."[6] To this, however, one might add a fourth condition: that effective relief, if developed, will be granted. Glassman then appraises the competitive consequences of various types of remedies in merger cases, revolving around two basic issues. In this discussion he focuses his attention upon the relative merits of spin-offs when compared with divestiture. Second, he discusses the relative merits of partial, full, and multiple divestitures. As he points out, both of these questions are crucial to any appraisal of the "success" of an antimerger enforcement policy.

Divestiture is the most common relief sought by antitrust agencies in merger cases. Glassman points out that there are two important questions which must be answered in each case, however. How much is to be spun off or divested? What form should the spin-off or divestiture take? It seems that for the most part the antitrust agencies—both economists and lawyers—have failed to provide answers to these questions in developing the framework for most cases. It also seems that answers to these questions should be provided by the staff prior to, or concurrent with, filing a complaint.[7]

It is generally assumed that if company A is purchased by company B (a competitor), then a remedy which requires company A to sell company B to company C (not a competitor) will result in restoring the industry involved to approximately the same competitive condition which existed prior to the initial acquisition. This is a ridiculous assumption. It is, of course, not possible to sell off company A to company C and restore the competitive conditions to those which existed prior to the merger, since the facilities of company A are now a part of a conglomerate firm (company C) and *are not* a separate economic entity of the type which existed prior to the merger. The only way in which one could assume that the purchase-resale process had no economic effect would be to assume that the impact of conglomerate mergers is neutral. This writer's opinion on this subject is already a matter of record[8] and unalterably in opposition to such an assumption.

An interesting and novel possibility which Glassman suggests is that competition might be enhanced by partial rather than full divestiture. In this vein he suggests that the commission might well have required Procter & Gamble to dispose of a portion of the Clorox assets rather than all of them. In this instance, as it worked out, a transition took place from a rather small one-product firm, Clorox, to a large diversified household cleaning supply firm, Procter & Gamble, and then back to a separate company. In this instance the product sold— Clorox—occupied a dominant place in the market. Assuming for the moment that the companies involved might be somewhat the same size, this might be advantageous. It is difficult to imagine, however, as Glassman does, that such partial divestitures will reduce the cost of litigation. It would seem that as long as a possibility exists for the company to retain the fruits of its acquisition, it will fight. Moreover, in the case of consumer products, particularly those like liquid bleach that have no scale economies of production, the important consideration is the product name. Without the name "Clorox," the production facilities for producing liquid bleach would be more or less useless insofar as P & G was concerned. Rather than advocating a partial divestiture in this case, it might be suggested that the production plants of the original Clorox Corporation be subdivided and that two or three firms be established. In this case, however, one would have to give serious consideration to the elimination of the "Clorox" trademark.[9]

Conglomerate mergers do not seem to present as serious problems to Glassman. He argues, for example, that total divestiture has no direct impact upon competitive conditions in the market. It would seem that he would have been better off if he had used the word *simple* rather than *direct* in this context. All conglomerate mergers result in substantial losses of information regarding profits, and so forth; as a consequence, they constitute perhaps the most significant of the many entry barriers which exist.

It is not so much a question of whether or not the acquiring company is a significant competitor as it is that the information loss associated with the merger reduces both the quality and the quantity of information available to all firms in and out of the industry. Glassman points out that almost all cases on conglomerate mergers have dealt with the primary question of potential competition, that is, that the acquiring firm was a potential competitor. This seems to "beg the question." In the case of conglomerate mergers one might view *all large firms* as potential competitors and therefore any significant merger—any merger eliminating a firm of large size—reduces the level of industry knowledge. The current approach to conglomerate mergers ignores this information loss problem directly.

One aspect of Glassman's argument pervading his study has considerable merit. Spin-offs are clearly superior to simple divestitures, be they partial, complete, or multiple. Furthermore, spin-offs, or divestitures for that matter, should include all capital invested and profits earned by the acquired corporation during the acquiring company's ownership tenure. There is obviously no reason why the acquiring company should make substantial financial gains which result from its illegal merger activity.

This comment concludes by addressing the single most distressing aspect of the study. In his discussion of developing an appropriate form of relief, Glassman states that:

One of the basic problems with specifying detailed relief is that the antitrust authority has limited expertise in the industry and does not and cannot respond quickly and accurately in a profit-maximizing fashion to the imperatives of the market. It is the participants in the industry who are best qualified to write efficient relief and carry out relief imposed upon them in a successful fashion. Thus, in theory one should create incentives to the provision of optimal relief and then say to the respondent, "Here are the ground rules; implement the relief in the manner that is best for you."[10]

In other words, Glassman argues that the antitrust agencies are not qualified to decide upon the particular form of the relief sought. If the antitrust agencies are so lacking in knowledge regarding the organization and operation of an industry, it is clear that complaints should not have been issued in the first place. Moreover, it is an open admission, if true, that the staff of the agency originating the complaint has not or cannot meet what should be the first principle of bringing a case—no complaint should be issued unless it is possible to define what is specifically wrong with the industry in question and what should or can be done about improving competitive conditions. It seems impossible that any knowledgeable member of an antitrust agency could recommend that the firm or firms involved in antitrust cases should develop the particular form of relief. It goes without saying that the firm or firms involved know more about the industry than the staff of an antitrust agency. It is not clear, however, that they *will* develop a relief that will present a plan which is consistent with the achievement of a maximum improvement of competitive conditions. This approach has all of the characteristics of asking the leader of a wolf pack for his expert assistance in developing a protection system for lambs. The net result of both of these approaches would be an unacceptably high level of carnage.

6 The Instruments of Antitrust Enforcement

William Breit and **Kenneth G. Elzinga**

One of the most predictable elements in any academic discussion of antitrust efforts is the oft-repeated claim that the penalties are too low and the enforcement efforts too small. Virtually every economist interested in antitrust heard this as a student and most continue to regale their students and spice up their writings with descriptions of the miniscule fines that have been assessed against antitrust violators, the virtually nonexistent examples of jailings of convicted business executives, and the pyrrhic monopoly and merger victories where the government wins the case but loses the relief decree. Moreover, students are instructed to be moderately scandalized upon learning that the combined budgets of the enforcement agencies could not buy one bomber and are much less than the current budget of some obscure government agency. The traditional response to this state of affairs is to recommend greater penalties, renewed attempts to secure structural relief, larger budgets for the enforcement agencies, and even institutional modifications designed to effectuate the above. Indeed, in antitrust this attitude has become so ingrained that despite a widespread and growing application of the tools of economics to law enforcement, the efficacy of the instruments of antitrust enforcement have, with few exceptions, remained largely unexamined.

The purpose of this chapter is to apply the tools of economic analysis to the instruments of antitrust. First the question of the optimal amount of antitrust enforcement will be analyzed by utilizing a cost-benefit framework. Then it will be suggested that the weapons of antitrust enforcement can be fruitfully reappraised and the adequacy of each penalty can be considered in the light of its deterrence impact and social cost. The economic theory of bureaucracy will also be brought to bear on the question of the adequacy of present penalties in deterring monopolistic behavior. Finally, the insights gained from this research will suggest reforms in the present structure of antitrust penalties.

The first task of an economic approach to antitrust activity attempts, above all, to answer the question: What is the optimal amount of antitrust enforcement? To put this another way, but more pertinently from the point of view of economic analysis, what is the optimal amount of illegal monopolistic behavior that society should permit if it is to be efficient in allocating its scarce resources? The answer to this question appears simple from the legal point of view: the optimal amount of illegal monopolistic activity is zero. Lawyers would argue, for

99

example, that any overt collusion to fix prices is a violation of the Sherman Act and should be detected and punished through fines and reparations to damaged parties. But a little reflection will indicate the inadequacy of this response. It is true that economists are generally agreed that competition is beneficial, that anticompetitive behavior reduces welfare and misallocates resources. Any reduction in such behavior involves a benefit to society in the form of greater output at lower prices. But this does not tell the whole story. For the economist must ask not only about the *benefits* to be gained from a particular policy, but also about the *costs* to be incurred in carrying it out. Precisely at this point the seemingly easy question of the optimal amount of antitrust enforcement is transformed into a more complex problem.

Consider, for example, a simple theoretical case in which a firm that is operating in a perfectly competitive market enters into a collusive arrangement whereby it agrees with its former rivals to charge a higher price and produce at a lower rate of output. Assuming that the cartel is successful, the usual misallocation of resources takes place. Part of the loss of consumer's surplus is a transfer of revenue to the cartel which must be subtracted in order to get the net loss to society caused by this individual member of the cartel. This net loss, the "welfare triangle" (or deadweight loss), represents the net loss to society from monopolistic behavior.[1]

It might seem, therefore, that antitrust policy should be directed toward the elimination of all such inefficiencies so that each and every welfare triangle could be captured for society. But economic theory provides two traditional demurrers to the perfectly competitive model as a guide to public policy, those of J.M. Clark and J.E. Meade.[2]

Clark's theory holds, in the first place, that if society wants socially desirable economic performance from some real-world industry, this will probably not be attained by imposing or requiring all of the structural and behavioral conditions of perfect competition. For example, if some industry were characterized by substantial economies of scale, then imposing perfect competition's structural condition of many independent firms upon that industry would in fact lower its economic efficiency. Then Clark went much further; he reasoned that enforcing any *one* of the conditions of perfect competition in some industry, where *all* of the conditions could not simultaneously be met, could conceivably harm the economic performance of that industry. Thus, if the exploitation of scale economies dictated the existence of only a few firms in a particular industry, then the imposition of the perfectly competitive *condition* of openly quoted prices could conceivably lower the industry's economic performance by serving to reduce competitive price cutting.[3]

In contrast to the theory of workable competition, the theory of second best demonstrates that if one of the industries in an economy does not generate the optimum *results* of perfect competition, then the attainment of (or movement towards) perfect competition in other industries may actually lessen overall economic welfare. For example, if one industry in an economy continues to exercise market power (or incurs any effect, such as external economies, which causes its price to diverge from marginal cost), then efforts by society to attain the results of perfect competition in other sectors of the economy, through antitrust policy, regulation, taxation, or whatever, may be counterproductive and in fact lower the value of total output.[4]

But the Clark-Meade objections are recognized as tributaries, not the mainstream of antitrust literature. That perfect competition is the appropriate goal of antitrust policy has remained the guidepost among economists from Cambridge to Cook County. The assertion herein is that in their enthusiasm for this model, economists have not recognized that even here as elsewhere there can be too much of a good thing. This proposition can be more directly formulated as a theorem: If a strictly laissez faire policy does not bring about perfect competition in all markets, then it is incorrect economic policy to attempt to achieve perfect competition through antitrust enforcement.

The theory of perfect competition as used in antitrust is preoccupied with the benefits to society from increased enforcement. This preoccupation is equivalent to attacking the problem of pollution by calculating only the benefits of antipollutants with no regard to their costs. However, an economic account of antitrust policy should consider not only the benefits from retrieved welfare triangles but also all the costs incurred by the Antitrust Division, the Federal Trade Commission, the costs of litigation and negotiation incurred by both plaintiffs and defendants, as well as the costs of maintaining and operating the courts. Such costs include all resources used by federal, state, and local governments and private parties in antitrust litigation, negotiation, and compliance. These costs are not inconsiderable.

The total welfare generated by antitrust enforcement is maximized when perfect competition is achieved. At that point the marginal benefit is zero and becomes negative with additional enforcement.[5] The total costs of enforcement, on the other hand, in principle could rise continuously without peaking as more and more resources are given over to public and private antitrust efforts. Even assuming that the total benefit curve lies above the total cost curve for the relevant range of antitrust activity, the derivatives of such functions would nevertheless be equal at a point short of perfect competition. This means, then, that if laissez faire did not automatically bring about perfect competition, it would be incorrect to move to achieve it through antitrust since there is obviously some point short of perfect competition where the marginal costs of antitrust enforcement exceed the benefits.

There is, however, one very special condition under which the theorem would not hold: when the degree of competition can be changed with no change in the amount of antitrust enforcement. If, for example, the budgets of the Antitrust Division and the Federal Trade Commission were held constant, and yet the competitive impact of antitrust could be increased, the theorem would be invalid. For in such a case the marginal costs to society of this antitrust enforcement would be zero and therefore would be equated with the marginal benefits at perfect competition. In that case, perfect competition might be the appropriate social goal because it would coincide with the maximization of net benefits to society from antitrust enforcement. It follows, therefore, that the desire to use antitrust efficiently to bring about something approximating perfectly competitive conditions must eventually involve a policy that does not use up scarce resources.

The antitrust tool kit contains an uneven assortment of policy instruments which for the most part were explicitly provided in the Sherman Act. This arsenal is the inevitable result of compromise emerging from the historical milieu of the period. It certainly does not contain the whole range of possible weapons. For example, some instruments originally proposed for inclusion in the Sherman Act were the suspension of tariffs on articles controlled by trusts, special taxation of their products, and prohibition for trusts to carry on interstate commerce. Bills containing these provisions were reported to various committees but none was ever reported back to Congress. Perhaps the most drastic proposal was that of Senator Turpie of Indiana who submitted a resolution which provided for government seizure of the goods of monopolistic conspirators and for their forfeiture, confiscation, and sale. Eight of the original bills introduced were based on the idea of tariff reductions or suspensions for goods controlled by trusts. Two bills proposed to tax trusts 25 percent of their capital assets and products. Two bills would deprive conspirators in restraint of trade of recourse to the courts for enforcement of contracts. Other bills wanted forfeiture of corporate charters. None of these proposals survived the compromise package that the Sherman Act represents.[6]

The present antitrust tool kit contains the following instruments for penalizing antitrust violations: (1) financial penalties paid to the state;[7] (2) treble damage payments to injured private parties;[8] (3) incarceration;[9] (4) injunctive directives such as the corporate surgery of dissolution, divorcement, and divestiture (hereafter dissolution);[10] and the efficacy of all these is affected by (5) the amount of resources devoted to the detection and conviction of anticompetitive behavior.[11]

It should be noted, however, that all of these penalties are more or less efficient depending upon (1) their relative deterrence impact; (2) their relative cost, in terms of resources used up; and (3) the extent to which the enforcement agencies are likely to use them wisely. These penalty variables shall now be considered in the light of each of these three categories.

One of the most fruitful lines of recent research in the economics of legal institutions has demonstrated the importance of offender's risk attitudes in assessing the deterrent impact of various penalties.[12] Any discussion of new approaches in antitrust must take account of these developments.

The point of departure is an examination of the motivations of the businessmen whose behavior antitrust policy is presumably designed to affect. This analysis can be generalized to include any anticompetitive action, but its development in the context of an example is serviceable. The decision to enter a cartel is illustrative. If the businessman is attempting to maximize his expected utility, then in its starkest form, this antitrust violation will occur if the expected utility from colluding exceeds the expected utility from competing. But the term "expected utility" used by economists is a portmanteau expression which requires unpacking.

The manager's expected utility simply refers to the average level of satisfactions experienced or gained from his business activities. They are "expected" because he operates under conditions of uncertainty and he cannot know in advance whether he will actually realize any particular amount of utility. Only a set of probabilities is known. There are essentially three items that must be taken into account in order to predict accurately a potential cartelist's behavior. First, the manager is interested in the profits he will realize from the cartel compared with those he realizes staying out of the cartel. But he is actually interested in the *expected value* of those profits. That is, he discounts the profits by the market rate of interest, the probability of his being detected and convicted of an antitrust violation, and by the risk of antitrust penalties he must pay. So, given the market rate of interest, the second item is the probability of detection and conviction as well as the magnitude of the penalties. This risk is part of his costs and reduces the expected value of his monopoly profits and therefore the capitalized value of his enterprise. Insofar as it is a deterrent, antitrust policy works by making the expected value of monopoly profits less by increasing the risk facing the potential and actual cartelist. Any increase in the height of the penalties or the probability of detection and conviction would increase the risk facing the firm. This increase would cause a rise in the firm's expected costs because shareholders would now insist on a higher return to offset the increased riskiness of the enterprise.[13] Some will sell their shares which will reduce the market value of the stock and increase its yield. This increased yield indicates a higher cost of capital to the firm. Consequently the rising probability of antitrust conviction or the risk of incurring higher financial penalties increases expected costs and reduces the expected value of the profit accruing to the firm. If the goal of antitrust activity was totally to deter collusion, then the best policy would be to increase this risk, making the firm's expected costs rise so high that the expected utility of monopoly profits would be zero. At that point there would be no incentive to collude since the expected utility of profits under perfectly competitive conditions would be the same as those under collusion.

How much any specific policy will actually deter illegal behavior therefore depends on the businessman's attitude toward risk. It will be argued that the more averse he is to risk, the more will he be deterred by any given reduction in the expected value of his monopoly profits resulting from increased risk. The more of a risk lover he happens to be, the less will he be deterred by any reduction in the expected value of his monopoly profits resulting from increased risk. His attitude toward risk determines the utility or satisfaction that he expects to get from his monopoly profits. So important are the risk attitudes of businessmen in determining their propensity to restrain trade that antitrust weaponry can be effective only if consistent with these attitudes.

By now it should be clear that Congress has affected the expected utility from anticompetitive behavior by imposing the penalties listed above. On the surface these four penalties (fines, reparations, incarceration, and dissolution) differ greatly. But as Gary Becker has noted:

The cost of different punishments to an offender can be made comparable by converting them into their monetary equivalent or worth, which, of course, is directly measured only for fines. For example, the cost of an imprisonment is the discounted sum of the earnings foregone and the value placed on the restrictions in consumption and freedom.[14]

This means that all of the antitrust penalties have a monetary counterpart. Obviously, they are more directly measured in the first two penalties, fines and reparations, but the third and fourth penalties of incarceration and dissolution also can be collapsed into a pecuniary equivalent.

Also, each of the four penalties has its efficacy affected by the fifth component of the antitrust tool kit: the amount of resources devoted to the detection and conviction of anticompetitive behavior. It is assumed that the probability of detection and conviction is a function of the amount of these resources. With these considerations in mind, the analysis focuses on how altering the penalties and the probabilities of their application has differing deterrent effects depending upon managerial psychology.

Obviously a risk-neutral businessman is indifferent between any increase in the probability of detection and conviction (P) which is offset by a decrease in the monetary penalty (M) if the expected value ($P \cdot M$) of the penalty remains the same, since all of his utility derives from the expected value of the monopoly profits. But for the risk-averse manager, the expected utility derived from the monopoly profit's expected value differs depending upon the value of the monetary counterparts of M and the level of P. He would prefer a lower M and a higher P rather than a high M and low P. The opposite is the case with the risk lover who prefers a high M in combination with a low P in this context. This means that if the conventional wisdom on managerial risk attitudes (as expressed, for example, by Galbraith and Marris[15]) is correct, antitrust policy seeking to deter should have greater emphasis placed on higher penalties with less concern for the probability of detecting and convicting each offense.[16]

Given this general framework, the deterrence impact of the specific penalties as they now exist and are applied must be considered. The general view of these penalties, with the recent exception of treble damage suits, is that they have been of *de minimus* deterrence value.

In the case of fines, this exaction was only $5000 per count until 1955. The present level of $50,000 per count remains a minor expense to all but the smallest of antitrust violators. Indeed, the average fine levied in Sherman Act cases from 1890-1954 was $38,479; in spite of the possible tenfold increase after 1955, the average fine in 1960-69 was $122,326. The total amount of fines levied from 1890-1969 was only $30.2 million.[17] One indication of the negligible deterrence value of this penalty is that antitrust observers of various persuasions have recommended its increase.[18]

From the standpoint of deterrence impact, the treble damage penalty seems promising. Treble damage suits languished for several decades under a moderately hostile judicial interpretation in which considerations of privity narrowed the scope of treble damage actions and therefore their preventive effect. More recent court decisions have eased the standing to sue requirements so that remoter parties damaged by monopolistic behavior can have their access to the court. The recent proliferation of class action suits is an indication that the trend is toward a more liberal interpretation of those who have suffered allowable damages. Without overstating the ease with which these reparations can be collected, it is certainly the case that potential antitrust violators fear, and are more deterred by, the financial costs of treble damage suits than the presently miniscule fines.

The electrical equipment cartel provides dramatic evidence of this point: the total fines levied against the cartel were slightly under $2 million. The treble damage suits cost the plaintiffs an estimated $500 million. In the more recent tetracycline conspiracy case, the defendant drug companies offered a pool of $100 million to be divided among the states, with accepting states then agreeing not to file treble damage actions against the producers should the latter lose the trial. This substantial sum was offered as a contingency settlement, *prior* to the completion of litigation, indicating that the expected value of the treble damage payments exceeded $100 million.

As in the case of fines, incarceration under the antitrust laws has had practically no prophylactic effects One of the notable features of this penalty is the infrequency of its application. Posner's important collection of data includes these statistics: from 1890-1969, there were 538 Sherman Act criminal convictions. Of these, only 26 sustained prison sentences and most of these 26 involved "either acts of violence or union misconduct." The few jail sentences that have been imposed are seldom of more than thirty days duration.[19]

The discussion of dissolution can be brief, since the same lack of vigor and infrequency of imposition found in the jail penalty exists in the case of this fourth penalty. Matthew Josephson ascribes to James Hill this statement about the government's first structural relief order separating the Great Northern Railway Company from the Northern Pacific Railway:

Two certificates of stock are now issued instead of one; they are printed in different colors, and that is the main difference.[20]

Whether the story is apochryphal or not, it does portray the general tenor of the government's past efforts to secure structural relief. The earliest scholarly study of dissolution was done by George E. Hale, who showed that the government did not get off to a promising start in the business of trust dissolution.[21] Nor did the situation change in ensuing periods. Walter Adams found the government's victories in litigated monopoly cases pyrrhic because of the lack of meaningful structural relief,[22] Milton S. Goldberg found the same situation in his survey of consent decrees,[23] and Kenneth G. Elzinga concluded that structural relief in antimerger cases was seldom accomplished, by either the Federal Trade Commission or the Antitrust Division.[24]

However much deterrent impact the foregoing weapons might entail, they have varying costs associated with their use. Any given amount of deterrence is therefore more or less efficient depending upon the costs incurred to achieve it. Or to put it simply, since each of the penalties has its monetary equivalent, which one is the cheapest to apply?

Strictly on the basis of costs, the first of the five mechanisms, fines paid to the state, is the least costly to effectuate. Like all of the other penalties, fines require the use of resources to prove the antitrust violation. But presumably this cost is the same regardless of the penalty imposed. The efficiency advantage of fines is that the marginal social cost of imposing a higher rather than a lower fine is virtually zero. Congress or the courts (whoever might be charged with levying the fine) could alter the level of the fine at practically no cost since, obviously, imposing the higher fine uses up no more resources than charging a lower fine.

Paradoxically, the instrument which currently receives the highest marks for deterrence is at the bottom of its class in respect to costs. The treble damage penalty, of course, involves the usual resource costs of detecting and proving violations. But its deterrence value comes through the identification and compensation of allegedly injured parties. It is this latter process, identification and compensation, that imposes not insubstantial costs on society.[25] These costs are imposed in the form of private pleadings and discovery, joinders, multidistrict litigation complexities, out-of-court negotiations and legal maneuverings, and, at times, massive class actions. The opportunity costs of court resources utilized by the remarkable increase in private damage suits provides a powerful incentive to economize and free the scarce resources for more productive uses elsewhere. This would be no mean accomplishment. Consider the benefits from reducing court congestion alone. In the decade 1960-70, the federal caseload increased 43 percent from 89,112 cases to 127,820. The backlog of cases pending was 68,842 in 1960; by 1970 this had risen to 114,117.[26] Chief Justice Burger in the first State of the Federal Judiciary Address outlines some of the reasons for the litigation, and his predecessor had earlier noted the backlog crisis.[27]

Recent court decisions and congressional legislation have had the effect of lowering the price of going to court for many citizens. In fact that was part of the intention. Some of the proposals for court reform and increased judicial efficiency will also serve to lower the price and increase the quantity of court services demanded. These changes lead to the prediction that even if a host of measures are taken, the queuing problem will remain. As long as this situation prevails, the benefits from devising more efficient antitrust enforcement methods will be substantial.

The costs of the incarceration penalty are obviously high. There are the apparent direct costs of buildings, supervisory staff, food and maintenance, as well as the offender's earnings foregone and the monetary equivalent of his loss of freedom. The magnitude of these costs has led Becker to recommend the virtual abolition of imprisonment as an efficient deterrent mechanism.[28] In recognition of these costs, the National Advisory Commission on Criminal Justice Standards and Goals recommended a general reduction of prison sentences and a total cutback of prison systems in the United States.[29]

The penalty of structural relief, like treble damage suits and incarceration, requires the use of posttrial resources to effectuate the penalty and "showcase" the deterrence effect to potential violators. Partly because the historical experience with structural relief has been so minimal, data on the resources used in completing a dissolution effort are not available.[30] But any dissolution order that is to be effective will generally involve at least a year's time from the enforcement agencies compliance staff (both lawyers and economists); the company management will incur much greater costs in the legal aspects of compliance, the seeking of an appropriate buyer (i.e., the advertising, showing, and negotiations concerning the to-be-divested properties), and the costs imposed upon management with regard to maintaining operations in the face of a dissolution requirement.

These costs should not be underestimated. The accounting and personnel problems of dividing a firm, after the assets have been scrambled, are frequently substantial, particularly where the assets have been mingled for a long period of time. The sale of a viable bundle of assets will have repercussions in the production, financial, and marketing sectors of the company. Problems of morale and uncertainty about future location and employment will inevitably impose some toll on companies under dissolution order. In merger cases, divestiture orders are often made complicated (and therefore more costly to effectuate) because the acquired assets have either been so depleted (or so modified and rebuilt) that to carve out the original acquisition would be extremely expensive.[31] In addition to the costs imposed upon the enforcement agencies in directing and monitoring the dissolution, and the costs imposed upon the company lawyers, accountants, management, and other personnel in complying with the order, effective dissolution (i.e., dissolution which will have spillover deterrence effects) will also require some third-party monitoring, either by the courts, Congress, or public interest law firms and consumer groups.

The fifth instrument of enforcement, the size of the enforcement effort, would impose incremental costs upon society if its deterrence impact is to increase. These costs consist of the expanded budgets of the Antitrust Division, the Federal Trade Commission, the courts (as more cases are brought), and the expanded managerial and litigative costs borne by companies attempting to avoid or circumvent antitrust prosecution (the largest category). As pointed out earlier, there are little data on the magnitude of these costs. The Antitrust Division presently has a budget of about $14 million; the Federal Trade Commission's antitrust budget is less than $9 million. No data are available on the magnitude of the costs generated by these budgets, much less the costs which would be generated by their increase. Such costs would include the increased expenses of legal and economic advice, management time spent on antitrust matters, expanded clerical costs, enlarged court costs, and increased efforts by the assorted hangers-on of the institution of antitrust: academics, journalists, detectives, congressional committee staff, lobbyists, conference promoters, and purveyors of legal reports.

In this section the instruments of antitrust will be assessed in light of the third standard, the likelihood with which they can avoid the impediments of bureaucratic inefficiency. In the case of three of the instruments, their virtues with regard to this standard are apparent. With fines, treble damages, and incarceration, the court (one of the simplest of government bureaucracies) straightforwardly issues an edict or sentence. There is then little room for bureaucratic discretion in the implementation of the order. The fine must be paid, the reparations award must be made, or the violator must serve his sentence.

But in the case of the remaining two instruments (dissolution and increasing the amount of enforcement resources), it is tautological that increasing reliance on them involves an increasing reliance on bureaucratic procedures and institutions—in other words, a burgeoning Antitrust Division and Federal Trade Commission. It might prove instructive, therefore, to examine the implications of bureaucratic behavior upon antitrust enforcement using models of bureaucracy which economists have developed in recent years.

There are two major theses of the modern theory of bureaucracy. The first is that a model of bureaucratic behavior yields better predictions when it is assumed that the bureaucrat is motivated by utility maximization which is satisfied when he directs his behavior toward ends that serve his self-interest. Secondly, there is a tendency in bureaus for information passing through the hands of individual officials to become distorted both qualitatively and quantitatively as it is forwarded up the hierarchy.[32]

An illustration is the implementation of a divestiture order by an agency's compliance section. The personnel of this section are the main point of contact with the businessmen affected by the divestiture decree. These bureaucrats must monitor and evaluate the efforts by company management to sell some portion of the assets. There is an asymmetry of interest between these two groups that is important to note. The obvious interest of the corporate management is to minimize the effect of the decree. In contrast, the interest of the compliance lawyer is not so concentrated. His utility function has many arguments and therefore his interests are dispersed. In addition to the public interest, loyalty to his agency, and the Veblenian "instinct of workmanship," the compliance lawyer is also interested in the pleasantness of his working conditions and the amount of harmony with those whom he meets on a day-to-day basis. The overlap of interest between the two may occur in constructing a final decree that barely unsheaths the corporate scalpel. The management would then be happy; and the compliance lawyer would have incurred less friction in his work. Because the final relief order will be checked and approved on the basis of information forwarded by the compliance official himself, and knowing that those above cannot evaluate an avalanche of information, there is an incentive to distort or minimize the information and thereby neglect the public interest.

In brief, deterrence and cost standards aside, considerations of the nature of bureaucracy itself weigh against the use of dissolution and expanding the antitrust agencies. Since the other instruments are wielded outside of any complex bureaucratic milieu, other things equal, they are to be preferred.

The foregoing discussion of the instruments of antitrust policy from the standpoint of the problems of deterrence, costs, and bureaucratic inefficiencies leads ineluctably to a rather sweeping recommendation for the streamlining of the antitrust tool kit. A severe monetary exaction paid to the state by violators should be the sole instrument of antitrust enforcement.[33] There is some fine capable in principle of being as effective as *any* other instrument of deterrence; in terms of additional scarce resources, the cost of such a fine (once a violation has been detected and convicted) is in fact zero. And there is no other instrument which involves so few and simple bureaucratic channels to implement. As contrasted with any other weapon, its advantages are clear and compelling: The conceptual and administrative problems of dissolution would be avoided, the political and judicial difficulties arising from the Draconian penalty which consigns businessmen to jail would be bypassed, and the additional scarce resources inevitably used up in the laudable but vain attempt to assess damages and recompense injured parties would be salvaged for alternative and more highly productive uses. Indeed, this weapon should appeal most agreeably to economists who have taken the traditional view of the monopoly problem. It is the only instrument that can justify on economic grounds a completely vigorous and single-minded antitrust policy, for no other weapon is consistent with an attempt to bring about conditions approximating perfect competition.[34]

Moreover, the case for increasing financial penalties as an alternative to increasing the volume of resources flowing into increased detection and conviction of antitrust violators is even stronger when placed in the context of the risk attitudes of American management.

What is still more, the use of a single high financial penalty in the corporate world of risk aversion could provide incentives for automatic deconcentration and a remedy for such structural maladies as shared monopoly and anticompetitive acquisitions. For example, a firm which is found guilty of holding an illegal market share and thereby suffers a high monetary toll under this proposal would seek to avoid a recurrence of the exaction by taking steps to lower its market share until it is well within the bounds of legality.

This program for antitrust reform would increase the efficiency of the American economy with all of the concomitant benefits that healthy economic rivalry provides. But it should be recognized that improving the efficacy of the antitrust statutes is no panacea for the monopoly problem itself. Antitrust is, after all, only one dwarfish program in the range of governmental policies that affect competition, and these others all too often have the effect of lessening free-market forces. The ultimate victory of antitrust will not be as a set of statutes, but as a *philosophy of statecraft* that affects areas impenetrable through antitrust enforcement alone. The most substantial welfare gains for consumers will be made not so much through the more efficient deterrence of private monopoly but through stopping government as a promoter of monopoly.[35] This means an end to government policies which protect vested interests from the chilling winds of competition and which enrich favored businesses with government largesse. Long ago David Cushman Coyle stated that the "price of free men is free prices." Free prices will result only after a vigorous application of the antitrust philosophy to curtail not only anticompetitive business practices but also our unfortunate experiment in economic statecraft, government regulation.

Comment

R. Dennis Murphy

The strength of this analysis lies in its generally lucid exposition and its careful detailing of the full social costs incurred by present antitrust penalties. There are, however, several questionable assumptions and oversights which require comment. In addition, Breit and Elzinga do not adequately support or explain their concluding recommendations.

One of the most unnerving weaknesses is the very narrow analysis of the social costs attributable to excess market power. One is continually led to believe that missing "welfare triangles" constitute the sole loss to society from monopolistic behavior. Certainly retardation in the rate of technological change and reduction in managerial efficiency at least deserve mention, particularly in view of the emphasis later placed upon bureaucratic inefficiencies.

On a more general level, the authors frequently fail to differentiate clearly between market structure and conduct. The confusion is particularly glaring in the authors' claim that economists from Cambridge to Cook County hold that "perfect competition is the appropriate goal of antitrust." Clearly one does not have to concur fully with J.M. Clark or J.E. Meade to doubt the desirability of a perfectly competitive market *structure* in the United States or to disagree totally with the assertion that "the total welfare generated by antitrust enforcement is maximized when perfect competition is achieved." At the same time, most economists probably would insist that otherwise imperfect competitors refrain from anticompetitive *conduct*, such as agreeing on prices or dividing markets. To cite an obvious example, "mainstream" economists would be fairly delighted with as few as seven or eight domestic automobile producers and yet condemn any trade agreements among them.

Thus it was unnecessary and distracting for the authors to state and prove the theorem that "it is incorrect economic policy to achieve perfect competition through antitrust enforcement." Without further clarification of the authors' interpretation of the term *perfect competition*, the entire discussion amounts to little more than a lengthy dismantling of a straw man. (The proof does, of course, establish the rather obvious principle that the marginal cost of antitrust enforcement should not be allowed to exceed the marginal benefit.)

On the other hand, the authors should have devoted greater space to their proof of the theorem that all current antitrust penalties have a monetary counterpart. How, for example, are economists to measure methodically the full impact of jail sentences on corporate vice-presidents? It is doubtful whether the deterrent power of the social disgrace attending incarceration could be matched by a simple monetary fine, no matter how large.

It is easy to sympathize with the study's amusing account of the bureaucratic

111

horrors likely to infest an expanded antitrust division. But as indicated earlier, these warnings should apply with equal force to the performance of overgrown dominant firms (such as United States Steel). In short, recognition of bureaucratic inefficiencies and distortions increases both the apparent costs and benefits of intensified antitrust enforcement.

The final point for discussion is whether or not the authors support their conviction that a monetary fine should be the sole instrument of antitrust enforcement. It is probably true that stiffer fines for per se Section I Sherman Act offenses will help deter future violations (though, for reasons already stated, Breit and Elzinga are not convincing when they argue that fines should supplant prison sentences). Further, the authors cogently defend their proposed elimination of treble damage suits. However, the authors' claim that the elevation of monetary fines will involve a marginal cost of zero is doubtful. Surely defendants will contest government charges more vigorously if faced with possible financial disaster, and judges and juries no doubt ponder the severity of mandatory punishments when assessing guilt.

The wisdom of relying strictly on fines in Section II cases eludes comprehension. According to Breit and Elzinga, "automatic" deconcentration will occur as errant monopolists disassemble themselves or curtail business operation to avoid payment of a "high monetary toll." (The authors apparently envision a series of fines continuing in effect until full compliance with the law is achieved, since a once-and-for-all penalty at the time of conviction would not affect the firm's market strategy.) At best this approach differs from traditional dissolution proceedings only in that officials of the guilty firm would have a somewhat greater voice in determining how best to reduce the firm's market power.[1] All of the other stumbling blocks, frustrations, and social costs of current structural antitrust cases would remain. Protracted and costly adjudication would still be required to establish that the Sherman Act had been violated. The proposed reform would then impose the added burden of determining a schedule of sufficiently odious fines. Once prodded to pursue voluntary deconcentration, the firm's management would be saddled with all of the details of dissolution outlined by the authors in their discussion of current dissolution orders: an appropriate buyer would still have to be sought, company staff would still have to weigh the merits of various dissolution schemes and changes in marketing practices, and a frazzled management would still feel the strain of conducting daily business operations in the face of difficult and detailed disentanglement proceedings. Nor would the burden placed upon government lawyers and economists be significantly reduced. Close and constant scrutiny of the monopolist's deconcentration efforts would still be required in order to determine when the financial penalties should be lifted. The authors quite rightly caution that "these costs should not be underestimated." Nor can they be avoided if meaningful deconcentration is to take place.

Similarly, it is questionable whether "a single high financial penalty in the corporate world of risk aversion" would constitute a satisfactory challenge to the problem of conscious parallelism. Structural problems require structural reforms, and the authors have not established that their penalty system leads to more complete or painless deconcentration than mandatory government-supervised dissolution. Perhaps there are advantages to the monetary penalty approach which have been overlooked; but, in any event, the authors should clearly have developed their structural antitrust program more fully. Possibly the scant attention paid to Section II Sherman Act questions reflects a belief on the authors' part that the government should confine its antitrust activities to detecting explicit price-fixing conspiracies. But surely a more concerted government attack on the structural front is long overdue. And the success of such efforts will probably depend more upon a clarification of Section II of the Sherman Act and a streamlining of the judicial process than on an overhaul of the current arsenal of penalties.

Part V
Economics and Politics of Antitrust Policy: An Overview

7

Current Policy Issues in Antitrust

Willard F. Mueller

Antitrust policy is in trouble. Or, more correctly, the U.S. market economy is in trouble and traditional antitrust efforts are not likely to correct the problem. It is no longer good enough to indulge in consolation at conferences by agreeing that things would be much worse were it not for the antitrust laws and the lackluster records of the enforcement agencies. Ben Lewis has aptly character- ized antitrust as "a kind of rearguard protection as we move slowly toward the next waterhole."[1] True, the diminishing flock of antitrust faithful can cite some victories in the last two decades. Certainly, the most notable example has been the enforcement of the Celler-Kefauver Act of 1950, which has become a powerful weapon for stopping horizontal mergers. Without the strict rules of law developed in this area, certainly many industries would be much more concen- trated than they are today.[2] But this result must be measured as a success mainly because it prevented things from getting worse, rather than because it brought about any notable improvement in competition. This also has been true of most legislative efforts involving antitrust. The Senate Antitrust and Monop- oly Subcommittee has fought a valiant and little appreciated rearguard action against a continuing onslaught by special interests seeking exemptions from the antitrust laws.

The Justice Department may point with pride to a growing number of successful conspiracy prosecutions and consent decrees; indeed, under the new chief of the Antitrust Division, Thomas E. Kauper, it appears the division will place even higher priority on these efforts, particularly in cracking down on local and regional conspiracies.[3] The most important new dimension on this front is the growing number of private treble damage actions brought in the aftermath of Justice Department actions. These have a potential for raising significantly the costs to conspirators. But again, conspiracy cases are partly a symptom of how bad things already are, that is, existing high levels of concentration are especially conducive to successful conspiracies. It is therefore easy to exaggerate the benefits resulting from such cases. There is mounting evidence that conspiracy pays, even when the white-collar criminal is found guilty and sentenced.[4] As a result, the deterrent effect of vigorous action in this area is probably exag- gerated. It is doubtful, for example, that the seven conspiracy cases brought against steel firms in the 1960s had any significant lasting impact on competition in the industry.

Most importantly, there has been little antitrust action in the mainstream of the market power problem. Fewer big Section 2 Sherman Act cases were brought in the last two decades than in the two decades following 1890, despite an enormous growth in the Antitrust Division. Also, there is considerable uncertainty regarding future merger enforcement policy, especially toward conglomerates since the infamous ITT settlement aborted the effort for an early Supreme Court decision in this area.[5] Nor is this all the bad news. Industrial market concentration appears to be creeping even higher (see Table 7-3), and an increasing share of U.S. and the Western world's industrial capacity is becoming dominated by a relatively few enormous conglomerate enterprises (see Table 7-1).

Given this dismal setting, what can be done? Others have addressed the question of how best to select particular cases. The emphasis in this chapter is on the danger in becoming preoccupied with optimum allocation of scarce antitrust resources. Such myopic preoccupation may lead to a search for the least soggy spot in a swamp, when one should be out surveying the high country. Time and personal preconceptions determine the issues which will be discussed. Although not exhausting the crucial problem areas, the following are believed to be among the most crucial issues calling for antitrust or related regulatory actions:

1. Public policy toward the large conglomerate corporation, both domestically and internationally
2. Industrial restructuring of concentrated industries
3. Problems that advertising creates for market structure, conduct, and performance
4. Needed reforms in certain procedures of the antitrust agencies

Industrial organization economists generally are preoccupied with market power created by horizontal market structure. This preoccupation reflects partly the state of price theory, which has developed an increasing number of models designed to explain imperfectly competitive markets. The seminal works of Chamberlain and Robinson dealt exclusively with horizontal market power, as did such subsequent refinements of those models as Bain's work on barriers to new competition.[6] Concomitant with, and partly as a result of, these new theories, economic data sources were developed—especially industry and product concentration ratios—that proved useful in testing these models. Despite many deficiencies in the data, empirical studies almost unanimously support the prediction of oligopoly theory that profit rates are positively related to the degree of market concentration and the height of entry barriers.[7] Industrial organizational economists can appropriately take pride in their accomplishments in this area over the past decade.

Ironically, just as meaningful insights into the intricacies of horizontal market power are being gained, this knowledge is becoming less relevant because of the changing organizational characteristics of business enterprise. This is not to say that such efforts have been wasted or that horizontal power is no longer a problem. Rather, the growing importance of large multiproduct, multimarket enterprises that straddle numerous markets and even nations create new dimensions of power.[8] But preoccupation with horizontal market power may have blinded many industrial organization economists and antitrust policy-makers to the potential problems posed by the modern conglomerate corporations that inhabit most of the economic landscape. Many economists seem to infer that there is no problem so long as the share of the top 100 or 200 corporations does not increase greatly from year to year.[9] But this misses the point that a fundamental transformation is occurring in the organizational characteristics and power of the typical large corporation, thereby making obsolete models focusing solely on horizontal market power in individual industries.

With each passing year, more of the financial and industrial sectors of the economy are becoming dominated by huge conglomerate enterprises. The relevant statistics here are not simply the share of total industrial activity held by a fixed number of the largest firms—say the top 200 industrial corporations—but the share held by an increasing number of very large conglomerate firms. The transformation to an industrial economy controlled by a few very large corporations is illustrated by Table 7-1, which measures the share of industrial assets held by corporations with assets exceeding $250 million. Admittedly, inflation explains some of the apparent growing importance of large corporations[10]—practically all of which also are multinational conglomerates—but, nonetheless, it is clear that huge conglomerates control a large and increasing share of total industrial activity.

Many economists have dismissed the entire issue as one of industrial bigness, unrelated to issues of competition. As M.A. Adelman is fond of saying, "absolute size is absolutely irrelevant."[11] But much more is involved than bigness per se. The enormous modern conglomerate is not merely a giant-sized version of a Marshallian "representative firm." Rather, it is more like a huge amalgamation of numerous Marshallian firms whose overall size is not limited by natural economic laws. A decade ago, E.G. Nourse aptly characterized the seemingly irrepressible process of conglomerate growth when he wrote:

There is no demonstrable or discernible limit, national or international, at which such concentration of economic power, once fully underway, would automatically cease. It has insidious ability even to frustrate attempts of the Central Government to check or reverse its growth through legislative action. There are many conflicts of political interest to be overcome.[12]

It appears clear that the competitive behavior of the vast conglomerate enterprise cannot be adequately explained by oligopoly theory. The pricing, output, and other market decisions of the large conglomerate are not con-

Table 7-1

Number of Manufacturing Corporations with Assets Exceeding $250 Million and $1 Billion, and Share of Total Assets of Corporations Engaged Primarily in Manufacturing, 1909-1972

	(Assets in Millions)					
	Firms with Assets Over $1 Billion			Firms with Assets Over $250 Million		
Year	Number	Assets	Share of Total Corporation Assets	Number	Assets	Share of Total Corporation Assets
1909	1	1,822	a	3	2,480	a
1919	1	2,366	a	16	7,900	a
1929	2	5,378	8%	31	18,390	27%
1935	3	5,132	9%	25	14,882	26%
1948	12	20,107	17%	59	39,692	33%
1959	24	61,207	27%	127	115,357	50%
1969	87	229,461	46%	293	330,592	66%
1972	115	321,158	52%	350	435,708	70%

aTotal asset data for all manufacturing corporations not available.

Sources: Number and assets of corporations for 1909 to 1948 are based on Norman Collins and Lee Preston, "The Size Structure of the Largest Industrial Firms, 1909-58," *American Economic Review* (December 1961), pp. 1005-1011. Total assets for these years are based on Internal Revenue data. Firm data and asset data for 1959-72 are for the first quarter of each year, respectively, as reported in FTC-SEC *Quarterly Financial Report for Manufacturing Corporations* for various years. Asset data are for corporations engaged primarily in manufacturing, both domestically and abroad. Therefore, some nonmanufacturing assets and assets of foreign operations are included among the assets of the largest corporations and by all corporations. The data do not include enormous amounts of nonconsolidated assets held by the largest corporations. See FTC Staff Report on *Corporate Mergers*, 1969, p. 175. Thus the figures for 1959 to 1972, at least, likely understate the largest corporations' share of total assets held by all corporations engaged primarily in manufacturing.

strained by the structure of a particular market, as is assumed by oligopoly theory.[13] As documented in a number of industry studies, the conglomerate has considerable discretion in making decisions in individual markets or submarkets.[14] But the problems posed by conglomerates extend beyond narrow issues of competition. The enormous financial resources of multinational conglomerate corporations give them the capacity to frustrate the monetary and fiscal policies of nation states. As the *Wall Street Journal* recently observed:

They can, and they do, force unwanted changes in the various values of national currencies. They strongly influence interest rates throughout the world. . . . It is increasingly argued that no nation nor any international monetary system can withstand the multinationals' financial power.[15]

The power of huge conglomerates extends into the political as well as the economic affairs of nations. Recent revelations regarding ITT's affairs in Chile as well as in the United States illustrates how economic power is transferred into political power.

Industrial organization economists have contributed little to our knowledge of the sources and significance of conglomerate market power. The best known textbook in the field, Joe S. Bain's, *Industrial Organization*, 1968, makes no reference to the conglomerate firm. The more recent and most comprehensive textbook, F.M. Scherer's, *Industrial Structure and Economic Performance*, 1971, surveys the literature on industrial conglomeration, concluding his chapter on the subject by observing that though there are "some grounds for apprehension concerning the consequences of conglomerate bigness, . . . the link between bigness and deficient performance are tenuous. . . . For this reason conglomerate bigness carried a relatively low priority on the industrial organization economist's list of public policy problems, at least up to the late 1960s. However, as the trend toward conglomerate bigness accelerates, concern over the issues it raises will appropriately grow apace."[16]

This is a serious indictment of industrial organization economists, for it is an admission that most research tends to lag, much less anticipate, important organizational changes in our economy. Some may place the blame for this failure on the absence of an adequate theory of conglomerate market power. The main problem, however, is not an absence of theory, since there are a number of plausible hypotheses worthy of testing. Certainly a major reason for the dearth of research is the absence of data for testing these hypotheses. But perhaps more important is the reluctance of most academic researchers to explore fully the available data because they do not lend themselves to refined quantitative techniques whose use some researchers consider prerequisites of "scientific" inquiry.

In view of the enormous difficulties in obtaining reliable data on conglomerate organization and behavior, the FTC's recent research efforts in this area are especially unfortunate. This reference is to the four-year study which ultimately was published as an FTC staff report entitled, *Conglomerate Merger Performance: An Empirical Analysis of Nine Corporations*, November 1972. First, the FTC failed to use effectively its authority to get the necessary data.[17] Second, the commission made a deal with the nine conglomerates assuring them that the commission would make public no data that would disclose the financial or other characteristics of *individual* corporations.[18] Finally, the staff report never addressed itself to the basic competitive issues involved, although its conclusions, if not its analysis, left the clear implication that conglomerates pose no competitive problems. Not surprisingly, critics of government merger and other policies toward conglomerates immediately took great solace from this conclusion. As *Fortune* put it, "In peerless bureaucracies, [the FTC economists] wrote: 'From a competitive standpoint, the effects of conglomerate diversification appear to be largely neutral.' "[19]

What makes the conclusion so incredible is that the report did not even test any of the leading hypotheses regarding a conglomerate's impact on competition, although the commission had directed the staff to do so.[20] The inference of neutrality was based primarily on a number of tables which *aggregated* the market shares of the conglomerates studied. One of the tables is reproduced here as Table 7-2, which, presumably, is one of the main factual bases from which the neutrality inference was drawn. It summarizes for six companies the changes in market shares for 286 product classes between 1963 and 1969.[21] In the *aggregate*, these companies' market shares increased by 1 percent or more for 62 products, declined for 39 products and remained unchanged for 125, whereas they reportedly dropped 50 products during the period. On the basis of this aggregate picture, the report concluded that "the pattern presented by [the table] is one of no substantial change in market shares in either direction. Thus conglomerates did not seem to be particularly successful in expanding the market positions they held in 1963."[22]

This analytical approach raises some serious questions. First, analytical problems arise by aggregating the results of the six companies. The companies in the FTC sample were a heterogeneous group, ranging from White Consolidated, a relatively small and specialized conglomerate, to ITT, an enormous multiproduct, multinational enterprise. Clearly some of the nine would be expected to have more economic clout than others, which suggests considerable differences in market power existed among the companies. For example, in 1969 ITT had assets (excluding Hartford Fire Insurance) greater than the combined assets of the five smallest conglomerate companies studied.[23]

An intriguing question is raised by the fact that conglomerate B (could it be ITT?) in Table 7-2 increased its market share in 30 products and experienced decreases in only 7. In contrast, company F experienced increases in 3 product classes and decreases in 6. The study does not even attempt to answer the crucial question of whether these differences are explained by organizational differences among the acquiring companies, the markets in which the acquired companies operated, or by other factors.[24] Additionally, the table gives no indication as to the importance of the products involved, the significance of the product classes dropped during the period, and whether the products reportedly "dropped" were discontinued lines or simply spun off to other firms. The point is that one cannot draw significant inferences from these kinds of aggregate comparisons. The purpose of the study was to determine which kinds of conglomerate mergers posed anticompetitive effects, the assumption being that *not all did*. Merely because most acquired firms were not leading firms in concentrated industries, or because conglomerates did not expand market shares in all or most product classes, does not warrant an inference that conglomerate mergers have a "neutral" effect and therefore pose no competitive problems.[25]

Table 7-2
Percentage Point Change in Manufacturing Product Class Market Shares of Sample Conglomerates, 1963-69

Conglomerate	Increases +5.0 or more	+3.0 to +4.9	+1.0 to +2.9	No Change +0.9 to -0.9	-1.0 to -2.9	Decreases -3.0 to -4.9	-5.0 or less	Product Dropped, 1963-69	Market Share Change Not Available	Total
				(Number of Product Classes)						
A	1	4	4	17	6	1	0	16	0	49
B	10	5	15	65	5	1	1	15	4	121
C	0	1	2	5	0	0	0	4	0	12
D	3	0	2	2	1	1	1	1	2	13
E	2	1	9	26	9	3	4	4	3	61
F	1	0	2	10	6	0	0	10	1	30
Total (6 cos.)	17	11	34	125	27	6	6	50	10	286
Percentage Total	5.9	3.8	11.9	43.7	9.4	2.1	2.1	17.5	3.5	100.0

Market Share Change (Percentage Points)

Source: Federal Trade Commission, Economic Report on Corporate Merger Performance: An Empirical Analysis of Nine Corporations, November 1972, p. 113.

Perhaps most amazing of all is the report's conclusions regarding the probable effects of reciprocity. It stated: "It is not clear, however, that conglomerate firms engage in widespread, systematic reciprocity."[26] Although the study did not attempt to gather information on the subject, "all of the sample conglomerates denied making significant changes in purchasing patterns of the firms they acquired."[27] It is not known whether or not the report's authors gave credence to these obviously self-serving statements. But readers of the report are not told that after it was initiated and before it was published, the Justice Department had brought and settled five merger cases in which reciprocity was a major issue.[28] Four of these cases involved two conglomerates studied by the Commission staff.[29] In the ITT cases, considerable evidence was developed on the practice of reciprocity, much of which was placed in the public record. However, in responding to the Commission's data requests, ITT apparently did not supply any information on the practice. Additionally, in the last few years both the Commission and the Justice Department have brought numerous other actions challenging the practice of reciprocity.

All the Commission data and most of the Justice Department's data could have been analyzed by the FTC's economics staff. Indeed, the FTC's 1969 staff report on mergers detailed the widespread practice of reciprocity, spelled out in case studies how the practice may affect competition, and demonstrated how conglomerate mergers created new reciprocity opportunities or added to existing ones.[30] The FTC's 1972 staff study made "no effort" to examine such central conglomerate hypotheses as reciprocity, cross-subsidization, or mutual forbearance.[31] It is perhaps fortunate that economic studies are not taken too seriously by antitrust lawyers, for the Justice Department has stated that the report will not alter the Department's conglomerate merger policy.[32] However, the report cannot help but have some adverse effect on enforcement policy, as defendants attempt to rely on its conclusions.

Although the report made an important contribution in its Chapter 5, dealing with information loss resulting from conglomerate expansion, this chapter was seriously weakened because the Commission forced the staff to suppress information on individual companies.[33] Consequently, viewed as a whole, the inquiry must be judged a disaster in the effort to obtain more reliable knowledge upon which to base responsible public policy toward conglomerates.

What then should be public policy toward conglomerates? With the settlement of the ITT cases, it will take years before getting definitive judicial guidelines. But even at best, it can be seriously questioned whether Section 7 will be adequate for the task. At most, rules that will prevent mergers among very large companies or the acquisition of a leading company in a concentrated industry may be developed. Yet the postsettlement experience of ITT illustrates how a conglomerate may absorb enormous amounts of assets through numerous small acquisitions. In the twenty months since the settlement, ITT has acquired at least fifty-five companies with a combined value (in ITT stock) of about $575 million.[34] This more than equals the assets ITT has divested to date pursuant to the ITT settlement.

In view of the mounting evidence that conglomerates pose political as well as economic dangers transcending the economist's narrow view of a merger's impact on an isolated market, there is need for new legislation that imposes much stricter rules for conglomerate mergers. Legislation should require that before a large conglomerate could make an acquisition of significant size, the Federal Trade Commission make an affirmative finding that (1) the merger does not have the effect of substantially lessening competition under the existing law and (2) the merger is in the public interest because it promises to increase competition, efficiency, or provide other economic benefits in which the public would share. For this purpose, a large conglomerate could be defined as one with sales in excess of $500 million and the acquired or merging company one with assets of $10 million. A conglomerate that acquired during a twelve-month period a number of smaller companies with combined assets of $10 million might also be required to obtain such approval. Evidence concerning the issues involved would be developed before the FTC in a public hearing to which the Antitrust Division of the Department of Justice could be a party. FTC decisions could be appealed by either the merging parties or the Department of Justice. The procedures should permit private parties to intervene in such proceedings. The purposes of these procedures are twofold: first, to establish special standards for mergers by large conglomerates that may pose serious economic and social dangers without offsetting benefits to the public interest and, second, to require the antitrust authorities to account publicly for their decisions to permit or reject such mergers.[35]

Placing stricter curbs on mergers will not solve problems posed by existing conglomerates. The major benefit will be insurance of a more decentralized industrial structure, which will be desirable on both economic and political grounds. But it is an inescapable fact of life that existing conglomerates will not wither away; on the contrary, in the decades ahead an increasing share of the Western world's financial and industrial resources will become controlled by multinational conglomerates. Control of much of the world economy by these enterprises raises important issues concerning their national citizenship and allegiance. Their multinational character make it difficult to perceive the American national interest in their dealings abroad. There may still be merit to Thomas Jefferson's observation that "merchants have no country. The mere spot they stand on does not constitute so strong an attachment as that from which they draw their gain." Today, because the largest multinational corporations operate worldwide, they may have no strong attachments to any land, as they freely transfer resources around the globe.

Obviously, the emergence of multinational corporations as the dominant business enterprise makes obsolete historical instruments of social control. Just as the huge multinational conglomerate transcends national boundaries, so must new methods of social control be multinational in scope. Although traditional antitrust will continue to have a role, additional instruments of control that deal more directly with corporate behavior must be created. The precise form of these new methods of control is not clear, but a first step would be enactment of a federal chartering statute that recognizes explicitly the public character of these corporations and imposes new responsibilities on them.[36] An essential prerequisite of such a statute is the requirement of extensive public disclosure of the affairs of large conglomerates. The need for such disclosure was emphasized in the FTC's 1969 merger report,[37] and, as Boyle has emphasized, this is the key recommendation of the 1972 report.[38] The need for more adequate disclosure of corporate financial affairs grows as American corporations grow in size and complexity. Economic intelligence about many aspects of business organization is worse today than it was around 1900, when Theodore Roosevelt made his plea for opening to public view the "mammoth" corporations of his day. In his first address to the Congress, Roosevelt declared that "great corporations exist only because they are created and safeguarded by our institutions; and it is therefore our right and our duty to see that they work in harmony with these institutions." He therefore argued that "the first requisite [of corporate accountability] is knowledge, full and complete; knowledge which may be made public to the world."

High market concentration pervades much of the American economy. Economists may quibble over precisely how much market concentration has risen or fallen over the last couple decades, but the indisputable fact of life is that in many industries production is concentrated in a few hands, has been highly concentrated in a few hands for many decades, and will in all probability remain so unless some explicit public policy initiatives are taken to change things. Depending on the data used, between one-quarter and one-third of American manufacturing occurs in industries where four firms control 50 percent or more of domestic output. Analysis of the most recent data indicates that, on average, market concentration rose slightly in the 1960s (Table 7-3). The greatest increases occurred in consumer goods industries, particularly those involving highly differentiated products.[39]

A debate continues among American economists as to the precise relationship between market concentration and economic power. But there can no longer be any serious doubt that high market concentration in an industry generally confers considerable market discretion to the firms in the industry, particularly as reflected in the ability to achieve and maintain noncompetitive profit rates.[40]

A consensus also appears to be emerging among economists that the existence of excessive market power in parts of the economy creates an inflationary bias. Put differently, when such market power exists, it is impossible to rely solely on monetary and fiscal policy to achieve and maintain full employment without excessive inflation. Although there are still unbelievers, especially in the bastion of laissez faire economics, the University of Chicago, events have forced most economists to discard theoretical models that assume away the problems posed by market power.

Credit for much of this change in attitude must go to President Nixon, who conducted a truly historic economic experiment. In January 1969, the president announced that he would bring about price stability without significantly increasing unemployment. He pledged that he would accomplish this without any government intervention in the marketplace. For the next twenty-seven months, despite active manipulation of monetary and fiscal policy, price inflation continued—indeed accelerated—and the unemployment rate rose from 3.3 percent to about 6 percent. The fatal flaw in the President's game plan was the fundamental assumption that "free" market forces were sufficiently powerful to discipline key price and wage decisionmakers in the economy. Were market forces truly competitive in all industries, as they are in many industries, the overall price level would have begun moderating shortly after fiscal and monetary policy had contracted aggregate demand.

After President Nixon's twenty-seven-month costly experiment with "free markets," he dramatically reversed course and adopted a new program, the first phase of which was a three-month wage-price freeze. The subsequent phases of his new program once again place great faith in the pervasiveness of competition. The whole world watches expectantly as the experiment continues.

As a result of experiences over the past decade, there appears to be a growing recognition of the significant relationships between market power and the effectiveness of monetary and fiscal policy. For example, President Johnson's Cabinet Committee on Price Stability concluded, "We recommend vigorous enforcement of the antitrust laws as essential for reducing further the inflationary effects of discretionary power. Only to the extent that we maintain effective market competition can we continue to place primary reliance on private decision makers in our quest for high employment, rapid economic growth and price stability."[41]

President Johnson's Cabinet Committee report reflected the views of men who had come to this conclusion after having struggled with the market power-inflation problem. More recently, other prominent public officials have come to share this view. For example, Arthur F. Burns, Chairman of the Federal Reserve System and earlier an intimate advisor to the president when he embarked on his famous experiment in January 1969, recently testified:

Improved policies of managing aggregate demand, important though they be, will not of themselves suffice to assure prosperity without inflation. Structural reforms are also needed. Not a few of our corporations and trade unions now have the power to exact rewards that exceed what could be achieved under conditions of active competition. As a result, substantial upward pressure on costs and prices may emerge long before excess aggregate demand has become a problem.[42]

These views assume that the extent of government involvement in price and wage decisions is directly related to the extent that competition restrains the discretionary power of key decisionmakers. The choice is therefore to either enlarge the area of competitive markets or enlarge the area of government involvement in business pricing decisions. Moreover, the extent of market power in business bears directly on the extent and use of power by labor. Market power in business begets market power in labor, as well as encourages labor to make maximum use of its power.

But perhaps even more importantly, where firms enjoy persistently exorbitant profits, as in the drug industry, such excess profits must be eliminated if labor unions are not to exercise their full power. It is not convincing to argue, as have many economists, that eliminating monopoly profits in a particular industry is not really very important because it will not improve significantly the allocation of resources or the distribution of income in the economy. The critical point missed by this argument is that it is unreasonable to expect some persons in the economy to exercise restraint in the use of discretionary market power unless an explicit national policy designed to place limits on market power in all segments of the economy is adopted. Thus, increasing competition in an industry serves the dual purpose of reducing the discretionary power of those in the industry and encouraging others in the economy to behave responsibly in using their power.

This immediately raises the question of how best to deal with the issue of market power in today's economy. As noted above, one of two areas must be enlarged; the area where competition is sufficiently effective to limit the pricing discretion of business firms or the area of price controls. Over the past decade, under three administrations, a decided preference has been shown for increasing price controls than for increasing competition. Perhaps the problem is that efforts to increase competition through structural reform necessarily are time-consuming and that many individual efforts are required to have a large overall effect.

Certainly over eighty years of experience with the enforcement of the Sherman Act make it clear that the traditional antitrust approach is not adequate to cope with the task. It can be seriously questioned whether the antitrust agencies have the capacity to do the job, even if they have the will. The revelations regarding the IBM case initiated by the Justice Department in January 1969 are instructive. In that case the Control Data Corporation (CDC), which had a private suit quite closely resembling the Justice Department's complaint, was carrying most of the burden of the case. When IBM and CDC reached a settlement in the matter, IBM destroyed a computerized index to the 27 million documents collected by CDC, allegedly hampering the Justice Department's efforts in the case. An indication of the costs involved in trying a case of this magnitude under existing law is that in its settlement with CDC, IBM agreed to pay CDC $15 million for attorney's fees and other expenses. This is greater than the annual budget of the Antitrust Division.

Donald I. Baker, head of the Antitrust Division's policy planning section, shares the view that the Justice Department cannot effectively cope with the concentrated industry problem. He recently stated:

My own view is that the Section 2 standard is probably inadequate as a practical matter to deal with the broad oligopoly situations we've got across the country. . . . The burden of proof on the Government will just turn out to be too great. . . . These Section 2 "big firm monopoly" cases are just enormously draining of our resources, . . . and we just simply do not have the kind of resources that would be needed to pursue the Section 2 standard against the broad range of oligopoly markets.[43]

To be serious about industry restructuring, new approaches are needed: (1) a new mandate from the Congress indicating that it does indeed support a public policy designed to improve the effectiveness of competition in the economy, and (2) a new statute that permits both effective and expeditious steps to bring this about. For these reasons, there is great merit in Senator Hart's recently introduced Industrial Reorganization Act.[44] America is at one of those unique turning points in history when, by action or inaction, she must decide which road she shall travel to achieve her national objectives.

Because of its length and complexities, only overall reactions to the proposal's various provisions will be discussed.

1. Its passage would constitute a clear mandate from the Congress that it supports a vigorous procompetition policy through judicious industrial restructuring in key industries.
2. It expedites the enforcement process by articulating standards that go to the heart of the matter: the possession of monopoly power. The existing case law focuses on issues of intent to monopolize, the abuse of monopoly power, and other aspects of conduct and business behavior rather than market power as such.
3. It establishes an organizational and procedural framework that could expedite relief in the most important segments of the economy by: (1) establishing an Industrial Reorganization Commission for the sole purpose of enforcing the Act; (2) directing it to give top priority to seven important industries, and (3) establishing a special Industrial Reorganization Court that would provide a panel of judges to deal specifically with cases originating under the act.
4. The act encourages the commission and court to explore a variety of ways for reorganizing an industry to enhance competition. The Industrial Reorganization Commission may explore methods of increasing competition beyond those available to the Industrial Reorganization Court. For example, in some cases it might recommend that government actions be taken to encourage new entry in an industry; in others, it might consider the desirability of establishing government-owned enterprises in highly concentrated industries much as Sweden has done with apparent success in the drug industry.

Perhaps the major criticism of the proposal will center on Section 101, which defines unlawful possession of monopoly power. The section provides that "there shall be a rebuttable presumption that monopoly power is possessed" (1) by any corporation that persistently earns after-tax profits exceeding 15 percent; (2) if there has been no substantial price competition among two or more corporations for a period of years, and (3) if four or fewer corporations account for 50 percent or more of sales in a relevant economic market. (The bill spells each of these out in some detail.) A corporation falling within these criteria would have the burden of rebutting the presumption that it had monopoly power. However, it would not violate the law if its power was due solely to patents, or if divestiture would result in loss of substantial economies.

Establishing precise standards of unlawful conduct is always one of the most troublesome tasks facing legislative bodies and the courts. Some economists may argue that the four-firm concentration standard is too strict. The Neal Report, for example, put the figure at 70 percent.[45] This author's view is that four-firm concentration of 70 percent is so blatantly excessive that the Industrial Reorganization Commission should begin action with industries in this class immediately, except where a patent defense exists. If the industry can demonstrate that economies of scale are responsible for the high concentration, which would mean, of course, that continued high concentration is inevitable, the Commission should recommend to the Congress that the industry be subject to price and other regulatory controls. After disposing of these industries, the Commission should proceed to less concentrated ones to determine the optimum mix of policies required to achieve more effective competition. Although the act seems to be aimed mainly at horizontal market power, it does not rule out the possibility of restructuring conglomerate enterprises if this were demonstrated to be essential to restoring competition in an industry. But the act would not do much about existing conglomerate power except, perhaps, that derived from vertical relationships.

Advertising poses a variety of antitrust and other trade regulation issues. It may increase market concentration, deceive consumers, and result in an enormous waste of resources spent for noninformational advertising. The evidence demonstrates that, since about the mid-1950s, advertising and related forms of product differentiation are the single most important causes of growing market concentration. Table 7-3 shows some preliminary results of a study of the latest market concentration data. Whereas average market concentration has held about constant for all producer goods industries since 1958, it has risen sharply for consumer goods. Although the most dramatic increases occurred in industries with moderate or highly differentiated products, concentration has increased even in industries with the least degree of product differentiation.

This dramatic increase in market concentration speaks ill for the future performance of these industries. Traditional antitrust approaches can accomplish little to deal with the problem. However, the FTC's trailblazing case challenging the shared monopoly power of cereal manufacturers may demonstrate what can

Table 7-3

Average Four-Firm Unweighted Concentration Ratios by Type of Industry for 166 Industries, 1947-70

	166 Industries	Producer Goods N = 97	Consumer Goods: Degree of Differentiation[a]			
			All N = 69	Low N = 20	Moderate N = 33	High N = 16
		Average Unweighted Four-Firm Concentration				
1970	42.7	42.8	42.4	28.2	41.4	62.3
1967	41.4	41.9	40.8	26.0	39.7	61.6
1963	41.3	42.4	39.9	25.8	38.8	59.8
1958	40.3	42.4	37.4	23.8	36.7	55.9
1954	40.6	43.3	37.1	25.3	35.8	54.6
1947	40.9	44.1	36.3	27.8	35.0	49.6
Change 1947-70	+1.8	−1.3	+6.1	+.4	+6.4	+12.7

[a]The classification of industries as between producer goods and consumer goods, as well as by the degree of product differentiation is based on the classification system developed in Bureau of Economics, Federal Trade Commission, *Comparable Concentration Ratios for 213 Manufacturing Industries Classified by Producer and Consumer Goods and Degree of Product Differentiation 1947, 1954, 1958, and 1963*, March 15, 1967.

Note: This table is based on an unpublished study by the author.

be accomplished by this route.[46] It presents a challenge to economists in helping to fashion meaningful relief. Certainly deconcentration alone will not accomplish the desired results. Relief must go to the heart of the problem: the extent and methods of advertising.

Relief for problems posed by advertising cannot be provided by antitrust alone. Over the past decade the FTC has developed a panoply of weapons for striking at the problem. Time permits only listing the various programs: (1) affirmative disclosure requirements; (2) corrective advertising; (3) substantiation of advertising claims; and (4) counteradvertising.[47] These approaches represent a useful kit of tools for striking at the monopoly as well as the deceptive aspects of advertising. But continued bold experimentation is required to truly insure that advertising plays a constructive role in our economy.

At the outset of the Kleindienst hearings regarding the circumstances surrounding the ITT settlement, President Nixon said, "We want the whole record brought out because [Kleindienst] wants to go in as Attorney General with no cloud over him."[48] Not only did the hearings fail to lift the cloud over Kleindienst, but the cloud darkened and grew until it overshadowed Pennsylvania Avenue from the Department of Justice to the White House. The hearings documented the process by which the large corporation brings its influence to bear on government and how government responds.[49]

Although the full story may never be known, the hearings developed disturbing facts concerning the operations of the Justice Department. The public had been misled in the summer of 1971 as to the actual reasons for the ITT settlement, and Kleindienst was not telling the truth when he said the entire settlement had been "handled and negotiated exclusively" by Antitrust Division Chief McLaren. Kleindienst and White House aides were very much involved in the entire process. The hearings also made public for the first time that Kleindienst and Mitchell had overruled other legal actions recommended by McLaren.

The handling of the ITT settlement and other antitrust matters inevitably reduce the public's confidence in the Department's integrity. How, then, can public confidence be restored? The answer, in part, is to eliminate the heavy blanket of secrecy that covers so much of the public's business. This requires opening more government and corporate behavior to public scrutiny.

One of the most disturbing aspects of the ITT settlement is that Kleindienst, Mitchell, and McLaren repeatedly insisted that the entire process followed in the ITT settlement negotiations was standard operating procedure at the Justice Department. Insofar as this is true, it is the essence of the public's lack of confidence in much antitrust enforcement. As the *New York Times* put it,

There is indeed a well-established precedent, under both Democratic and Republican administrations, by which top Government officers talk privately with big businessmen about out-of-court settlements. . . . But this is precisely what is wrong with the way the antitrust laws are enforced . . . the entire secret process substitutes rules by men for rule by law. Such a process always creates the danger that a case will be determined by political and personal influence—or financial and economic influence—rather than by the merits as judged by impartial jurists.[50]

This problem can be solved only if officials of the Department of Justice and the Federal Trade Commission[51] are held more publicly accountable. This is especially true in the over 80 percent of the antitrust cases that end in out-of-court settlements. Legislation (S. 782) recently introduced by Senator John V. Tunney would go far toward opening up the consent settlement process to wider public and judicial scrutiny. It would, among other things, require the Justice Department to document publicly the considerations that influence the terms of a settlement, including an evaluation of the impact of the settlement. In this respect, it is similar to the environmental impact statements required of the National Environmental Protection Act. Additionally, the bill would require that corporate defendants list all oral or written communications between themselves and any member of government.[52] Although such legislation is no cure-all for political corruption or administrative bungling, it could be an important step in restoring the public's confidence that ours is a government run according to rules of law rather than by arbitrary decisions of men.

Since 1890, economists have repeatedly lamented that antitrust has never been given a fair chance to prove what it could accomplish. True, there have been no grand experiments comparable to those of the New Deal—the NRA, AAA, or WPA—or, more recently, comparable to President Nixon's ill-fated twenty-seven-month game plan which tested the efficacy of "free markets" in the application of fiscal and monetary policy. If antitrust has not been given a fair test in the last eight decades, can anyone reasonably expect that it will be given one in the future? The answer is an obvious categorical no. But this does not rule out the possibility of meaningful antitrust reform.

Just over a decade ago Ben Lewis summed up the seemingly impregnable place big business had built for itself by the late 1950s. As he saw it:

The behavior of bigness today is spotless—at least no spots remain unremoved for long; and its appearance and demeanor are attractive and ingratiating. Tutored by its attorneys, bathed, barbered, and cosmeticized by Madison Avenue, nourished and sanctified by war and cold war, and enthroned by public opinion which sees only "goodness" in bigness that is well mannered and well behaved, bigness exhibits the supreme confidence and gracious assurance that bespeak stature, status, and a clear conscience. Bigness was once the bad boy in Sunday school; now it sits on the vestry.[53]

But breezes of reform have been blowing across America since Lewis wrote these discouraging words. The big business image has been badly tarnished. GM's blatant efforts to intimidate Ralph Nader left spots that have not yet been removed. Many consumers have revolted against Madison Avenue's hard sell, and no longer accept shoddy products as inevitable. The revelations of ITT's affairs at home and abroad have taught a new generation, and refreshed the memories of an older one, that economic and political power are fellow travelers. Allegations of international financial manipulations have made multinational corporations seem more menacing than the legendary gnomes of Zurich.

These and other events have created a sense of disquietude among the people, an environment conducive to reform. To date its major manifestations have been to place more direct constraints on big business performance in such matters as product safety, greater truth in packaging and lending practices, environmental protection standards, minority hiring practices, and a growing trend toward direct intervention in wage and price decisions. To the true believer in "free" markets, much of this smacks of heresy and a fear of heading down Hayek's "road to serfdom."[54] Realistically, of course, these actions simply reflect a widespread disenchantment with the kind of *performance* generated by "free" markets.

Rather than deplore these developments, one should readily admit that even effectively competitive markets cannot be expected to insure socially optimum performance in many areas. As Joan Robinson recently observed, "The distinction that Pigou made between private costs and social costs was presented by him as an exception to the benevolent rule of *laissez-faire*. A moment's thought shows that the exception is the rule and the rule is the exception."[55] Thus many aspects of industrial performance require state intervention. But this is not an argument for abandoning competitive market forces as a planner and regulator of economic activity in as many areas as possible. Whenever the government assumes a new responsibility, the more essential it becomes that as much of the economy as possible is regulated by the market rather than by the government. Wherever the market system works effectively, it is possible to avoid government intervention into the economically and politically hazardous thicket of specifying complex dimensions of economic performance.

Antitrusters should therefore hitch themselves to the reform movement. Society should accept a realistic view of what can and cannot be accomplished by the market, and instruct others as to how more competition and less centralization of economic power serves the public good. Critics may then become participants in the reform movement rather than be ignored as a curious group of zealots clamoring for a return to an age that never existed. If such a strategy successfully broadens their constituency, the reforms discussed herein—and more—may yet come to pass.

Notes

Notes

Chapter 1
Allocative and Distributive Effects
of Monopoly

1. Reviews of past empirical studies of the concentration-profitability association are found in Leonard W. Weiss, "Quantitative Studies of Industrial Organization," in *Frontiers of Quantitative Economics*, ed. by M.D. Intriligator (Amsterdam: North Holland Publishing, 1971); and James A. Dalton and David W. Penn, *The Quality of Data as a Factor in Analyses of Structure-Performance Relationships* (Washington: Government Printing Office, 1971). Chapter 2 of this volume contains a commentary on findings of a negative association.

2. The preparation of this discussion owes much to earlier discussions with Michael Glassman.

3. The value of the last unit is the price the consumers were willing to pay. In this case, only 4/10 of an additional M was sold at a price of $12. Thus the extra value was $4.80.

4. The assumption is that long-run average costs are constant. Therefore, in perfect competition, the change in price is zero.

5. The monopoly profits rectangle is also eliminated. This aspect is considered later in the discussion of the distributive effects of monopoly power.

6. This static model ignores the possibility that imperfectly competitive industries may be more progressive than competitive industries. If so, the allocative costs of monopoly would be reduced. The evidence does not support this proposition, as in F.M. Scherer, *Industrial Market Structure and Economic Performance* (Chicago: Rand McNally, 1970), Chapter 15. The welfare triangle analysis also ignores the effects of monopoly profits on the distribution of income. The latter effects will be discussed later.

If the M producer's long-run average cost curve is U shaped and the firm is operating on the downward-sloping portion of the curve, the welfare triangle will *understate* the deadweight loss. With less than optimum operations, there is an additional welfare loss that accrues neither to the producer nor to the consumer. This is also discussed in Shou-Eng Koo, "A Note on the Social Welfare Loss Due to Monopoly," *Southern Economic Journal* 37 (October 1970): 212-14.

7. If the slope of the demand function were known, and equal for both C and M markets, the benefits would be a quadratic function of the output distortion and linearly related to the slope. In such a case the demand function is:

$$P \quad = a - mQ. \tag{a}$$

138

The monopoly and competitive prices would then be

$$P_M = a - mQ_M, \text{and} \qquad \text{(b)}$$

$$P_C = a - mQ_C. \qquad \text{(c)}$$

The price distortion would be

$$P_M - P_C = m(Q_C - Q_M). \qquad \text{(d)}$$

Substituting (d) into (4) for Δp yields

$$B = 1/2(Q_C - Q_M)m(Q_C - Q_M). \qquad \text{(4a)}$$

$$B = 1/2m(Q_C - Q_M)^2. \qquad \text{(4b)}$$

8. The initial theoretical work was introduced by Harold Hotelling, "The General Welfare in Relation to Problems of Taxation and of Railway and Utility Rates," *Econometrica* 6 (July 1938): 242-69. For further elaboration on the interpretation of Equation (1.9), the reader can see *Industrial Market Structure*, pp. 401-02; George J. Stigler, "Statistics of Monopoly and Merger," *Journal of Political Economy* 64 (February 1956): 34; James M. Buchanan and Gordon Tullock, "The 'Dead' Hand of Monopoly," *Antitrust Law and Economics Review* 1 (Summer 1968): 85-96; and Charles E. Mueller, "Lawyer's Guide to the 'Welfare Loss' Concept: An Introduction," *Antitrust Law and Economics Review* 5 (Spring 1972): 75-96.

9. Arnold C. Harberger, "Monopoly and Resource Allocation," *American Economic Review* 44 (May 1954): 77-87.

10. David Swartzman, "The Burden of Monopoly," *Journal of Political Economy* 68 (December 1960): 627-30; and David Schwartzman, "The Effect of Monopoly on Price," *Journal of Political Economy* 67 (August 1959): 352-62.

11. It should be noted that if the proportionate welfare loss remains constant, an economy with a GNP growing at a faster rate than the population will experience increasing losses per capita over time.

12. Stigler, "Statistics of Monopoly and Merger," *Journal of Political Economy* 64 (February 1966), p. 18. © 1974 by The University of Chicago. For other weaknesses see Scherer, *Industrial Market Structure*, pp. 402-04; Dean A. Worcester, Jr., *Monopoly, Big Business and Welfare in the Postwar United States* (Seattle: University of Washington Press, 1967), pp. 210-227; and Dean A. Worcester, "Innovations in the Calculation of Welfare Loss to Monopoly," *Western Economic Journal* 7 (September 1969), pp. 234-43.

13. D.R. Kamerschen, "An Estimation of the 'Welfare Losses' from Monopoly in the American Economy," *Western Economic Journal* 4 (Summer 1966):

221-37. Kamerschen employed the Lerner Index of Monopoly Power $[(P - MC)/P]$, which is equivalent to Π/S, as the surrogate for E. Equation (1.4) would be $B = 1/2\Pi$.

Another study, employing $E = 1.5$, found the welfare loss to be in the Harberger-Swartzman range; F.W. Bell, "The Effect of Monopoly Profits and Wages on Prices and Consumers' Surplus in American Manufacturing," *Western Economic Journal*, 6 (June 1968): 233-41.

14. Scherer, *Industrial Market Structure*, pp. 402-403.

15. The following analysis has been adapted from William S. Comanor and Harvey Leibenstein, "Allocative Efficiency, X-Efficiency and the Measurement of Welfare Losses," *Economica* 36 (August 1969): 304-309. The analysis would differ somewhat if the added costs were due to overhead expenses and thus did not affect marginal costs. But the introduction of this consideration would not alter substantively the "cost effect" analysis. This is discussed in M.A. Crew and C.K. Rowley, "On Allocative Efficiency, X-Efficiency and the Measurement of Welfare Loss," *Economica* 38 (May 1971): 199-203.

16. This latter loss has been termed "X-inefficiency" by Professor Leibenstein in Harvey Leibenstein, "Allocative Efficiency vs. 'X-Efficiency'," *American Economic Review* 49 (June 1966): 392-415. Further illustrations of this concept are presented by Weiss, *Quantitative Studies*, pp. 370 ff.; F.M. Scherer, *Industrial Market Structure*, p. 407; O.E. Williamson, "A Dynamic Stochastic Theory of Managerial Behavior," in *Prices: Issues in Theory, Practice and Public Policy*, A. Phillips and O. Williamson, eds. (Philadelphia: University of Pennsylvania Press, 1968); and Tibor Scitovsky, "Economic Theory and the Measurement of Concentration," in *Business Concentration and Public Price Policy*, NBER (Princeton University Press, 1955), pp. 106-108.

17. Richard Caves et al., *Britain's Economic Prospects* (Washington: Brookings Institution, 1968), pp. 12-13, 279-323 and 491-93. There are additional references cited in Scherer, *Industrial Market Structure*, fn. 17, p. 405.

18. O.E. Williamson, "Managerial Discretion and Business Behavior," *American Economic Review* 53 (December 1963): 1032-57.

19. Scherer, *Industrial Market Structure*, p. 403. Scherer's estimate also includes an estimate of the distortions caused by upstream monopoly power.

20. Not all of the acquired market power may be capitalized, as pointed out by Harold Bierman, Jr. and Robert Tollison, "Monopoly Rent Capitalization and Antitrust Policy," *Western Economic Journal* 8 (December 1970): 385-89.

21. It would appear that over time the value of the acquired monopoly power would be fully amortized. At some point, therefore, the reported economic profits should rise because of the write-off of the capitalized market power.

22. This argument is developed at some length by Gordon Tullock in "The Welfare Costs of Tariffs, Monopolies, and Theft," *Western Economic Journal* 5 (June 1967): 224-32.

23. A discussion of additional costs stemming from externalities of such

efforts is found in E.J. Mishan, "A Note on the Costs of Tariffs, Monopolies and Thefts," *Western Economic Journal* 7 (September 1969): 230-33.

24. The analysis of the welfare loss attaching to the welfare triangle also ignores such problems as externalities in production and consumption and the effects of monopsonistic power.

25. One only has to maintain a given triangle and mentally move the demand curve back and forth, maintaining a given slope, to witness different areas in the rectangle.

26. Scherer, *Industrial Market Structure*, p. 409.

27. William S. Comanor and Robert H. Smiley, "Monopoly and the Distribution of Wealth," *Quarterly Journal of Economics*, forthcoming.

28. By increasing the costs of assaulting the market power, these companies reinforce the insulation stemming from influence in the political sphere. If the battle must be waged on political as well as economic and legal fields, the costs rise considerably. Therefore, in a benefit-cost framework, the net *economic* benefits may be low when attacking the worst offenders.

29. Some specific aspects of this solution are developed by Mann and Meehan in Chapter 2. A more comprehensive approach is taken by Roger G. Noll, *Reforming Regulation* (Washington, D.C.: Brookings Institution, 1971).

30. William J. Baumol, "Informed Judgment, Rigorous Theory, and Public Policy," *Southern Economic Journal* 32 (October 1965): 137-45.

Chapter 2
Policy Planning for Antitrust Activities:
Present Status and Future Prospects

1. The core of the criticism is that the Commission has been more concerned with the arbitration of equity disputes among businessmen (protecting competitors) than with economic or allocative efficiency. Rather than cite all of the critics, we refer the reader to the citations found in two of the more recent studies of the Commission. See Richard A. Posner, "The Federal Trade Commission," *University of Chicago Law Review* 37, no. 1 (Autumn 1970): 47-89, fn. 1; and *Report of the ABA Commission to Study the Federal Trade Commission*, 1969, p. 10, fns. 22, 23, and 24.

The same criticisms have been made of the Department of Justice's enforcement of antitrust laws. See Richard A. Posner, "A Statistical Study of Antitrust Enforcement," *Journal of Law and Economics* 13, no. 2 (October 1970): 365-419; Richard A. Posner, "A Program for the Antitrust Division," *University of Chicago Law Review* 38, no. 2 (Winter 1971): 500-536; and Mark J. Green et al., *The Closed Enterprise System* (New York: Grossman, 1972).

2. The work at the Commission has proceeded much further in antitrust than in consumer protection, largely because economic theory is more readily applicable and better data exists for measurement.

3. F.M. Scherer, *Industrial Market Structure and Economic Performance* (Chicago: Rand McNally, 1970), p. 402.

4. In using deadweight welfare loss as the criterion for defining antitrust priorities, the explicit assumption is that the primary goal of the antitrust agencies should be to promote allocative efficiency, subject to a budget constraint. This goal is consistent with the view of others. For example, see Richard Posner, "A Program for the Antitrust Division," p. 505 and Robert Bork, "Legislative Intent and the Policy of the Sherman Act," *Journal of Law and Economics* 9 (October 1966): 7-48.

5. Excess profit is net income minus the amount necessary for a competitive return.

6. Using a criterion as unrestrictive as that only 30 percent of a firm's sales has to be accounted by one four-digit product, 189 of the *Fortune 500* in 1967 could not be assigned to any industry. Statement of H. Michael Mann before the Monopoly Subcommittee of the Select Committee on Small Businesss, U.S. Senate, March 8, 1973.

7. The method for the computation of partial changes in the deadweight loss triangle is complex. For present purposes, it suffices to assert that there is a link between changes in the profit margin and the equations necessary to calculate partial increments (or decrements) in the triangle. It is possible to estimate changes in the profit margin if we know precisely how a particular practice influences concentration, barriers to entry, or the effectiveness of collusion.

8. Leonard Weiss, "Quantitative Studies of Industrial Organization," *Frontiers of Quantitative Economics*, ed. M.D. Intriligator, (Amsterdam: North Holland Publishing, 1971), pp. 362-411.

9. Yale Brozen, "Bain's Concentration and Rates of Return Revisited," *Journal of Law and Economics* 14 (October 1971): 351-69.

. 10. This position was originally advanced by Yale Brozen, "Significance of Profit Data for Antitrust Policy," in J. Fred Weston and Sam Peltzman, *Public Policies Toward Mergers* (Pacific Palisades: Goodyear Publishing Co., 1969), pp. 110-127. Brozen followed this paper with further analysis in "The Antitrust Task Force Deconcentration Recommendation," *Journal of Law and Economics* 13 (October 1970): 279-92.

11. Brozen asserts that in concentrated industries where larger firms earn higher returns than smaller firms, high concentration reflects the efficient organization of the industry. Yale Brozen, "Bain's Concentration and Rates of Return Revisited," pp. 361-66. Also Stanley I. Ornstein, "Concentration and Profits," *Journal of Business* 45, no. 4 (October 1972): 519-41. Ornstein finds that economies of scale, rather than concentration, explain high profitability.

12. Posner, "A Program for the Antitrust Division," pp. 506-531.

13. Brozen argues that certain accounting conventions bias rates of return upward in concentrated industries, "Significance of Profit Data for Antitrust Policy," pp. 115-18. However, Sam Peltzman believes that many of the conventions have the same impact on firms in unconcentrated industries:

"Therefore, a positive relationship between measured profitability and concentration implies a positive relationship between the latter and true profitability." Sam Peltzman, "Profit Data and Public Policy," p. 130. Weiss suggests that firms in concentrated markets have an incentive to understate their true profitability. Leonard Weiss, "Quantitative Studies," p. 370. We see no reason to presume that the biases work any more strongly in favor of a positive relationship than against finding a positive relationship.

14. The one study is George Stigler's *Capital and Rates of Return in Manufacturing Industries* (Princeton, N.J.: Princeton University Press, 1963). However, Robert W. Kilpatrick, in an article titled, "Stigler on the Relationship between Industry Profit Rates and Market Concentration," *Journal of Political Economy* 76, no. 3 (May/June 1968), pp. 474-88, pointed out a statistical flaw in Stigler's work. When this flaw is corrected, Stigler's results coincided with those of other studies.

15. Leonard Weiss, "Quantitative Studies," p. 371.

16. Joe Bain, "Relation of Profit Rate to Industry Concentration: American Manufacturing," *Quarterly Journal of Economics* 65, no. 3 (August 1951): 293-324.

17. It is important to note that "nonsignificant evidence quite literally fails to signify *anything*; it leaves us in our original state of ignorance." Daniel B. Suits, *Statistics: An Introduction to Quantitative Economic Research* (Chicago: Rand McNally, 1963), p. 128. Brozen forgets this lesson when he asserts: "We can stop trying to explain the existence of the relationship (between concentration and profitability) since there is none." "Concentration and Structural and Market Disequilibria," *Antitrust Bulletin* 16, no. 2 (Summer 1971): 248. A null hypothesis cannot be proven to be true.

18. Bain, "Relation of Profit Rate"; George Stigler, "A Theory of Oligopoly," *Journal of Political Economy* 72, no. 1 (February 1964), pp. 44-61; H. Michael Mann, "Seller Concentration, Barriers to Entry, and Rates of Return in Thirty Industries, 1950-1960," *Review of Economics and Statistics* 48, no. 3 (August 1966): 296-307.

19. Brozen, "Antitrust Task Force Deconcentration Recommendation," Table 1, p. 282.

20. Ibid., Table 5, p. 89.

21. Ibid., Table 6, p. 291. The mean rate of return for the high barrier class in the years 1961-66 is significantly higher, at the 0.01 level, than the mean of the substantial and moderate-to-low barrier classes.

22. Weiss, "Quantitative Studies," p. 370.

23. "Comments," in M.D. Intriligator, *Quantitative Economics*, p. 409.

24. Ornstein's evidence indicates that, by his measure, economies of scale explain about 40 percent of the variation in concentration. This suggests that optimal scales do not fully explain dominant market positions. The fact that larger firms earn more than smaller firms in concentrated industries does not

necessarily mean that high concentration is the product of superior efficiency, as Brozen argues. In fact, the evidence indicates that "in many and perhaps most American industries high concentration is not a technological, marketing, or financial imperative" Scherer, *Market Structure*, p. 103. Rather, the large firm profitability in concentrated industries is the likely result of forces, not related to efficiency, which impede the growth of smaller firms.

25. A recent study indicates that the observed positive association between an industry's higher average rate of return and the dispersion in returns around the mean does not mean a greater frequency of unsatisfactory returns, the sign that the higher return contains a risk premium. In fact it appears that both the higher return and the greater dispersion are related to high barriers to entry. Richard W. McNally and Lee A. Tavis, "'Spatial Risk' and Return Relationships: A Reconsideration," *Journal of Risk and Insurance* 39, no. 3 (September 1972): 351-67.

26. F.M. Scherer, *Market Structure*, pp. 377-78.

27. Posner, "Program for the Antitrust Division," pp. 516-25.

28. A particularly persuasive analysis is contained in Joe Bain, *Industrial Organization* (New York: John Wiley and Sons, 1968), pp. 332-48. Bain demonstrates that detailed descriptions of interseller coordination in six industries did not permit a prediction of pricing performance, but that knowledge about structure did.

29. Roger Sherman and Robert Tollison, "Public Policy Toward Oligopoly: Dissolution and Scale Economics," *Antitrust Law and Economics Review* 4, no. 4 (Summer 1971): 82.

30. In particular, Richard A. Posner, "A Program for the Antitrust Division"; Carl Kaysen and Donald F. Turner, *Antitrust Policy: An Economic and Legal Analysis* (Cambridge, Mass.: Harvard University Press, 1959), and Green et al., *The Closed Enterprise System*. All of the above authors differ as to what will cause a loss in economic efficiency but none disagree that economic efficiency should be the primary goal of antitrust enforcement.

31. The reader is referred to the discussion above.

32. Some of the more important papers are Oliver E. Williamson, "Managerial Discretion and Business Behavior," *American Economic Review* 53, no. 5 (December 1963): 1032-57; R. Joseph Monsen, Jr. and Anthony Downs, "A Theory of Large Managerial Firms," *Journal of Political Economy* 73 (June 1965): 221-36; Armen A. Alchian, "Corporate Management and Property Rights," in *Economic Policy and Regulation of Corporate Securities*, ed. by Henry Manne (Washington, D.C.: American Enterprise Institute, 1969), pp. 337-60; J. Newhouse, "Toward a Theory of Nonprofit Institutions: An Economic Model of a Hospital," *American Economic Review* 60, no. 1 (March 1970): 64-74; Roger G. Noll, "The Behavior of Regulatory Agencies," *Review of Social Economy* 29, no. 1 (March 1971), pp. 15-19; Ross V. Eckert, "The Los Angeles Taxi Monopoly: An Economic Inquiry," *Southern California Law*

Review 43 (Summer 1970): 407-53; and Roland N. McKean, "Differences between Individual and Total Costs within Government," *American Economic Review* 54 (May 1964): 243-57.

33. The economic organizations can be firms in the private sector, nonprofit organizations, and government agencies.

34. The discussion in this part is merely a review and an expansion of a number of insightful points made previously by Richard Posner, "The Federal Trade Commission," pp. 82-87.

35. Actually Posner argues that only those areas of Commission responsibility which would promote economic efficiency would be turned over to the Antitrust Division and the remaining responsibilities, such as the enforcement of the Robinson-Patman Act, should be left to private parties. Ibid., pp. 48-61. A careful reading of other studies by Posner indicate that he has a number of reservations of his own about the performance of the Antitrust Division. See, for example, Posner, "A Statistical Study of Antitrust Enforcement," esp. pp. 410 and 416; and Posner, "A Program for the Antitrust Division," p. 502.

36. In particular, see the studies by Noll, Eckert, and Posner cited in note 32 above.

37. Ross V. Eckert, "Taxi Monopoly," p. 442.

38. Ibid., pp. 442-43.

39. Posner, "Federal Trade Commission," p. 83.

40. Anthony Downs, "An Economic Theory of Political Action in a Democracy," *Journal of Political Economy* 65, no. 2 (April 1957): 148-49.

41. Posner considered only those commissioners since 1949 who are not presently in service (Posner, "The Federal Trade Commission," p. 86). Eighteen commissioners have been appointed since 1949 and have since left the Commission. Ten of the eighteen have returned to the private practice of law or have been appointed judges.

42. One student of regulation has suggested that regulators "make decisions that minimize the chance of unfavorable external judgments. . . ." When an issue is raised which is likely to be a radical departure, the commissioners will try to shift the responsibility to Congress. Roger Noll, "Regulatory Agencies," pp. 17-18.

43. Since Congress wrote the present laws, they will have no incentive to pressure the Commission into a radical departure from the current interpretation of the laws unless they feel that the courts have strayed very far from their original intention. Since there have been very few congressmen and senators who have sought new legislation which would put heavier weight on economic efficiency, we must assume that Congress is relatively happy with the courts' interpretation that the antitrust laws are to arbitrate disputes among businessmen.

44. U.S. Senate, *Hearings on Agriculture-Environmental and Consumer Protection Appropriations*, 92nd Congress Fiscal 1973 (Washington, D.C.: U.S. Government Printing Office), p. 1502.

45. Richard Posner, "The Federal Trade Commission," p. 86. Posner also points out that the value of experience at the FTC comes about because inexperienced attorneys can gain trial experience much more rapidly than they could in private practice. (Ibid.)

46. The reader only has to look at the history of the Antitrust Division's IBM case or the FTC's cereal or Xerox cases. Both the cereal and the IBM cases took approximately three years from conception to complaint. This is usually followed by another six month to a year delay until trial. The IBM case has been around for a much longer period and it has still not reached the trial stage.

47. Posner has argued, reasonably, that "the value of their trial experience to future employers is unaffected whether the cases tried promote or impair the welfare of society." Richard Posner, "The Federal Trade Commission," p. 86.

48. The reader is referred to the discussion at the beginning of the chapter.

49. This argument is not new, as in William A. Niskanen, Jr., *Bureaucracy and Representative Government* (Chicago: Aldine-Atherton, 1971), p. 26.

50. Posner, "Federal Trade Commission," p. 54.

51. Green, *Closed Enterprise System*, p. 119.

52. Robert H. Bork, "Legislative Intent and the Policy of the Sherman Act," *Journal of Law and Economics* 9 (October 1966): 7-48.

53. Bork does concede that the protection of small business was a concern of Congress but he argues the value is considered complementary rather than in conflict with the goal of economic efficiency (ibid., p. 10). If this is true, the courts that had to interpret the statute, which was intentionally written in vague language, seem to have gotten the wrong impression. Bork himself points out a number of cases where judges considered other values, especially Judge Learned Hand in the *Alcoa* 148 F. 2nd 416 (1945), and *Associated Press*, 326 U.S. 1 (1945), cases. Ibid., pp. 8-11, esp. fn. 3.

54. Thomas E. Kauper, "The 'Warren Court' and the Antitrust Laws: of Economics, Populism, and Cynicism," *Michigan Law Review* 67 (December 1968): 288.

55. 328 U.S. 781, 1946.

56. Almarin Phillips, "The Objectives of Economic Policy—The Contribution of Antitrust," unpublished version, pp. 10-11. Even if all price-fixing cases are concerned with economic efficiency, the gains to society from bringing these cases are not likely to be very large. One study of the Antitrust Division's price-fixing cases from 1955 to 1968 found a disproportionate frequency (i.e., the probability is less than 5 in 100 that the distribution occurred by chance) of cases in industries with four-firm concentration ratios below 35 percent. James M. Clabault and John F. Burton, Jr., *1968 Cumulative Statistical Supplement to Sherman Act Indictments 1955-1965* (New York: Federal Legal Publications, 1968), Table 5, p. 47. In industries with concentration this low, one would not expect the price-fixing agreements to be effective, and therefore the loss in economic efficiency due to price fixing is not expected to be very large. The Antitrust Division brings these cases because they are easy to win, and thus the

division can improve its appearance as a vigorous enforcer of the laws. The reader is referred to the discussion of the "numbers game" below.

57. Thomas E. Kauper, "Warren Court."

58. 370 U.S. 294 (1962).

59. 384 U.S. 270 (1966).

60. Morris A. Adelman, "Problems and Prospects in Antitrust Policy-II," in *Perspectives on Antitrust Policy*, ed. by Almarin Phillips (Princeton, New Jersey: Princeton University Press, 1965); Jesse W. Markham, "The Effectiveness of Clayton Act Section 7," also in *Perspectives on Antitrust Policy*; Thomas E. Kauper, "Warren Court," to mention a few.

61. A number of cases the Antitrust Division has brought in the past few years have had a strong emphasis on injury to competitors. See Kauper's discussion of *Arnold, Schwinn and Co.*, 388 U.S. 365 (1967), *White Motor*, 372 U.S. 253 (1963), and *Von's Grocery*, 384 U.S. 270 (1966), to mention a few cases of dubious value brought by the Antitrust Division. Thomas E. Kauper, "Warren Court." For a discussion of the conditions under which vertical restrictions will injure competition as well as competitors, the readers should see William S. Comanor, "Vertical Territorial and Customer Restrictions: White Motor and Its Aftermath," *Harvard Law Review* 81, no. 7 (May 1968): 1419-38.

62. The experience of the authors and discussions with attorneys at the Antitrust Division indicate that the young lawyers consider their experience as training for their future careers in private practice.

63. Green, *Closed Enterprise System*, p. 123.

64. The Nader Study Group indicated that Congressman Rooney slashed the division's budget by 25 percent in 1952 because of the decline in the won/loss record of the Division. Ibid., pp. 122-24.

65. Donald I. Baker, the Director of the Policy Planning Office for the Antitrust Division, in a recent interview, stated that he recommended that the Division not move against shared monopolies of any kind of broad scale because of the amount of resources which are required to develop a case of this type. Baker also provided another bit of evidence which suggests that lawyers at the Division are likely to be conservative in extending the law to concentrated industries: he argued that if Congress wanted a broad scale attack on concentrated industries it should pass new legislation: *Antitrust and Trade Regulation Report* no. 606 (March 27, 1973), pp. AA-2-AA-6.

66. The authors are presently working on a study to provide systematic empirical support for the hypothesis that the incorporation of economic efficiency as a goal for antitrust policy will probably not occur.

Chapter 2
Comment

1. A summary of the author's views is given in John M. Blair, "Planning for Competition," *Columbia Law Review* 64 (March 1964): 524-54.

2. Arnold C. Harberger, "Monopoly and Resource Allocation," *American Economic Review* 44 (May 1954): 77-87. See also F.M. Scherer, *Industrial Market Structure and Economic Performance* (Chicago: Rand McNally, 1970), p. 402.

3. Statement of H. Michael Mann before the Monopoly Subcommittee of the Select Committee on Small Businesses, U.S. Senate, March 8, 1973.

4. See 85th Cong., 2nd sess., Senate Subcommittee on Antitrust and Monopoly, *Report on Administered Prices, Automobiles*, (1958), Appendix A, pp. 184-94, by Marc Nerlove.

5. Edward H. Chamberlin, *The Theory of Monopolistic Competition*, 4th ed. (Cambridge: Harvard University Press, 1942), pp. 126-27.

6. Norman R. Collins and Lee E. Preston, *Concentration and Price-Cost Margins in Manufacturing Industries* (Berkeley: University of California Press, 1968), p. 56.

7. Howard N. Ross, "Illusions in Testing for Administered Prices," *Journal of Industrial Economics* 21 (April 1973): 187-95.

Chapter 3
An Analysis of the Allocation of
Antitrust Division Resources

1. Richard A. Posner, "A Statistical Study of Antitrust Enforcement," *Journal of Law and Economics* 13, no. 2 (October 1970): 355-420.

2. G.E. and R.D. Hale, "Cost Benefit in Court," *George Washington Law Review* 39 (1969-1970): 83-92.

3. F.M. Scherer, *Industrial Market Structure and Economic Performance* (Chicago: Rand McNally, 1970), Ch. 17.

4. U.S. Congress, Joint Committee on Internal Revenue Taxation, "Staff Study of Income Tax Treatment of Treble Damage Payments under the Antitrust Laws," November 1, 1965, p. 39.

5. Federal Trade Commission, *Report on the Baking Industry*, 1967, pp. 66-73.

6. W.B. Erickson, "Economics of Price Fixing," *Anti-Trust and Economics Review* 2 (Spring 1969): 102.

7. In general one would expect collusion to be more successful the more concentrated the industry, the more uniform the product and the more accurate the information available about current rivals' prices. All three markets involved here were concentrated. Information about rivals' prices was openly available where government agencies made bids public (electrical equipment and bleachers) or in retail sales at posted prices (the level at which the Seattle bread conspiracy operated). The antitrust actions in these cases may not have been the most important reasons for the collapse of some of these conspiracies. For instance, in the Seattle bread case, the market shares of the six leading bread

brands fell from 81 percent to 44 percent between 1956 and 1966. FTC, *Baking Industry*, p. 71.

8. As summarized in L.W. Weiss, "Quantitative Studies in Industrial Organization," in Intriligator, *Frontiers in Quantitative Economics* (Amsterdam: North-Holland Publishing, 1971).

9. Strictly speaking, this holds only if the acquiring firm is among the top n firms and the acquired firm is not. If both firms are in the top n or if neither is, ΔCR will usually be less than VS_a/VS. Where both are in the top n, this defect can be remedied by simply choosing a smaller n. In fact, since b varies inversely with n, our procedure is likely to understate the effect of such a merger. Where neither is in the top n, our procedure is apt to overstate the merger's effect. Horizontal merger suits where neither firm is in the top n would rarely be "strong" cases if $n > 8$, but one can imagine some if $8 \geqslant n > 4$.

10. Based on L.E. Preston and N.R. Collins, *Concentration and Price-Cost Margins in Manufacturing Industries* (Berkeley: University of California Press, 1968), p. 99. This value of b is for all industries where their index of geographic dispersion is 90 or greater with no control for the capital-output ratio. When they do control for the ratio, b rises to 0.173, but the coefficient for the capital output ratio is nonsignificant and has the wrong sign. Using all industries, the value of b ranges from 0.122 to 0.153 depending on the two-digit industries covered and the other variables considered.

11. The duration of collusion is expected to be less, however. The reader should see the subsequent discussion of this point.

12. Fritz Machlup and Martha Taber, "Bilateral Monopoly, Successive Monopoly, and Vertical Integration," *Economica* 27, no. 106 (May 1960).

13. G. Stigler, "A Theory of Oligopoly," *Journal of Political Economy* 72, no. 1 (February 1964): 44-61, and L. Telser, "Some Determinants of the Returns to Manufacturing Industries," report no. 6935, Center for Mathematical Studies in Business and Economics, University of Chicago, unpublished.

14. Task Force on Competition and Productivity, *Report, Antitrust Law and Economics Review* 2 (1968-69): 51-52.

15. In the twenty-two criminal collusion complaints filed by the Justice Department in 1968-1970 that contained statements of the time period covered, the mean duration was 7.5 years. Derived from Commerce Clearing House, *Trade Regulation Reporter*, pt. 5, "New U.S. Antitrust Cases," ¶45,068-45,070, covering 1968-70.

16. R.A. Smith, "The Incredible Electrical Conspiracy," *Fortune* 63 (April 1961).

17. Using a discount rate of 10 percent, a ten-year restraint has a present value 3.6 times that of a two-year restraint of the same annual value and 68 percent of a restraint of the same annual value that lasted forever.

18. One reason may be that one person did not consider appeals while the others did. Leaving that person's estimates out does not change the average estimated chances of a win substantially much, however.

149

19. Based on complaints listed in the Commerce Clearing House, *Trade Regulation Reporter*, pt. 5, "New U.S. Antitrust Cases," ¶45-068-45,070, covering 1968-70. The Bureau of the Budget, *Budgets of the United States, Fiscal Year 1970, 1971, and 1972 Appendixes*, Government Printing Office, 1969, 1970, and 1971, show 162 cases for fiscal 1968, 1969, and 1970. These do not include the regulatory cases. The tabulation here shows only 117 cases for calendar years. The difference is partially due to the exclusion of nonstructural monopoly cases and may reflect some difference between calendar and fiscal year data, but the main difference seems to be that the Justice Department counts civil and criminal suits in the same case as two suits while this study counts them as one. The Justice Department *Annual Reports of the Attorney General*, Government Printing Office, 1968 and 1969, for fiscal 1968 and fiscal 1969 allocate the cases for those two years as 20 percent (vs. 23 percent in our tabulation) criminal collusion, 16 percent (vs. 27 percent) civil collusion, 56 percent (vs. 41 percent) merger, and 8 percent (vs. 9 percent) monopolization (including leverage), but few of the last group are structural monopoly cases.

20. Donald I. Baker, "The Antitrust Division, Department of Justice: The Role of Competition in Regulated Industries," *Boston College Industrial and Commercial Law Review* 11, no. 4 (May 1970): 571-93.

21. The reader is referred to note 19.

22. Membership in the Section of Antitrust and the estimated coverage of ABA membership were supplied the writer in correspondence from the ABA.

23. Antitrust and legal staff is from Baker, "Antitrust Division." FTC Bureau of Competition staff was supplied by an FTC official.

24. Posner, "Antitrust Enforcement," pp. 369-74.

25. Actual outlays listed in the U.S. Bureau of the Budget, *Budgets of the United States*, for fiscal 1970, 1971, and 1972, Government Printing Office, 1969, 1970, and 1971.

26. Sizes are cited in only about half the complaints listed. Other cases are ignored in these averages. Where both total sales and affected sales are cited, the latter figure is used. In many of the other cases, affected sizes are probably exaggerated. This is particularly likely in structural monopoly and leverage cases. Where the action derived from a case initiated before 1968, the values of sales were taken from the earlier complaints. Regulation-practice case sizes were estimated using a list of cases in Baker, "Antitrust Division," using guesses on the extent of business affected based on the U.S. Bureau of the Census, *Statistical Abstract of the United States, 1969*, Government Printing Office, 1969, and national income by industry. Regulation-merger cases were based on a list prepared in consultation with one of the Division attorneys and statistics from *Moody's Manuals.*

"Sales size" of acquired banks was estimated at 5 percent of their assets. In 1965 the national income accruing in banks ($9.0 billion) was 2.4 percent of bank assets ($379 billion). Value added is roughly half of sales in most of the other industries considered, so this number was doubled and then rounded to 5 percent to yield a "sales size" roughly comparable to that in manufacturing. The sales sizes of horizontal and potential entry merger cases are probably unrepresentatively low because of the large number of banking cases included in 1968-70.

27. A. Harberger, "Monopoly and Resource Allocation," *American Economic Review* 44, no. 2 (May 1954): 77-87.

28. Market shares were taken from those complaints that give such a figure in the Commerce Clearing House, *Trade Regulation Reporter*, pt. 5, "New U.S. Antitrust Cases," ¶ 45,068-45,070 (1968-70).

29. The reader is referred to note 28.

Chapter 3
Comment

1. Oliver E. Williamson, "Economies as an Antitrust Defense: The Welfare Tradeoffs," *American Economic Review* 58 (March 1968): 18-36.

2. George A. Stigler, "A Theory of Oligopoly," *The Organization of Industry* (Homewood: Richard D. Irwin, 1968), pp. 39-63.

3. It is not clear that the incipiency cases have been eliminated. Weiss states that to be a strong merger case, among other things, it must be "where there are strong indications that concentration will become serious in the near future. The parties to the merger also must be of at least minimum efficient scale." See text, p. 36.

Chapter 4
Antitrust Cases as a Guide to
Directions in Antitrust Research
and Policy

1. *Chicago Board of Trade* vs. *United States*, 246 U.S. 231, 38 Sup. Ct. 242 (1918). This account is taken from an unpublished manuscript by Richard O. Zerbe, entitled, "The Chicago Board of Trade Case and the Grain Trade" (1970).

2. After 1939 known as the "To Arrive Rule" and later again as the "Call Rule." The more relevant sections of the rule were:

A. A board of directors is hereby empowered to establish a public "call" for corn, oats, wheat and rye to arrive, to be held in the exchange room, immediately after the close of the regular session of each business day.
B. Contracts may be made upon the "call" only in such articles and upon such terms as have been approved by the "call" committee.
C. The "call" shall be under the control and management of a committee consisting of five members appointed by the president with the approval of the board of directors.

D. Final bids on the "call" *less the regular commission charges for receiving and accounting for such property may be forwarded by dealers.* [Emphasis added.]

E. Any transaction of members of this association made with intent to evade the provisions of this rule shall be deemed uncommercial conduct, and upon conviction such member shall be suspended from the privilege of the association for such time as the board of directors may elect.

3. Milton Handler, *Cases and Other Materials on Trade Regulation*, 3rd ed. (Brooklyn: Foundation Press, 1960), pp. 185-86.

4. Ibid., p. 186.

5. Ibid., p. 187.

6. Ibid.,

7. Ibid.

8. *National Association of Window Glass Manufacturers et al.*, vs. *United States*, 263, U.S. 403 (1923).

9. Ibid., p. 412.

10. Compare *Appalachian Coals, Inc.* vs. *U.S.*, 288 U.S. 344, 54 S. Ct. 471 (1933) for a similar instance in which the depressed state of the industry probably influenced the decision.

11. This suggestion was originally made to the author by John S. McGee.

12. *National Association of Window Glass Manufacturers et al.*, vs. *United States*, 263, U.S. 403, 411-12.

13. *United States* vs. *Aluminum Company of America*, 148 F. 2d, 416 (1945).

14. Ibid., pp. 424-25.

15. See *U.S.* vs. *Columbia Steel Company*, 334 U.S. 495, 527-28, 68, Sup. Ct. 1107, 1124 (1948). "We do not undertake to prescribe any set of percentage figures by which to measure the reasonableness of a comparative enlargement of its activities by the purchase of the assets of a competitor. The relative effect of percentage command of a market varies with the setting in which that factor is placed."

16. R.H. Coase, "Durability and Monopoly," *Journal of Law and Economics* 15 (April 1972): 143.

17. Handler, *Trade Regulation*, p. 391.

18. *United States* vs. *E.I. DuPont De Nemours and Company*, 351 U.S. 377 (1956).

19. Ibid., p. 394.

20. George W. Stocking and Willard F. Mueller, "The Cellophane Case and the New Competition," *American Economics Review* 45 (March 1955): 63.

21. *F.T.C.* vs. *Procter and Gamble Company*, 386 U.S. 568 (1967).

22. The facts in the Clorox case as presented here are taken from John L. Peterman, "The Clorox Case and the Television Rate Structure," *Journal of Law and Economics* 12 (October 1968): 321.

23. *F.T.C.* vs. *Morton Salt Company*, 334 U.S. 37, 68 Sup. Ct. 822 (1948).

24. The material for this discussion of Brown Shoe is taken from material by John Peterman, forthcoming in the *Journal of Law and Economics*.

25. *U.S.* vs. *Brown Shoe Company*, 370 U.S. 294 (1962).

26. *F.T.C.* vs. *Brown Shoe Company*, 384 U.S. 316 (1966).

27. *U.S.* vs. *Brown Shoe Company*, 370 U.S. 294, 344 (1962).

Chapter 4
Comment

1. It can be called a minor restructuring because the assets and the markets to be divided can be delineated easily.

2. John A. Menge, "Style Change Cost as a Market Weapon," *Quarterly Journal of Economics*, 76 (November 1962): 632-47.

3. Bradford C. Snell, "Annual Style Change in the Automobile Industry as an Unfair Method of Competition," *Yale Law Journal* 80, no. 3 (January 1971): 567-613.

4. "Unfair Competition," *Iowa Law Review* 21 (January 1936). Reprinted in *Readings in the Social Control of Industry*, ed. by E.M. Hoover and Joel Dean (Philadelphia: Blakiston Co., 1949), p. 178.

Chapter 5
The Role of the Economist in
Developing Antitrust Remedies

1. That is not to say that economists have not made recommendations about relief in specific cases or about relief of a particular type. Rather, it is to say that a systematic approach to the question of antitrust relief in general has not been attempted. William Breit and Kenneth Elzinga apparently are making an effort in this direction with their forthcoming papers.

2. Some examples of this sort of work include: William H. Nichols, "The Tobacco Case of 1946," *American Economic Review* 39 (May 1949): 284-96; James W. McKie, "The Decline of Monopoly in the Metal Container Industry," *American Economic Review* 45 (May 1955): 499-508; and Carl Kaysen, *United States* vs. *United Shoe Machinery Corporation* (Cambridge, Mass.: Harvard University Press, 1956). See esp. pp. 271-344. Many other examples could be cited, but it is striking how long a list of articles and books about antitrust cases could be when assembled in which little or no mention of remedy is made.

3. See George J. Stigler, "Mergers and Preventive Antitrust Policy," *University of Pennsylvania Law Review* 104 (November 1955): 176-84; and George J. Stigler, "The Economic Effects of Antitrust Laws," *Journal of Law and Economics* 9 (October 1966): 225-38.

4. Costs can be imposed in a variety of ways. Some relief designed to end price discrimination undoubtedly raises consumer prices. A poor divestiture order may lead to the destruction or dimunition of valuable assets. In general, relief which leads to an incorrect quantity-price configuration imposes additional costs upon society.

5. Walter Adams, "Dissolution, Divorcement, Divestiture: The Pyrrhic Victories of Antitrust," *Indiana Law Journal* 27 (Fall 1951): 1-37; and Kenneth Elzinga, "The Antimerger Law: Pyrrhic Victories?" *Journal of Law and Economics* 12 (April 1969): 43-78.

6. An interesting theoretical problem is presented by what appears to be an asymmetry in the treatment of costs by the government and private firms. The government should be willing to pursue an antitrust case so long as the *total cost* is less than the amount by which action can reduce deadweight losses. The respondent, however, will be willing to pursue the matter so long as its *private costs* are less than the expected value of monopoly profits lost through losing the case. Since monopoly profits usually exceed deadweight losses by substantial amounts, respondents are in a position to deter all antitrust activity by indicating a willingness to spend an amount such that *total costs* (private and public) will always exceed the expected value of deadweight loss reduction. In short, does it ever pay to bring an antitrust case? Perhaps this question deserves serious examination.

7. Elzinga, "Antimerger Law," pp. 54-61.

8. In view of substantial reservations about the efficacy of conduct orders by many economists, one may be surprised at their enthusiasm for attacking price-fixing which is invariably treated with cease and desist orders. Perhaps the paradox is resolved by hypothesizing that economists believe that antitrust fines and imprisonments have been effective.

9. This means a remedy has no impact because it is irrelevant or evadable. Respondents might be expected to eagerly consent to such relief, saving substantial litigative costs.

10. Not everyone accepts this underlying crucial hypothesis. See Yale Brozen, "Bain's Concentration and Rates of Return Revisited," *Journal of Law and Economics* 14 (October 1971): 351-69.

11. For a description of market characteristics that make collusion more or less likely, see George J. Stigler, "A Theory of Oligopoly," *Journal of Political Economy* 72 (February 1964): 44-61.

12. *FTC* vs. *Procter and Gamble Co.*, 386 U.S. 568 (1967).

13. Elzinga, "Antimerger Law."

14. Of course, it is also possible that the name "Clorox" was such a valuable asset that Procter and Gamble would not have consented or appealed less. A trademark licensing order provision might be called for in that case.

15. The discussion of spin-offs and the spin-off of monopoly rents owes much to James M. Folsom.

16. This conclusion should be modified to some extent. Stockholders will

seek to create a viable entity so long as the reduction in monopoly rents as a result of creating an effective new competitor is less than the capital losses incurred by creating a nonviable spin-off.

17. Such a provision would act as a fine, and as a serious deterrent to merger activity.

18. This definition is not meant to be precise. It is clear that much needs to be done to determine how similar behavior by monopolists and tight oligopolists is. If such behavior is almost identical, then perhaps price-fixing should be attacked with structural orders.

19. See the following discussion on conduct remedies.

20. Brozen, "Bain's Concentration and Rates of Return Revisited," p. 366. "First, it seems that his [Bain's] sample of more concentrated industries was weighted with those in process of expanding toward a new, long-run equilibrium.... Rates of return in this group of industries moved toward the average rate in subsequent years...." Regression fallacies aside, what are the policy implications of Brozen's findings? Should antitrust authorities wait for many years while the market slowly eradicates welfare losses? A similar question about monetary and fiscal authorities waiting for the operation of the Pigou Effect in deep depressions has generally been answered in the negative.

21. Harold Demsetz, "Why Regulate Utilities?" *Journal of Law and Economics* 11 (April 1968): 55-65.

22. Dealing with monopoly through sale of rights or through fines also violates the spirit of the discussion of this study. Those approaches are attempts *to extract monopoly profits* from business firms, but the explicit goal of relief in this study is *to eliminate deadweight losses* occasioned by the existence of monopoly power.

23. One of the best illustrations of this problem is found in Don Patinkin, *Money, Interest and Prices*, 2nd ed. (New York: Harper and Row, 1965). Patinkin goes into great detail specifying a model which has "manna from heaven," great auctions with renegotiation of contracts, weekly time horizons, and other.equally realistic ingredients. He finds, however, that the model is deficient in the sense that there is nothing to stop people from borrowing virtually infinite amounts. His solution is "imperfect capital markets," but he spares the reader any detailed description of the nature of *this* assumption.

24. In second-best worlds, moving one variable toward its competitive value may decrease welfare if other variables depart from competitive values. See J.M. Clark, "Toward A Concept of Workable Competition," *American Economic Review* 30 (June 1940): 241-56.

25. Such arguments are economically naive since the theoretical linkage between advertising intensity and barriers to entry has not been rigorously defined.

26. Between 1970 and 1971 advertising to sales ratios (A/S) for the five leading producers of cigarettes declined sharply as shown in the table below. Measured advertising to sales fell even more.

Company	A/S 1970	A/S 1971
R. J. Reynolds	3.42%	2.51%
Phillip Morris, Inc.	4.40	3.30
American Brands	2.43	1.94
Liggett and Myers	3.84	4.77
Brown and Williamson	6.79	5.96
Average	4.18%	3.70%
% decrease	9.09%	

27. That is so because the discriminating monopolist continues to sell incremental units until price equals marginal cost but that is at the point of competitive output. Of course, a discriminating monopolist may cause massive income redistribution.

28. What lawyers call vertical price-fixing, economists usually call resale price maintenance.

Chapter 5
Comment

1. These comments do not deal with the sections concerning "monopoly" relief and the treatment of conduct problems. Much of what is said with respect to merger relief can be applied to merger problems.

2. *U.S.* vs. *I.T.T.*

3. By "inside" is meant those actually involved in providing economic advice and guidance as a part of their everyday activity. Glassman, in terms of this definition, is an "inside" economist. Academic economists are for the most part "outside" economists.

4. See the text, p. 81, emphasis added. The text of the paper does not indicate what is meant by a systematic approach, and successive rereadings of the paper have shed little light on that aspect.

5. See text, p. 82.

6. See text, p. 82.

7. This is analogous to the advice given this writer by his undergraduate statistics teacher who kept insisting that one should have a relatively clear idea of how one is going to tabulate and use data asked for by questionnaire.

8. Stanley E. Boyle, "A Critical Review of FTC's Report on Conglomerates," *New York Law Journal*, January 29, 1973.

9. Some careful thought might well be given to antitrust remedies which eliminate the property rights inherent in the use of a name like Clorox which represents a product trade name rather than the output of a firm trade name. The same might be said of product trade names such as Chevrolet, Cadillac,

Buick, Pontiac, and Oldsmobile. The list of such products could be extended considerably. Prohibitions of this sort seem of greater economic significance and likely to lead to the reduction of unnecessary "entry barriers" than senseless wringing of hands about the magnitude of advertising expenditures and the like.
  10. Ibid., p. 9.

Chapter 6
The Instruments of Antitrust Enforcement

  1. Most economists now agree that this underestimates the actual welfare loss since it does not take into account the investment of resources in the activity of monopolizing and in policing the cartel agreement. On this, see Gordon Tullock, "The Welfare Costs of Tariffs, Monopolies, and Theft," *Western Economic Journal* 5 (June 1967) and Harvey Leibenstein, "Allocative Efficiency vs. 'X'-Efficiency," *American Economic Review* 56 (June 1966).
  2. J.M. Clark, "Toward a Concept of Workable Competition," *American Economic Review* 30 (June 1940), reprinted in E.M. Hoover and J. Dean, eds., *American Economic Association Readings in the Social Control of Industry* (Philadelphia: Blakiston Company, 1942); J.E. Meade, *The Theory of International Economic Policy, Trade and Welfare* (London: Oxford University Press, 1955), vol. 2.
  3. Clark's theory is not noted for precision and its application is not without difficulties. Stephen Sosnick has surveyed the vagaries of much of the early literature of workable competition, for example, Stephen Sosnick, "A Critique of Concepts of Workable Competition," *Quarterly Journal of Economics* 72 (August 1958). Proponents of strong antitrust enforcement feared that implementation of the theory of workable competition into antitrust policy would provide a "cornucopia of escape hatches." Walter Adams, "The 'Rule of Reason': Workable Competition or Workable Monopoly," *Yale Law Journal* 63 (January 1954).
  4. Later mathematical formulations of the theory of second best have shown the decision rules for attaining optimality are so complex and the data necessary to implement these rules are so costly and uncertain (if not totally unavailable) that Scherer branded the theory a "counsel of despair." F.M. Scherer, *Industrial Market Structure and Economic Performance* (Chicago: Rand McNally, 1970), p. 25.
  5. Ideally the total benefit curve would be concave from below. This is particularly realistic if the policy planners in the Antitrust Division and Federal Trade Commission rely more heavily on concentration ratios as a starting point for information on questions of competition and monopoly. As the Census Bureau's concentration ratios increasingly become the hunting guide for detecting possible antitrust violations, the welfare losses from monopolistic behavior

will tend to be reduced at a decreasing rate. A high official in the Justice Department, in referring to the Census Bureau data, has been quoted as asserting, "We are going to use it quite a bit. Concentration data are tremendously important in our thinking process, picking which cases to bring and which to not." Cited in "Business Gets a New Measure of Bigness," *Business Week*, January 27, 1973, pp. 80-81.

6. Hans B. Thorelli, *The Federal Antitrust Policy* (Stockholm: Kungl. Boktryckeriet P.A. Norstedt and Söner, 1954), pp. 170-210.

7. 15 U.S.C. 1-2 (1970).

8. 15 U.S.C. 15 (1970).

9. 15 U.S.C. 1-2 (1970).

10. 15 U.S.C. 4 (1970) allows courts to use injunction to "prevent and restrain" antitrust violation. While injunctive relief can take many forms, such as barring an antitrust violator from making future acquisitions or requiring that a certain percentage of his output be sold to small, independent firms, the analysis is confined to the injunctive relief directing dissolution, divorcement, and divestiture. Since injunctive relief other than corporate surgery generally involves the government in the actual management of the firm, it is a bastard form of antitrust regulation. Corporate surgery remains the *sine qua non* of injunctive relief. The technical distinctions between dissolution, divorcement, and divestiture are discussed in S. Chesterfield Oppenheim, "Divestiture as a Remedy Under the Federal Antitrust Laws," *George Washington Law Review* 19 (December 1950): 120-21.

11. Section 6 of the Sherman Act provides for forfeiture of property owned by an antitrust violator when "in the course of transportation from one state to another, or to a foreign country. . . ." This dead letter section of the law will be ignored in this analysis. Any antitrust penalties located outside the antitrust statutes, such as the provision in the Panama Canal Act barring Sherman Act violators from use of the canal, also are ignored (15 U.S.C. 31 (1964)).

12. Gary S. Becker, "Crime and Punishment: An Economic Approach," *Journal of Political Economy* 76 (March/April 1968) reprinted in W. Breit and H. Hochman, *Readings in Microeconomics* (New York: Holt, Rinehart and Winston, 1971); William Breit and Kenneth G. Elzinga, "Antitrust Penalties and Attitudes Toward Risk: An Economic Analysis," *Harvard Law Review* 86 (February 1973).

13. For some empirical evidence and a sophisticated model of the effect of risk on corporate profits, see I.N. Fisher and G.R. Hall, "Risk and Corporate Rates of Return," *Quarterly Journal of Economics* 83 (February 1969).

14. Becker, "Crime and Punishment," pp. 346-47.

15. John Kenneth Galbraith, *The New Industrial State*, 2nd ed. (Boston: Houghton Mifflin, 1971), Chapters 2-15; Robin Marris, *The Economic Theory of "Managerial" Capitalism* (New York: Basic Books, 1964), Chapters 1-2, 5-7.

16. A diagrammatic proof of this argument is in Breit and Elzinga, "Antitrust Penalties."

17. Richard A. Posner, "A Statistical Study of Antitrust Enforcement," *Journal of Law and Economics* 13 (October 1970): 390-92.

18. Mark J. Green, Nader Study Group, *The Closed Enterprise System* (New York: Grossman, 1972), pp. 129-30; President Nixon's *Task Force on Productivity and Competition*, report of Chairman George Stigler reprinted in *Antitrust Law and Economics Review* (Spring 1969); "Tough Trust Laws Proposed by [Arthur F.] Burns," *Washington Post*, p. A1, February 21, 1973.

19. Posner, "Statistical Study," pp. 389-91.

20. Matthew Josephson, *The Robber Barons* (New York: Harcourt, Brace, 1962), p. 450.

21. George E. Hale, "Trust Dissolution: 'Atomizing' Business Units of Monopolistic Size," *Columbia Law Review* 40 (April 1940): 617-23.

22. Walter Adams, "Dissolution, Divorcement, Divestiture: The Pyrrhic Victories of Antitrust," *Indiana Law Journal* 27 (Fall 1951).

23. Milton S. Goldberg, *The Consent Decree: Its Formulations and Use* (East Lansing: M.S.U., Bureau of Business and Economic Research, Occasional Paper no. 8, 1962).

24. Kenneth G. Elzinga, "The Antimerger Law: Pyrrhic Victories?" *Journal of Law and Economics* 12 (April 1969).

25. A much fuller discussion of the costs and inefficiencies of private treble damage suits is in William Breit and Kenneth G. Elzinga, "Antitrust Enforcement and Economic Efficiency: The Uneasy Case for Treble Damages," *Journal of Law and Economics* (October 1974).

26. From Senate Judiciary Committee, *The Federal Judicial System*, S. Rep. no. 134, 92nd Cong., 1st sess., 29, Table 16, 37 (1961) as quoted in Tom C. Clark, "Use of 'Parajudges' and the Administration of Justice," *Vanderbilt Law Review* 24 (November 1971): 1167-69.

27. Warren E. Burger, "The State of the Judiciary—1970," *American Bar Association Journal* 56 (October 1970), p. 929 and Earl Warren Address at Harvard Law School Sesquicentennial reprinted in *Judicature* 51 (January 1968): 196.

28. Becker, "Crime and Punishment," pp. 356-59.

29. *Report*, National Advisory Commission on Criminal Justice Standards and Goals (1972).

30. Data on the costs of *any* legal institution are virtually nil. The antitrust authorities gather little data on their internal operations and information on the costs incurred by private parties in defending antitrust suits is practically nonexistent.

31. Finding the right buyer, carving out a viable business unit, and appropriately dividing the inventory, work force, cash, and current customers seem to be problems perennial to dissolution attempts. This is discussed in George E. Hale, "Trust Dissolution," pp. 628-29.

32. The most general exposition incorporating these two aspects is that of

Gordon Tullock, *The Politics of Bureaucracy* (Washington: Public Affairs Press, 1965). More recent theoretical treatments, based heavily on the work of Tullock, are William A. Niskanen, Jr., *Bureaucracy and Representative Government* (Chicago: Aldine-Atherton, 1961), and Anthony Downs *Inside Bureaucracy* (Boston: Little, Brown, 1967).

33. Elsewhere the authors have spelled out the details of a suggested financial penalty which in their judgment will deter risk averse management. Breit and Elzinga, "Antitrust Penalties."

34. As indicated earlier, the debates in Congress leading to the passage of the Sherman Act indicated some interest in a weapon that would increase competition at minimal cost. The suggestion by a number of sagacious legislators at that period of reducing protective tariffs on the goods of antitrust violators would have resulted in sharply increased competition with little administrative costs. Unluckily, this instrument is not part of the antitrust arsenal at present. In terms of deterrence, costs, and avoiding bureaucratic inefficiency, tariff reduction deserves high marks. But it is a rather blunt instrument which cannot be used with as much precision as can the more direct weapon of fines. After all, reducing tariffs on homogeneous products would penalize the innocent along with the guilty.

35. Walter Adams and Horace M. Gray, *Monopoly in America: The Government as Promoter* (New York: Macmillan, 1956).

Chapter 6
Comment

1. And at worst, reduced government participation in the formulation of detailed dissolution plans may increase the already high likelihood that Section 2 cases will end in cosmetic structural reform.

Chapter 7
Current Policy Issues in Antitrust

1. Ben W. Lewis, "Power Blocs and the Operations of Economic Forces," *American Economic Review* 49, no. 2 (December 1958): 384.

2. Willard F. Mueller, *The Celler-Kefauver Act: Sixteen Years of Enforcement*, A Staff Report to the Antitrust Subcommittee on the Committee on the Judiciary, House of Representatives, 90th Congress, 1st sess., House Committee Print, October 16, 1967.

3. Remarks of Thomas E. Kauper to Annual Corporate Council Institute, Northwestern University, October 4, 1972, and Bruce B. Wilson, Deputy Assistant Attorney General of the Antitrust Division, "New Directions in Antitrust Policy," Boca Raton, Florida, March 29, 1973.

4. Walter B. Erickson, "The Profitability of Violating the Antitrust Laws: Dissolution and Treble Damages in Private Antitrust," *Antitrust Law and Economics Review* 2, no. 3 (Spring 1969): 101-118. Alfred L. Parker, "Treble Damage Action—A Financial Deterrent to Antitrust Violations?" *Antitrust Bulletin* 4, no. 4 (Summer 1971): 483-505.

5. For a discussion of the ITT settlement, see Willard F. Mueller, "The ITT Settlement: A Deal With Justice?" *Industrial Organization Review* 1 (1973).

6. Joe S. Bain, *Barriers to New Competition* (New York: John Wiley and Sons, 1962).

7. A comprehensive review of this literature is found in Leonard Weiss, "Quantitative Studies of Industrial Organization," in M.D. Intriligator, ed., *Frontiers of Quantitative Economics* (Amsterdam-London: North-Holland Publishing, 1971), Chapter 9.

8. The first comprehensive effort to demonstrate the unique character of this new business form and the special problems it posed for competitive and other dimensions of industrial organization was Corwin Edwards; "Conglomerate Bigness as a Source of Power," in *Business Concentration and Price Policy*, National Bureau of Economic Research (Princeton: Princeton University Press, 1955), pp. 331-59.

9. Actually the share of the top 200 corporations engaged primarily in manufacturing has risen substantially since World War II. Between 1947 and 1968 the top 200 corporations' share of these assets—which include some assets of their international holdings and some nonmanufacturing assets—rose from 47.2 percent to 60.9 percent. Staff Report of the Federal Trade Commission on *Corporate Mergers*, 1969, p. 173. Preliminary estimates indicate that this share rose further between 1968 and 1972. Importantly, however, this is a minimum estimate of these corporations' share of such assets because the leading companies control enormous amounts of assets that are not consolidated in their reported balance sheets. According to this author's best estimates, the top 200 corporations control close to two-thirds of *total* assets of all corporations engaged primarily in manufacturing. According to Census Bureau figures, the top 200 manufacturing corporations' share of total value added by all *domestic* manufacturing corporations rose from 30 percent in 1947 to 43 percent in 1970. Bureau of the Census, *Annual Survey of Manufacturers: 1970: Value of Shipment Concentration Ratios, 1972*, p. 3. Although "value-added" and "asset" series are not directly comparable, the Census Bureau value-added series increased by a greater percent—43 percent—than did the FTC asset series—31 percent.

10. Between 1909 and 1972 wholesale prices increased about fourfold. Adjusting 1909 assets of corporations accordingly would have increased to only three the number of $1 billion corporations expressed in 1972 prices.

11. Morris A. Adelman, "The Antimerger Act, 1950-1960," *American Economic Review* 51, no. 2 (May 1961): 243.

12. Edwin G. Nourse, "Government Discipline or Private Economic Power," in *Administered Prices: A Compendium on Public Policy*, Subcommittee on Antitrust and Monopoly of the Committee on the Judiciary, U.S. Senate, 88th Congress, 1st sess. (Committee Print, 1963), p. 255.

13. Edwards, "Conglomerate Bigness"; Fritz Machlup, *The Political Economy of Monopoly* (Baltimore: Johns Hopkins Press, 1952), pp. 111-13; John D. Blair, *Economic Concentration* (New York: Harcourt, Brace, 1972), Chapter 3; Willard F. Mueller, "Firm Conglomeration as a Market Structure Variable," *Journal of Agricultural Economics* 51, no. 5 (December 1969); F.M. Scherer, *Industrial Market Structure and Economic Performance* (Chicago: Rand McNally, 1971), pp. 273-83.

14. FTC Economic Staff, *Report on Corporate Mergers* (Washington, D.C.: Government Printing Office, 1969), pp. 321-472; Blair, *Economic Concentration*, Chapter 3. Often large "monopoly" cases actually involve aspects of conglomerate power, as discussed in, for example, Samuel M. Loescher, "A Sherman Act Precedent for the Application of Antitrust Legislation to Conglomerate Mergers—Standard Oil, 1961," in J.W. Markham and G.F. Papanek, *Industrial Organization and Economic Development* (Boston: Houghton Mifflin, 1970), pp. 154-215. The recent Justice Department complaint charging IBM with violating Section 2 of the Sherman Act alleges competitive practices possible only because the firm operates in a number of separate economic markets.

15. "Many Critics Charge Multinational Firms Create Money Crisis," *Wall Street Journal*, April 19, 1973, p. 1. Reprinted with the permission of The Wall Street Journal © Dow Jones & Company, Inc., 1973. A. U.S. Tariff Commission study states U.S.-based multinational corporations controlled $190 billion in short-term assets at the end of 1971. In contrast, the world's major central banks had combined foreign exchange reserves below $68 billion. *Implications of Multinational Firms for World Trade and Investment and for U.S. Trade and Labor*, Report by the U.S. Tariff Commission to the Committee on Finance, United States Senate, 93rd Cong., 1st sess., February 1973, p. 540.

16. Scherer, *Market Structure*, p. 283.

17. The commission relied exclusively on data submitted by the companies in response to data requested under compulsory process. The commission settled for only partial responses to many questions. Moreover, some requests encouraged self-serving responses which the commission did not bother to verify. The staff abandoned the in-depth case-by-case approach and use of investigational hearings as was contemplated by those originating the inquiry. The reader is referred to the testimony of Harrison F. Houghton, the Acting Director of the Bureau of Economics, at the time the inquiry was initiated—Hearings on Corporate Secrecy: Conglomerate Mergers, before the subcommittee on Monopoly, Select Committee on Small Business, U.S. Senate, March 8, 1973.

18. Stanley Eugene Boyle, one of the authors of the report, stated: "Unfortu-

nately, the Commission saw fit to withhold the publication of these detailed data with the result that much of the information which would prove interesting and useful was deleted. This agreement was made by one of the Commissioners without informing or consulting with the staff or other members of the Commission. The net result of this blunder was to substantially reduce the detail and value of the information contained in the version of the Report which was approved for publication by the Commission." Stanley E. Boyle, "A Critical Review of FTC's Report on Conglomerates," *New York Law Journal*, January 29, 1973, pp. 2-3.

19. Lewis Beman, "What We Learned from the Great Merger Frenzy," *Fortune* 87, no. 4 (April 1973): 68. *The Economist*, January 13, 1973, p. 40, concluded, "By and large, it [the FTC Report] defends conglomerates . . . from both their friends and foes."

20. November 3, 1969, FTC Chairman Paul Rand Dixon wrote to Senator Philip Hart: "The Commission has directed its staff to continue its study of . . . the economic performance of conglomerate firms in the *specific markets* into which they acquire, the effect of conglomerate mergers on the competitive vigor of enterprises by their change in status from independent firms to subsidiaries or divisions of conglomerates, and the impact of such structural changes on long run competitive activity." Letter from Chairman Paul Rand Dixon to Senator Philip Hart, in FTC Staff Report on *Corporate Mergers*, 1969, p. VIII (emphasis added).

21. Data were not available for three of the nine companies studied. This is an example of the incompleteness of the data received by the commission.

22. Stanley E. Boyle and Philip W. Jaynes, *Conglomerate Merger Perform-ance: An Empirical Analysis of Nine Corporations*, pp. 112-14. Hereafter cited as *Conglomerate Merger Performance*, "FTC Staff Report," 1972.

23. Ibid., p. 26. The nine conglomerates studied were FMC, G & W, ITT, LTV, Litton, Norton Simon, Rapid-American, Textron, and White Consolidated.

24. That is to say, in this and other analyses the staff did not attempt to answer the question the commission directed it to answer, i.e., "the economic performance of conglomerate firms in the *specific markets* into which they acquire. . . ." FTC Staff Report on *Corporate Mergers*, 1969, p. VIII (emphasis added).

25. The report stated that after acquisition, market shares declined for 127 products and increased for 91. Included among the declines were products dropped by the conglomerate. *Conglomerate Merger Performance*, 1972, p. 122. No explanation is given whether the "dropped" products were discontinued by the conglomerate or whether they were sold to another firm.

26. Ibid., p. 7.

27. Ibid.

28. One of these cases, involving Northwest Industries, is not being actively litigated. The other four were settled by consent decrees.

29. Three of the cases involved complaints involving three large mergers by ITT and another involved LTV.

30. FTC Staff Report on *Corporate Mergers*, 1969, pp. 323-98.

31. These criticisms are not directed at Stanley E. Boyle, one of the authors of the report. Boyle has criticized severely the final draft, alleging that the FTC suppressed some of the most important data received from the nine corporations investigated, Stanley E. Boyle, *New York Law Journal*, and testimony of Boyle before the Monopoly Subcommittee of the Selected Committee on Small Business, U.S. Senate, March 8, 1973. Moreover, had not Boyle consented to serve as a consultant to put together a draft of the report, the FTC would, perhaps, never have completed the report at all. That only a few resources were allocated to prepare the report illustrates the low priority the "new" FTC gave the study, which originally was intended to be a definitive work on the subject. The reader is referred to note 20 above.

32. "Conglomerate Merger Report," *Commerce Clearing House* January 8, 1973, p. 55268.

33. This is discussed in note 17 above.

34. Thirty of the acquisitions involved U.S. companies and the remainder were foreign.

35. For example, although 210 manufacturing companies with assets over $10 million were acquired in 1968, 89 of these were not examined either by the FTC or Justice Department. Moreover, under existing procedures there is no way for the public to learn why the agencies challenged only a dozen or so of the 121 that were investigated.

36. This is discussed in papers by Ralph Nader, Willard Mueller, John Flynn, Walter Adams in Ralph Nader and Mark Green, eds., *Corporate Power in America*, 1973, pp. 67-150.

37. FTC Staff Report on *Corporate Mergers*, 1969, pp. 20-24.

38. Boyle, *New York Law Journal.*

39. When industries are weighted by their value of shipments, the overall trend in concentration is the same as that shown in Table 7-3.

40. Weiss, "Quantitative Studies."

41. Cabinet Committee on Price Stability, *Report to the President on the Committee's Activities with Recommendations for Future Action*, December 28, 1968, p. 7.

42. Testimony of Arthur F. Burns before the Joint Economic Committee, February 20, 1973. Burns also wrote Senator Hart that he wished him well in his efforts to enact the Industrial Reorganization Act discussed below. Letter to Senator Philip Hart from Arthur F. Burns. Hearings on the Industrial Reorganization Act, Senate Subcommittee on Antitrust and Monopoly, United States Senate, March 27, 1973.

43. Interview of Donald I. Baker, *Antitrust and Trade Regulation Report*, Bureau of National Affairs, Washington, D.C., March 27, 1973, p. AA-2. Asked

if the Antitrust Division favored new legislation Baker responded, "I do not think that we have an absolutely fixed answer to that question. I think that it is our position that if you are going to start moving against oligopolies on a broad scale, you are going to need new legislation. But the second point of whether in fact we need a broad program to break up oligopolies is a harder one to come to terms with, because what we are concerned with primarily is the performance of particular industries. Breaking up enterprises on a broad scale across the economy involves some real cost, and isn't the kind of undertaking that would be lightly embarked on either by us or the Congress, and I would guess that some thought to less-sweeping measures should be given before you undertake vast restructuring." Ibid., p. AA-3. One alternative he suggested was freer international trade in concentrated industries.

44. Industrial Reorganization Act, S.1167.

45. Report of the White House Task Force on Antitrust Policy, July 5, 1968. This report is commonly referred to as the Neal Report, after its chairman, Phil C. Neal.

46. Federal Trade Commission, *In the Matter of Kellogg Company et al.*, File No. 711004, January 15, 1972.

47. A discussion of these programs is found in Willard F. Mueller, "Marketing Competition in Oligopolistic Industries: The Attack on Advertising," American Marketing Association Conference on Marketing Practices and Public Policy Issues, June 12-13, 1972.

48. President's News Conference, March 24, 1972, as reported in the *New York Times*, March 25, 1972, p. 13. © 1972 by The New York Times Company. Reprinted by permission.

49. A discussion of the Kleindienst hearings is found in Willard F. Mueller, "The ITT Settlement: A Deal with Justice?" *Industrial Organization Review* 1, no. 1 (1973).

50. "Antitrust as Usual," *New York Times*, March 19, 1972.

51. In recent years the FTC has made public more of its operations and taken some steps to eliminate both actual political interference and the appearance thereof. For example, as a general policy commissioners inform other commissioners when they receive communications from other government officials (executive or congressional) or private parties expressing interest in matters before the commission or its staff. However, the legal reforms made in the text should apply to the commission as well as the Justice Department.

52. Although Antitrust Division Chief Thomas Kauper generally opposed the Tunney bill, the New York City Bar Association's Committee on Trade Regulation supported it, including the section requiring disclosure of communications. It stated: "It is important to subject contacts between government decision makers and representatives of powerful corporations to this kind of therapeutic ventilation." As reported in Bureau of National Affairs, *Antitrust and Trade Regulation Report*, March 20, 1973, p. A-11.

53. Ben W. Lewis, "Power Blocs and the Operation of Economic Forces: Economics of Admonition," *American Economic Review* 49, no. 2 (December 1958): 392.

54. F.A. Hayek, *The Road to Serfdom* (Chicago: University of Chicago Press, 1944).

55. Joan Robinson, "The Second Crisis of Economic Theory," *American Economic Review* 62, no. 2 (May 1972), p. 7.

Bibliography

Bibliography

Adams, Walter. "Dissolution, Divorcement, Divestiture: The Pyrrhic Victories of Anti-Trust." *Indiana Law Journal* 27 (Fall 1951): 1-37.

_____. "The 'Rule of Reason': Workable Competition or Workable Monopoly?" *Yale Law Journal* 63 (January 1954): 348-70.

_____, and Gray, Horace M. *Monopoly in America: The Government as Promoter.* New York: Macmillan, 1966.

Adelman, Morris A. "The Antimerger Act, 1950-1960." *American Economic Review* 51, no. 2 (May 1961): 236-54.

_____. "The Measurement of Industrial Concentration." *Readings in Industrial Organization.* Edited by R.B. Heflebower and G.W. Stocking for the American Economic Association. Homewood, Illinois: Richard D. Irwin, 1958, pp. 3-46.

American Bar Association. *Report of the ABA Commission to Study the Federal Trade Commission.* 1969.

The American Economy—Prospects for Growth to 1985. New York: McGraw-Hill Publications, Economics Department, 1972.

Ando, Albert, and Modigliani, Franco. "The 'Life Cycle' Hypothesis of Saving." *American Economic Review* 53 (March 1963): 55-84.

"Antitrust as Usual." *New York Times.* March 19, 1972, p. 14.

Bain, Joe S. *Barriers to New Competition.* New York: John Wiley and Sons, 1962.

_____. *Industrial Organization.* New York: John Wiley and Sons, 1968.

_____. "Relation of Profit Rate to Industry Concentration: American Manufacturing." *Quarterly Journal of Economics* 65 (August 1951): 293-324.

Baker, Donald I. "The Antitrust Division, Department of Justice: The Role of Competition in Regulated Industries." *Boston College Industrial and Commercial Law Review* 11 (May 1970): 571-93.

_____. Interview, *Antitrust and Trade Regulation Report*, no. 606 (March 27, 1973), pp. AA-1 to AA-6.

Becker, Gary S. "Crime and Punishment: An Economic Approach." *Journal of Political Economy* 76 (March/April 1968): 169-217.

Bell, F.W. "The Effect of Monopoly Profits and Wages on Prices and Consumers' Surplus in American Manufacturing." *Western Economic Journal* 6 (June 1968): 223-41.

Beman, Lewis. "What We Learned from the Great Merger Frenzy." *Fortune* 87, no. 4 (April 1973): 70-73.

Bierman, Harold, Jr. and Tollison, Robert. "Monopoly Rent Capitalization and Antitrust Policy." *Western Economic Journal* 8 (December 1970): 385-89.

Blair, John D. *Economic Concentration.* New York: Harcourt Brace, 1972.

Blair, John M. "Planning for Competition." *Columbia Law Journal* 64 (March 1964): 524-54.

Bork, Robert H. "Legislative Intent and the Policy of the Sherman Act." *Journal of Law and Economics* 9 (October 1966): 7-48.

_____ "The Rule of Reason, and the Per Se Concept: Price Fixing and Marketing Division." *Yale Law Journal* 74 (April 1965): 775-847.

Boyle, Stanley E. "A Critical Review of the FTC's Report on Conglomerates." *New York Law Journal* (January 29, 1973): 2-3.

Breit, William, and Elzinga, Kenneth G. "Antitrust Penalties and Attitudes Toward Risk: An Economic Analysis." *Harvard Law Review* 86 (February 1973): 693-713.

Bronfenbrenner, Martin. "A 'Middlebrow' Approach to Economic Methodology." *The Structure of Economic Science*. Edited by Sherman Roy Krupp. Englewood Cliffs, New Jersey: Prentice-Hall, 1966.

_____. *The Theory of Income Distribution*. Chicago: Aldine-Atherton, 1973.

Brozen, Yale. "The Antitrust Task Force Deconcentration Recommendation." *Journal of Law and Economics* 13 (October 1970): 279-92.

_____. "Bain's Concentration and Rates of Return Revisited." *Journal of Law and Economics* 14 (October 1971): 351-69.

_____. "Concentration and Structural and Market Disequilibria." *Antitrust Bulletin* 16, no. 2 (Summer 1971), pp. 241-48.

Buchanan, James M., and Tullock, Gordon. "The 'Dead' Hand of Monopoly." *Antitrust Law and Economics Review* 1 (Summer 1968): 85-96.

Bureau of the Budget, *Budgets of the United States*. Appendixes, 1970, 1971, 1972.

Burger, Warren E. "The State of the Judiciary—1970." *American Bar Association Journal* 56 (October 1970): 929-34.

Burns, Arthur F. *Hearings on S.1167 before the Subcommittee on Antitrust and Monopoly of the Senate Committee on the Judiciary, 93rd Congress, 1st Session*. March 27, 1973.

"Business Gets a New Measure of Bigness." *Business Week* (January 27, 1973): 80-81.

Cabinet Committee on Price Stability. *Report to the President on the Committee's Activities with Recommendation for Future Action*. Washington, D.C.: Government Printing Office (December 28, 1968), pp. 1-10.

Caves, Richard. *American Industry: Structure, Conduct, Performance*. 3rd ed. Englewood Cliffs, New Jersey: Prentice-Hall, 1972.

_____. *Britain's Economic Prospects*. Washington: Brookings Institution, 1968.

Chamberlin, Edward H. *The Theory of Monopolistic Competition*. 4th ed. Cambridge: Harvard University Press, 1942.

Clabault, James M. and Burton, John F. *1968 Cumulative Statistical Supplement to Sherman Act Indictments 1955-1965*. New York: Federal Legal Publications, 1968.

_____. *Sherman Act Indictments. 1955-1965*. New York: Federal Legal Publications, 1966.

Clark J.M. "Toward a Concept of Workable Competition." *American Economic Review* 30 (June 1940): 241-56.

Clark, Tom C. "Use of 'Parajudges' and the Administration of Justice." *Vanderbilt Law Review* 24 (November 1971): 1167-79.

Comanor, William S. "Vertical Territorial and Customer Restrictions: White Motor and Its Aftermath." *Harvard Law Review* 81, no. 7 (May 1968): 1419-38.

_____, and Leibenstein, Harvey. "Allocative Efficiency, X-Efficiency and the Measurement of Welfare Losses." *Economica* 36 (August 1969): 304-309.

_____, and Wilson, Thomas A. *Advertising and Market Power.* Cambridge: Harvard University Press (forthcoming).

Crew, N.A. and Rowley, C.K. "On Allocative Efficiency, X-Efficiency and the Measurement of Welfare Loss." *Economica* 38 (May 1971): 199-203.

Dalton, James A. and Penn, David W. *The Quality of Data as a Factor in Analyses of Structure-Performance Relationships.* Washington: Government Printing Office, 1971.

David, Martin. *Alternatives Approaches to Capital Gains Taxation.* Washington, D.C.: Brookings Institution, 1968.

Demsetz, Harold. "Why Regulate Utilities?" *Journal of Law and Economics* 11 (April 1968): 55-65.

Downs, Anthony. "An Economic Theory of Political Action in a Democracy." *Journal of Political Economy* 65, no. 2 (April 1957): 135-50.

_____. *Inside Bureaucracy.* Boston: Little, Brown, 1967.

Eckert, Ross V. "The Los Angeles Taxi Monopoly: An Economic Inquiry." *Southern California Law Review* 43 (Summer 1970): 407-453.

Edwards, Corwin. "Conglomerate Bigness as a Source of Power." *Business Concentration and Price Policy.* National Bureau of Economic Research, Princeton: Princeton University Press, 1955.

Elzinga, Kenneth G. "The Antimerger Law: Pyrrhic Victories?" *Journal of Law and Economics* 12 (April 1969): 43-78.

Epstein, Ralph C. *Industrial Profits in the United States.* New York: National Bureau of Economic Research, 1934.

Erickson, Walter B. "Economics of Price Fixing." *Antitrust Law and Economics Review* 2, no. 3 (Spring 1969): 102.

_____. "The Profitability of Violating the Antitrust Laws: Dissolution and Treble Damages in Private Antitrust." *Antitrust Law and Economics Review.* Vol. 2 (Spring 1969): 101-118.

The Federal Individual Income Tax: Revising the Rate and Bracket Structure. New York: Tax Foundation, 1959.

Federal Trade Commission. *Economic Report on the Baking Industry,* 1967.

_____. *In the Matter of Kellogg Company* et al., File No. 711004, January 15, 1972.

_____. Economic Staff Report on *Conglomerate Merger Performance.* Washington, D.C.: Federal Trade Commission, 1972.

Federal Trade Commission. Economic Staff Report on *Corporate Mergers*. Washington, D.C.: Government Printing Office, 1969.

Fisher, I.N. and Hall, G.R. "Risk and Corporate Rates of Return." *Quarterly Journal of Economics* 83 (February 1969): 79-92.

Friedman, Milton. "The Methodology of Positive Economics." *Essays in Positive Economics*. Chicago: University of Chicago Press, 1953.

Galbraith, John Kenneth. *The New Industrial State*. 2nd ed. Boston: Houghton Mifflin, 1971.

Gallman, Robert E. "Trends in the Size Distribution of Wealth in the Nineteenth Century: Some Speculations." *Six Papers on the Size Distribution of Wealth and Income*. Edited by Lee Soltow. New York: Columbia University Press, 1969.

Goldberg, Milton S. *The Consent Decree: Its Formulations and Use*. Occasional Paper no. 8. East Lansing: Michigan State University, Bureau of Business and Economic Research, 1962.

Goldsmith, R.W. *A Study of Saving in the United States*. Princeton: Princeton University Press, 1955 and 1956.

Green, Mark J. *The Closed Enterprise System*. New York: Grossman, 1972.

Hale, George E. "Trust Dissolution: 'Atomizing' Business Units of Monopolistic Size." *Columbia Law Review* 40 (April 1940): 615-32.

_____, and Hale, R.D. "Cost Benefit in Court." *George Washington Law Review* 39 (1969-1970): 83-92.

Handler, Milton. *Cases and Other Materials on Trade Regulation*. 3rd d. Brooklyn: Foundation Press, 1960.

Harberger, Arnold C. "The Measurement of Waste." *American Economic Review* 54 (May 1964): 58-76.

_____. "Monopoly and Resource Allocation." *American Economic Review* 44, no. 2 (May 1954): 77-87.

_____. "Three Basic Postulates for Applied Welfare Economics: An Interpretative Essay." *Journal of Economic Literature* 9 (September 1971): 785-97.

Hayek, F.A. *The Road to Serfdom*. Chicago: University of Chicago Press, 1944.

Hicks, John R. "Annual Survey of Economic Theory: The Theory of Monopoly." *Econometrica* 3 (January 1935): 1-20. Reprinted in *Readings in Price Theory*. Edited by G.J. Stigler and K.E. Boulding for the American Economic Association. Homewood, Illinois: Richard D. Irwin, 1952, pp. 361-83.

Holmes, George K. "The Concentration of Wealth." *Political Science Quarterly* 8 (September 1893): 589-600.

Hotelling, Harold. "The General Welfare in Relation to Problems of Taxation and of Railway and Utility Rates." *Econometrica* 6 (July 1938): 242-69.

Houghton, Harrison F. *Hearings on Corporate Secrecy: Conglomerate Mergers, Before the Subcommittee on Monopoly of the Senate Select Committee on Small Business, 93rd Congress, 1st Session*. March 8, 1973.

Industrial Reorganization Act, S.1167, 93rd Congress, 1st Session. 1973.

Josephson, Matthew. *The Robber Barons.* New York: Harcourt, Brace, 1962.

Kamerschen, David R. "Changes in Concentration in American Manufacturing Industries." *Zeitschrift fur die gesamte Staatswissenchaft* 127 (October 1971): 621-39.

_____, with Richard Wallace. "The Costs of Monopoly." *The Antitrust Bulletin* 17 (Summer 1972): 489-96.

_____. "The Determination of Profit Rates in 'Oligopolistic' Industries." *Journal of Business of the University of Chicago.* 42 (July 1969): 293-301.

_____. "An Empirical Test of Oligopoly Theories." *Journal of Political Economy* 76 (July/August 1968): 615-34. Reprinted in *Journal for Reprints for Antitrust Law and Economics* 1 (Winter: 1969): 1207-1226.

_____. "An Estimation of the 'Welfare Losses' from Monopoly in the American Economy." *Western Economic Journal* 4 (Summer 1966): 221-37.

_____. "Market Growth and Industry Concentration." *Journal of the American Statistical Association* 63 (March 1968): 228-41.

_____. "Monopoly and Welfare." *Zeitschrift fur Nationalokonomie* 31 (December 1971): 507-510.

_____. "Recurrent Objections to the Theory of Imperfect Competition." *Zeitschrift fur die gesamte Staatswissenschaft.* 125 (October 1969): 688-94.

_____. "Trends in Concentration." *Journal of Business Administration* 3 (Spring 1972): 37-53.

Katzner, Donald W. *Static Demand Theory.* New York: Macmillan, 1970.

"Kauper Testifies Tunney Bill Would Provoke 'Undefined' Consent Decree Review." *Antitrust Trade and Regulation Report.* No. 605 (March 20, 1973), pp. A-9 to A-11.

Kauper, Thomas E. *Remarks to Annual Corporate Council Institute.* Northwestern University, October 4, 1972.

Kauper, Thomas E. "The 'Warren Court' and the Antitrust Laws: Of Economics, Populism, and Cynicism." *Michigan Law Review* 67 (December 1968): 269-88.

Kaysen, Carl. *United States* vs. *United Shoe Machinery Corporation.* Cambridge, Mass.: Harvard University Press, 1956.

_____, and Turner, Donald F. *Antitrust Policy: An Economic and Legal Analysis.* Cambridge, Mass.: Harvard University Press, 1959.

Kilpatrick, Robert W. "The Choice among Alternative Measures of Industrial Concentration." *Review of Economics and Statistics.* 49 (May 1967): 258-60.

_____. "Stigler on the Relationship between Industry Profit Rates and Market Concentration." *Journal of Political Economy* 76, no. 3 (May/June 1968): 474-88.

King, W.I. *The Wealth and Income of the People of the United States.* New York: Macmillan, 1915.

Kou, Shou-Eng. "A Note on the Social Welfare Loss Due to Monopoly." *Southern Economic Journal* 37 (October 1970): 212-14; and his "Reply" idem, 38 (January 1972): 424-25.

Lampman, Robert J. *The Share of Top Wealth-Holders in National Wealth, 1922-1956.* Princeton: Princeton University Press, 1962.

Lansing, John B. and Sonquist, John. "A Cohort Analysis of Changes in the Distribution of Wealth." *Six Papers on the Size Distribution of Wealth and Income.* Edited by Lee Soltow. New York: Columbia University Press, 1969.

Leibenstein, Harvey. "Allocative Efficiency vs. 'X'-Efficiency." *American Economic Review* 56 (June 1966): 392-415.

Lerner, Abba P. "The Concept of Monopoly and the Measurement of Monopoly Power." *Review of Economic Studies* 1 (June 1934): 157-78.

Lewis, Ben W. "Power Blocks and the Operation of Economic Forces: Economics of Admonition." *American Economic Review* 49, no. 2 (December 1958): 384-98.

Loescher, Samuel M. "A Sherman Act Precedent for the Application of Antitrust Legislation to Conglomerate Mergers—Standard Oil, 1911." Found in J.W. Markham and G.F. Papanek, *Industrial Organization and Economic Development.* Boston: Houghton Mifflin, 1970, pp. 154-215.

Lorie, J.H. and Fisher, L. "Rates of Return on Investment in Common Stocks." *The Journal of Business* 37 (January 1964): 1-21.

Lydall, Harold. "The Life Cycle in Income, Saving, and Asset Ownership." *Econometrica* 23 (April 1955): 131-50.

Machlup, Fritz. *The Political Economy of Monopoly.* Baltimore: Johns Hopkins Press, 1952.

————, and Taber, Martha. "Bilateral Monopoly, Successive Monopoly, and Vertical Integration." *Economica* 27 (May 1960): 101-119.

Mann, H. Michael. "Seller Concentration, Barriers to Entry, and Rates of Return in Thirty Industries, 1950-1960." *Review of Economics and Statistics* 48, no. 3 (August 1966): 296-307.

Manne, Henry, ed. *Economic Policy and Regulation of Corporate Securities.* Washington, D.C.: American Enterprise Institute, 1969.

"Many Critics Charge Multinational Firms Create Money Crisis." *Wall Street Journal.* April 19, 1973, p. 1.

Markham, Jesse W. "Market Structure, Business Conduct, and Innovation." *American Economic Review* 55 (May 1965): 323-32. Reprinted in David R. Kamerschen, *Readings in Microeconomics.* New York: John Wiley and Sons, 1969, pp. 344-78.

Marris, Robin. *The Economic Theory of "Managerial" Capitalism.* New York: Basic Books, 1964.

McGee, John S. *In Defense of Industrial Concentration.* New York: Praeger Publishers, 1971.

McKean, Roland N. "Differences between Individual and Total Costs within Government." *American Economic Review* 54 (May 1964): 243-57.

McKie, James W. "The Decline of Monopoly in the Metal Container Industry." *American Economic Review* 45 (May 1955): 499-508.

McNally, Richard W. and Ravis, Lee A. " 'Spatial Risk' and Return Relationships: A Reconsideration." *Journal of Risk and Insurance* 39, no. 3 (September 1972): 351-67.

Meade, J.P. *Efficiency, Equality and the Ownership of Property.* Cambridge: Harvard University Press, 1965.

Meade, J.E. *The Theory of International Economic Policy, Trade and Welfare.* London: Oxford University Press, 1955.

Menge, John A. "Style Cost Change as a Market Weapon." *Quarterly Journal of Economics* 76 (November 1962): 632-47.

Mishan, E.J. "A Note on the Costs of Tariffs, Monopolies and Thefts." *Western Economic Journal* 7 (September 1969): 230-233.

Modigliani, Franco and Brumberg, Richard. "Utility Analysis and the Consumption Function: An Interpretation of Cross-Section Data." *Post-Keynesian Economics.* Edited by Kenneth K. Kurihara. London: Allen and Unwin, 1955.

Monsen, R. Joseph, Jr. and Downs, Anthony. "A Theory of Large Managerial Firms." *Journal of Political Economy* 73 (June 1965): 221-36.

Mueller, Charles E. "Lawyer's Guide to the 'Welfare Loss' Concept: An Introduction." *Antitrust Law and Economics Review* 5 (Spring 1972): 75-96.

Mueller, Willard F. *The Celler-Kefauver Act: Sixteen Years of Enforcement.* A Staff Report to the Antitrust Subcommittee on the Committee on the Judiciary, House of Representatives, 90th Congress, 1st sess. (House Committee Print, 1967).

_____. "Firm Conglomeration as a Market Structure Variable." *Journal of Agricultural Economics* 51, no. 5 (December 1969): 1488-94.

_____. "The ITT Settlement: A Deal with Justice?" *Industrial Organization Review* 1, no. 1 (1973): 67-86.

_____. "Marketing Competition in Oligopolistic Industries: The Attach on Advertising." In *American Marketing Association Conference on Marketing Practices and Public Policy Issues.* June 12-13, 1972.

_____, and Stockings, George W. "The Cellophane Case and the New Competition." *American Economic Review* 45 (March 1955): 29-63.

Nader, Ralph; Mueller, Willard; Flynn, John; and Adams, Walter. *Corporate Power in America.* Edited by Ralph Nader and Mark Green. New York: Grossman, 1973.

National Bureau of Economic Research. *Business Concentration and Public Policy.* Princeton: Princeton University Press, 1955.

Newhouse, J. "Toward a Theory of Nonprofit Institutions: An Economic Model of a Hospital." *American Economic Review* 60, no. 1 (March 1970): 64-74.

Nichols, William H. "The Tobacco Case of 1946." *American Economic Review* 39 (May 1949): 284-96.

Niskanen, William A. *Bureaucracy and Representative Government.* Chicago: Aldine-Atherton, 1971.

176

Noll, Roger G. "The Behavior of Regulatory Agencies." *Review of Social Economy* 29, no. 1 (March 1971): 15-19.

Nourse, Edwin G. "Government Discipline or Private Economic Power." In *Administered Prices: A Compendium on Public Policy*, Subcommittee on Antitrust and Monopoly of the Senate Committee on the Judiciary, 88th Congress, 1st sess. (Committee Print 1963), pp. 245-61.

Oppenheim, S. Chesterfield. "Divestiture as a Remedy under the Federal Antitrust Laws." *George Washington Law Review* 19 (December 1950): 119-31.

Ornstein, Stanley I. "Concentration and Profits." *Journal of Business* 45, no. 4 (October 1972): 519-41.

Parker, Alfred L. "Treble Damage Action—A Financial Deterrent to Antitrust Violations?" *Antitrust Bulletin* 4, no. 4 (Summer 1971): 483-505.

Patinkin, Don. *Money, Interest and Prices.* 2nd ed. New York: Harper and Row, 1965.

Peterman, John L. "The Brown Shoe Cases." Unpublished manuscript. Chicago, Ill.: University of Chicago, 1973.

_____. "The Clorox Case and the Television Rate Structure." *Journal of Law and Economics* 12 (October 1968): 321-422.

Philips, Almarin. "The Objectives of Economic Policy—The Contribution of Antitrust." Unpublished.

_____, ed. *Perspectives in Antitrust Policy.* Princeton, New Jersey: Princeton University Press, 1965.

Posner, Richard A. "A Program for the Antitrust Division." *University of Chicago Law Review* 38, no. 2 (Winter 1971): 500-536.

_____. "A Statistical Study of Antitrust Enforcement." *Journal of Law and Economics* 13, no. 2 (October 1970): 355-420.

President's News Conference. *New York Times.* March 24, 1972, p. 13.

Preston, Lee E. and Collins, Norman R. *Concentration and Price-Cost Margins in Manufacturing Industries*, Berkeley: University of California Press, 1968.

Projector, Dorothy S. *Survey of Changes in Family Finances*, Federal Reserve Technical Paper, 1968.

_____, and Weiss, Gertrude S. *Survey of Financial Characteristics of Consumers.* Federal Reserve Technical Paper, 1966.

Pryor, Frederick L. "Simulation of the Impact of Social and Economic Institutions on the Size Distributions of Income and Wealth." *American Economic Review* 63 (March 1973): 50-72.

Rader, Trout. *Theory of Microeconomics.* New York: Academic Press, 1972.

Report of the White House Task Force on Antitrust Policy (Neal Commission). July 5, 1968.

Robinson, Joan. "The Second Crisis of Economic Theory." *American Economic Review* 62, no. 2 (May 1972): 1-10.

Ross, Howard N. "Illusions in Testing for Administered Prices." *Journal of Industrial Economics* 21 (April 1973): 187-95.

Scherer, F.M. *Industrial Market Structure and Economic Performance.* Chicago: Rand McNally, 1970.

Schwartzman, David. "The Effect of Monopoly on Price." *Journal of Political Economy* 67 (August 1959): 352-62.

Shepherd, A. Ross. "The Social Welfare Loss Due to Monopoly: Comment." *Southern Economic Journal* 38 (January 1972): 421-24.

Shepherd, William G. "Trends of Concentration in American Manufacturing Industries, 1947-1958." *Review of Economics and Statistics* 46 (May 1964): 200-212.

Sherman, Roger and Tollison, Robert. "Public Policy Toward Oligopoly: Dissolution and Scale Economies." *Antitrust Law and Economics Review* 4, no. 4 (Summer 1971): 77-90.

Smith, R.A. "The Incredible Electrical Conspiracy." *Fortune* 63 (April 1961): 132 ff.

Snell, Bradford C. "Annual Style Change in the Automobile Industry as an Unfair Method of Competition," *Yale Law Journal* 80, no. 3 (January 1971): 567-613.

Sosnick, Stephen H. "A Critique of Concepts of Workable Competition." *Quarterly Journal of Economics* 72 (August 1958): 380-423.

Spahr, Charles V. *An Essay on the Present Distribution of Wealth in the United States.* New York: Thomas Y. Crowell, 1896.

Spengler, Joseph J. "Vertical Integration and Antitrust Policy." *Journal of Political Economy.* 58 (August 1950): 347-52.

Stigler, George J. "Mergers and Preventive Antitrust Policy." *University of Pennsylvania Law Review* 104 (November 1955): 176-84.

_____. *Capital and Rates of Return in Manufacturing Industries.* Princeton, New Jersey: Princeton University Press, 1963.

_____. "A Theory of Oligopoly." *Journal of Political Economy* 72, no. 1 (February 1964): 44-61.

_____. "The Economic Effects of Antitrust Laws." *Journal of Law and Economics* 9 (October 1966): 225-38.

_____. *The Organization of Industry.* Homewood: Richard D. Irwin, 1968.

_____, chairman. "President Nixon's *Task Force on Productivity and Competition.*" *Antitrust Law and Economics Review* 13 (Spring 1969): 13 passim.

Stiglitz, J.E. "Distribution of Income and Wealth among Individuals." *Econometrica* 37 (July 1969): 382-97.

Suits, Daniel B. *Statistics: An Introduction to Quantitative Economic Research.* Chicago: Rand McNally, 1963.

Task Force on Competition and Productivity. *Report, Antitrust Law and Economics Review.* Vol. 2 (1968-1969).

Telser, Lester. "Some Determinants of the Returns to Manufacturing Industries." Unpublished. Report No. 6935. Chicago, Ill.: University of Chicago, Center for Mathematical Studies in Business and Economics.

Thorelli, Hans B. *The Federal Antitrust Policy.* Stockholm: Kungl. Boktryckeriet P.A. Norstedt and Soner, 1954.

"Tough Trust Laws Proposed by [Arthur F.] Burns." *Washington Post*, February 21, 1973.

Tullock, Gordon. *The Politics of Bureaucracy.* Washington: Public Affairs Press, 1965.

————. "The Welfare Costs of Tariffs, Monopolies, and Theft." *Western Economic Journal* 5 (June 1967): 224-32.

U.S. Bureau of the Census. *Annual Survey of Manufacturers: 1970, Value of Shipment Concentration Ratios*, Washington, D.C.: Government Printing Office, 1972.

U.S. Congress. "Staff Study of Income Tax Treatment of Treble Damage Payments under the Antitrust Laws." Joint Committee on Internal Revenue Taxation, November 1, 1965.

U.S. Department of Commerce, Bureau of the Census. *Current Population Reports—Population Characteristics, Household and Family Characteristics.* Series P-20, no. 125. Washington, D.C.: Government Printing Office, 1963.

————. *Historical Statistics of the United States from Colonial Times to 1957*, 1958.

U.S. Department of Health, Education and Welfare, Public Health Service. *Vital Statistics of the United States—1962.* Vol. 2, Mortality, Part A, 1964.

U.S. Department of the Treasury, Internal Revenue Service. *Fiduciary, Gift and Estate Tax-Returns, Statistics of Income 1962.*

United States Federal Reserve System. *Federal Reserve Bulletin.* Various issues.

U.S. Tariff Commission. Report on the *Implications of Multinational Firms for World Trade and Investment and for U.S. Trade and Labor.* Report to the Committee on Finance of the U.S. Senate, 93rd Congress, 1st sess., (Committee Print 1973).

Warren, Earl. "Address at Harvard Law School Sesquicentennial." *Judicature* 51 (January 1968), 196 ff.

Weiss, Leonard. "Quantitative Studies of Industrial Organization." In M.D. Intriligator, ed. *Frontiers of Quantitative Economics.* Amsterdam-London: North-Holland Publishing, 1971, Chapter 9.

Wells, Anita. "Legislative History of Treatment of Capital Gains under Federal Income Tax, 1913-1948." *National Tax Journal* 2 (March 1949): 12-32.

Weston, J. Fred and Peltzman, Sam. *Public Policies Toward Mergers.* Pacific Palisades: Goodyear Publishing Co., 1969.

Williamson, Oliver E. "Economics as an Antitrust Defense: The Welfare Trade-offs." *American Economic Review* 58 (March 1968): 18-36.

————. "Managerial Discretion and Business Behavior." *American Economic Review* 53, no. 5 (December 1963): 1032-1057.

————, and Phillips, Almarin, eds. *Prices: Issues in Theory, Practice and Public Policy.* Philadelphia: University of Pennsylvania Press, 1968.

Wilson, Bruce B. "New Directions in Antitrust Policy." *Antitrust Trade and Regulation Report.* No. 607, April 3, 1973, pp. D-1 to D-4.

Worcester, Dean A., Jr. *Monopoly, Big Business and Welfare in the Postwar United States*, Seattle: University of Washington Press, 1967.

Zerbe, Richard O. "The Chicago Board of Trade Case and the Historical Structure of the Grain Trade." Unpublished manuscript. Chicago, Ill.: University of Chicago, 1971.

Index

Index

118; and the economy, 30, 119;
minor, 16; oligopolistic, 12;
organization of, 81, 118, 121;
performance, 88, 134; and producer
goods, 130; regulation of, 37, 42;
resources of, 125; structure and
restructuring of, 93, 129
Inefficiency: allocative, 8, 17, 24;
bureaucratic, 108-112; of
companies, 85
Inflation, excessive, 8, 57, 119,
126-127
Injunctions, directives on, 102
Innovation, record of, 18-19, 29
Integrated firms, 40
Interest, asymmetry of, 108; market
rate of, 103, 120; public, 109
Internal Revenue Service (IRS), 16
International Business Machines
(IBM), 50, 53-54, 56, 58, 91, 128
International monetary system, 120
Interstate commerce, 37, 76, 102
Invention, pace of, 29
Investigations, antitrust, 48. *See also*
specific cases by name
ITT Case, 11, 37, 95, 122, 124-125;
affairs in Chile, 121; settlement of,
118, 131-133

Jail sentences, impact of, 105, 111.
See also Incarceration
Jefferson, President Thomas, 125
Johnson, Lyndon B., Cabinet
Committee on Price Stability, 127
Joint selling agents, establishment of,
92-93
Josephson, Matthew, cited, 105
Judges and the judiciary process, 12,
63, 75, 88, 107, 112-113. *See also*
Court System; Supreme Court
Justice, Department of, antitrust
activities of, 55, 57, 72-73, 117,
124; complaints received by, 45;
costs of, 47-48; as a deterrent force,
43; and ITT settlement, 131-132;
lawyer-years in, 45-48, 53; and
public confidence, 131-132

Kamerschen, David R., cited, 7
Kauper, Thomas E., cited, 23, 117
Kinney Shoe Stores, 72-73

Kleindienst, Attorney General
Richard, 131-132

Labor, 76; allocation practices, 67;
sharing arrangements, 67; unions,
76, 128
Labor Statistics, Bureau of, 30
Laissez-faire, policy of, 101, 126, 133
Law and laws: antitrust, 22, 35-36,
54-57, 76, 93, 95, 105, 117, 127,
132; and economics, 63;
interpretation of, 21; violation of,
86
Lawyer-years: allocated, 60-62;
antitrust, 48, 57; per area, 59;
expected gains, 49-51, 54, 56;
Justice Department, 45-48, 53
Lawyers, 11, 15, 20, 24, 88; antitrust,
27, 47, 54, 124; compliance, 83,
109; government, 47, 86; private
company, 47, 107
Legal staffs, 9, 12, 21, 24. *See also*
Litigation
Lending, truth in, 133
Lever Brothers Company, 71
Leverage cases, 12, 37-38, 41-46,
49-56, 60-62
Levin, Stanford L., cited, 3-12
Lewis, Ben, cited, 117, 133
Licenses, 90
Litigation, 35, 81, 83; antimerger,
86-87; antitrust, 24-25, 101; cost of,
45-48, 87, 101, 108; multidistrict,
106
Lobbying and lobbyists, effectiveness
of, 9, 11, 20-22, 28, 91-92, 108
Losses, welfare, 86-87

Maintenance: resale price, 36; retail
price, 19
Management and managers, company,
8-9, 18, 103-104, 107, 109, 111,
126
Mann, H. Michael, cited, 11-12, 15-25,
27-28
Margins and marginal improvements,
54, 70, 76, 82
Market: basket, 77; behavior, 95;
capital, 89-90; concentration, 36,
42, 118, 126, 130; concepts of, 64,
89; consumer, 41; and the economy,
16, 117; free, 110, 127, 133;

Market (cont.)
geographical, 40, 87; growth of, 18; money, 77, 103, 120; place, 95, 127; power, 9, 41, 93, 101, 111, 118, 127-128; practices, 112; sales, 53; sharing, 19, 36, 41, 52, 69, 72-73, 110, 122; size, 19, 48; structure, 19, 29, 37, 83, 118
Marris, Robin, cited, 104
Materials and supplies, cost of, 31
McGee, John S., cited, 63n
McLaren, Chief of Antitrust Division, 132
Meade, J.E., cited, 100-101, 111
Media, effectiveness of, 90. *See also* Communications industry
Meehan, James W., cited, 11-12, 15-25, 27-28
Menge, John A., cited, 77
Mergers and merger cases, 12, 35-38, 41-46; 49-56, 59-61, 83, 86-87, 92, 96, 98, 124-125. *See also* specific type of merger
Microeconomic theory, 63, 74-76, 81, 89
Mining activities, 91
Minority hiring practices, 133
Mitchell, John, cited, 132
Monetary system, 77, 103-104, 113, 120
Monopoly and monopolistic activities, 16, 83, 99, 106; behavior, 88, 100, 105, 111; bilateral, 41; cost effect of, 9; disadvantage of, 3; discriminating, 90-93; industrial, 5; innovative, 21; power of, 3, 6, 8, 57, 64, 93, 129; practices, 55, 57; pricing, 4, 18; private, 110; profits of, 10, 103, 128; rents, 82-83, 86-87; sale of rights, 88-89; single price, 88, 91; spin-off, 86-87; structural, 58, 60; traditional, 88, 92
Morale, problems of, 107
Morton Salt Case, 72
Motion pictures, distribution of, 69
Mueller, Willard F., cited, 12-13, 70-71, 117-135
Multidistrict litigation, 106
Multimarket enterprises, 119
Multinational conglomerates, 118-119, 125; corporations, 11-12, 125-126, 133

Murphy, R. Dennis, cited, 111-113

Nader, Ralph, 133; Study Group of, 22, 24
National Advisory Commission on Criminal Justice Standards and Goals, 107
National Environmental Protection Act, 132
National Recovery Act (NRA), 133
Neal Report, The, 130
New Deal Program, 133
New York Times, 132
Nixon, President Richard M., 127, 131, 133
Noncompetitive structures, 77, 126
Noninformational advertising, 130
Nonintegrated firms, 37, 40-41
Nonprofit maximizing level of advertising, 90
Nonsubstitutable products, 28
Nonviability, problem of, 85
Northern Lines Case, 37
Northern Pacific Railway, 105
Nourse, E.G., cited, 119

Oligopoly and oligopolies, 11, 24, 30, 88-89; bilateral, 41; and competition, 7; and industry, 12, 42; theory of, 118-120
Organization, industrial, 8, 81, 118, 121
Out-of-court settlements, 106, 132
Output restrictions, 3, 19
Ownership tenure, 98

Pacific Northwest Pipeline Company, 75
Packaging, truth in, 133
Parameter estimation, 58, 62
Patents, 40, 85, 90, 130; divestiture of, 89
Patinkin cartel, 67
Penalty system, 11-12, 113; antitrust, 99, 103; monetary, 104, 113; must fit the crime, 93; and structural relief, 107
Penn-Central Case, 37
Personnel problems, company, 69, 107
Peterman, John, cited, 63n, 71
Pharmacology, 29
Phillips, Alamarin, cited, 23

About the Editors and Contributors

James A. Dalton received the Ph.D. in economics from Boston College in 1969. Associate Professor of Economics at the University of Southern Florida, he has also been employed by Southern Illinois University at Edwardsville and by the Bureau of Economics of the Federal Trade Commission. Professor Dalton's research and publications are concerned with market structure, industry performance, and antitrust policy.

Stanford L. Levin is Assistant Professor of Economics at Southern Illinois University at Edwardsville; he is also a consultant to the Land of Lincoln Legal Assistance Corporation, Inc., working on behalf of low income people in utility rate hearings. He received the Ph.D. in economics in 1974 from the University of Michigan. Professor Levin's research is concerned with market structure and economic policy.

Richard J. Arnould received the Ph.D. in economics in 1968 from Iowa State University and is Associate Professor of Economics at the University of Illinois. His articles in the area of industrial organization have appeared in several professional journals.

John M. Blair received the Ph.D. from American University. He is Professor of Economics at the University of South Florida and has held several positions with the federal government. His publications include books and articles in economics and several government reports.

William Breit was educated at Michigan State University (Ph.D., 1961). Since 1965 he has been a member of the faculty of the University of Virginia, where he is Professor of Economics. His publications include books and articles in professional journals.

Stanley E. Boyle is Professor of Economics at Virginia Polytechnic Institute and State University. He has held several positions with the government, most recently with the Senate Subcommittee on Antitrust and Monopoly. He has authored several articles dealing with industrial organization and antitrust and is Managing Editor of *Industrial Organization Review*.

Kenneth G. Elzinga, Associate Professor of Economics at the University of Virginia, received the Ph.D. from Michigan State University in 1967. In 1970-71 he was the Special Economic Assistant to the head of the Antitrust Division. He has published articles in several professional journals.

Michael Glassman is a candidate for the Ph.D. in economics at the University of Chicago. Formerly at McMurray College, he is currently Chief of the Division of Economic Evidence in the Bureau of Economics at the Federal Trade Commission.

H. Michael Mann, Professor of Economics at Boston College, received the Ph.D. from Cornell University in 1962. He has also held positions as Special Economics Assistant to the Assistant Attorney General in Charge of Antitrust, and Director of the Bureau of Economics at the Federal Trade Commission. Professor Mann has published articles and comments in several professional journals.

James W. Meehan, Jr. received the Ph.D. from Boston College in 1967. He has held positions as a Staff Economist at the Antitrust Division of the U.S. Department of Justice, and Assistant to the Director, Bureau of Economics, Federal Trade Commission. Since Fall 1973 he has been Assistant Professor of Economics at Colby College. Professor Meehan has published articles and comments in several professional journals.

William F. Mueller is William F. Vilas Research Professor at the University of Wisconsin. Among his many professional activities he has been Director of the Bureau of Economics at the Federal Trade Commission. He has published several articles and books in the field of industrial organization and antitrust.

R. Dennis Murphy received the Ph.D. in economics from the University of Michigan. He is Assistant Professor of Economics at the University of Michigan-Dearborn, currently on leave to be Assistant to the Director of the Bureau of Economics, Federal Trade Commission. He is coauthor of a forthcoming book dealing with the economics of multiplant operations.

Charles G. Stalon received the Ph.D. from Purdue University and is Associate Professor of Economics at Southern Illinois University at Carbondale. He has served as an economist for the Federal Power Commission; his research has been in the areas of oligopolistic rivalry and price level movements.

Leonard W. Weiss is Professor of Economics at the University of Wisconsin and was Special Economic Assistant to the head of the Antitrust Division, Department of Justice. He has published numerous articles in various professional journals in the areas of industrial organization and antitrust.

Richard O. Zerbe received the Ph.D. from Duke University. He is Associate Professor of Economics at Roosevelt University and Visiting Associate Professor at Northwestern University. Professor Zerbe has contributed numerous articles to professional journals.